TABLE OF CONTENTS

Introduction, by Sandra Lee Kerman   i

CAPTAIN JOHN KIDD, Executed for Piracy   1

MARY YOUNG, *alias* JENNY DIVER, Executed for Street Robbery   7

WILLIAM JOHNSON AND JANE HOUSDEN, Executed for the Murder of Mr. Spurling   23

MATTHEW CLARKE, Executed for Murder   25

JOHN SHEPPARD, Executed for Highway Robbery   28

JONATHAN WILD, Executed for Feloniously Conniving with Thieves   44

NATHANIEL HAWES, Tortured, and Afterwards Executed, for Robbery   97

MARGARET DIXON, Murderer   111

FRANCIS CHARTERIS, Convicted of Using Violence to the Person of Ann Bond   114

CAPTAIN JOHN PORTEOUS, Convicted of Murder, and Murdered by the Mob   122

JOHN COLLINS, Executed for Murder   131

JONATHAN BRADFORD, Executed for a Supposed Murder   132

LYDIA ADLER, Convicted of Manslaughter   134

EUGENE ARAM, Executed for Murder   136

JOHN PRICE, COMMONLY CALLED JACK KETCH, Executed for the Murder of Elizabeth White   155

RICHARD TURPIN, Executed for Horse-Stealing   158

JOHN SMITH, Convicted of Robbery   174

LAURENCE EARL FERRERS, Executed for Murder   177

THOMAS ANDREWS, Convicted of an Unnatural Crime   192

MARY HAMILTON, *alias* CHARLES HAMILTON, *alias* GEORGE HAMILTON, *alias* WILLIAM HAMILTON, Whipped for Marrying with her own Sex   195

THOMAS COLLEY, Executed for Murder   196

THE REVEREND MR. WHEATLEY, Sentenced to do Public Penance for Adultery   206

—M'CANNELLY AND — MORGAN, Executed for Burglary   213

WILLIAM STROUD, Whipped for Swindling   216

WILLIAM YORK, Convicted of Murder   220

BENJAMIN TAPNER, JOHN COBBY, et al., Executed for Murder   222

ANN WILLIAMS, Executed for the Murder of her Husband   235

NICHOL BROWN, Executed for the Murder of his Wife   238

CHARLES PRICE, Apprehended on a Charge of Forgery   242

WILLIAM WARD, Convicted of Manslaughter   257

THE REVEREND BENJAMIN RUSSEN, Executed for a Rape   262

JOHN HOLMES AND PETER WILLIAMS, Whipped for Stealing Dead Bodies   265

JOHN RANN, COMMONLY CALLED SIXTEEN-STRING JACK, Executed for Highway Robbery   267

THE DUCHESS OF KINGSTON, Convicted of Bigamy   275

THE REVEREND JAMES HACKMAN, Executed for Murder   305

RENWICK WILLIAMS, COMMONLY CALLED 'THE MONSTER,' Convicted of a Brutal and Wanton Assault on Miss Anne Porter   312

FREDERIC LORD BALTIMORE, ELIZABETH GRIFFENBURG, AND ANNE HARVEY, The Former Tried for Committing a Rape of Sarah Woodcock, and the Two Latter as Accessories Before the Fact   321

JOHN MILLS, Executed for Murder   343

HANNAH DAGOE, Executed for Robbing a Poor Woman   348

JOHN CROUCH AND WIFE, Tried for Offering to Sell a Young Girl   350

ELIZABETH BROWNRIGG, Executed for Torturing her Female Apprentices to Death   351

INTRODUCTION

The appreciation of the prevalence and characteristic nature of crime is significant to an understanding of any society; it is necessary to an understanding of eighteenth-century England. The unprecedented quantity—and expertise—of criminal activities in the eighteenth century reflects the social disorder which underlay the hard veneer of propriety which characterized the political life of that conservative age. It also provides an accurate index of the profound economic and social dislocations which altered the face of England during her transformation into an urban and industrial society. The contemporary methods of dealing with crime, and the dominant theory of crime prevention, however, revealed no awareness that crime could be caused by anything but the sinfulness of the human soul.

The Newgate Calendar is a chronicle of the lives and exploits of noteworthy eighteenth-century criminals told with strong moral and exhortatory overtones. It is valuable in two capacities: as a document rich in facts, personalities and flavor, and as an example of the popular opinion and working morality of the time. The thought it reveals is rationalistic, but not "enlightened," and is typical of the average, middle-class—and official—opinion of the period. *The Newgate Calendar* is also a prime example of the popular secular literature which was first distributed on a large scale during this time. Like the popular literature of today, of which it is

i

the precursor, its two major selling points were its sensationalism and its guaranteed authenticity. This "human interest" is hardly resistable today; the fascination of violent and extraordinary lives still accounts for our initial attraction to *The Newgate Calendar*. But for the modern reader, the first level of the book's interest offers more than excitement. The realism and immediacy of the narratives gives us a living sense of the time and heightens our sensitivity to the more enduring historical values of a vital social document of eighteenth century England.

I

The Newgate Calendar derives its title from Newgate, the chief prison in the largest city of the realm, and an annex of the Old Bailey, the largest court of common law in England. The material included in *The Newgate Calendar* has two major sources. Called 'the calendar,' the Sessions papers of trials held at the Old Bailey (available from about 1730) provided complete records of all the legal proceedings: the official account of the crime, the activities in court, and the final judicial disposition of the case. The character and behavior of the criminal in prison and his confessions and last words were recorded by the prison chaplains—the Ordinaries of Newgate.

The genre of *The Newgate Calendar* is biography, but instead of the usual praise given to great and famous men, the lives and destinies of the criminals are cited as examples to the young of the wages of sin. *The Newgate Calendar* itself was anticipated by earlier volumes, and by a multitude of ballads, broadsides, True Confessions and Last Dying Words, which were always in great demand during the trials and executions of important criminals. These continued to be published in equal volume into the 1820's, long after the publication of the large collections of biographies.

The first collection of the lives of criminals was *Tyburn Calendar, or Malefactor's Bloody Register,* published shortly after 1700 by George Swindell's of Hanging Bridge, London—an appropriate address. (Tyburn, situated about two miles from Newgate, was the traditional place of execution in London, and *Tyburn* became the generic name for these locations.) The stated purpose of the first compilers, although differently worded in subsequent editions, is typical of the introductions to all the contemporary versions of the Calendar: "to fully display the regular progress from Virtue to Vice, interspersed with striking reflections on the conduct of those unhappy wretches who have fallen a sacrifice to the injured laws of their country. The whole tending to guard young minds from the allurements of vice and the paths that lead to destruction." *The Tyburn Calendar* was followed by many other books of its kind, culminating in the deluxe five-volume edition of *The Newgate Calendar* from which the present selection was made. It was not the last of these compilations, but it remained the most complete, and the standard text upon which future editions were based. Published in 1771,[1] it included accounts of the lives of the most important criminals of nearly three quarters of a century. It was a veritable national biography of crime, well designed, encyclopedic in scope, and characteristically moral in tone. The frontispiece of the original edition, which unfortunately could not be reproduced in this edition, is a good illustration of the theme of the Editors. It is a domestic scene in a well-to-do, happy home. A mother is seated near the window addressing her young son. One of her hands holds the *Newgate Calendar;* with the other she points out the window to the body of an executed criminal hanging from a gibbet, and her expression is one of loving but anxious concern. The moral is clear enough.

[1] Or possibly 1773; the accounts differ.

The authors of *The Newgate Calendar* chose to term themselves, ambiguously, "editors," and to remain anonymous. The evidence indicates that the prison Ordinaries were responsible for writing and publishing the *Calendar*, as well as providing some of its most important information. (The modesty of the 'editors' would thus be explained by the Chaplains' reluctance to be identified with a commercial venture made possible by their offices.) The reports on the behavior of condemned prisoners required of them by the Lord Mayor were turned to their own interest in a private financial venture, and the prison Chaplains were not more famous for their selfless dedication to their work than were other officials. The overwhelmingly moral tone of every narrative, the intimate knowledge of the last words and reactions of the condemned, and particularly of their repentance (or lack of it), point to the probability of the Chaplains' authorship. Although it was not difficult to acquire access to either the court or the prison, only the Ordinaries were in such close, constant and often confidential contact with so many prisoners.

The authors of *The Newgate Calendar* no doubt hoped to discourage crime; they may have succeeded to some small extent by helping to inform the public of the lesser-known capital offences. But their view toward the criminal and his punishment was entirely in harmony with the system which so badly aggravated a problem which could hardly be worse. The criminal was considered to be an unregenerate miscreant who, due to laziness and greed, renounces the virtuous life, and becomes a menace to society. His richly deserved punishment serves to prove that the ways of evil lead to evil ends. Society can only be repaid by its just revenge upon him, which also serves as a warning to anyone contemplating a similar career. His evil is in his heart; if, at the end, he sees the error of his ways and repents, so much the better for the repose of his soul. His execution is thus for his own good as well as for that of society.

The popularity of *The Newgate Calendar* was surpassed only by the popularity of public executions and other forms of public punishment. The spectacle of execution day in London has few peers in the annals of officially sanctioned mob brutality. The hero of the day was the condemned man who, unless his crime was of a particularly perverse or unpopular nature, was judged posthumously by the public according to the gameness with which he met his death. Christmas, Easter and Execution Days were the only legal holidays, and each was in its own way great cause for mirth and celebration. Great crowds including men, women, and children of all classes lined the road from Newgate to Tyburn on Execution Day. Enterprising apartment dwellers rented window and roof space along the route at high rates. The prisoner or prisoners (on a good day as many as seven or eight might have been executed at the same time), accompanied by the Ordinary, rode in a cart sitting on his own coffin. All along the road he received the encouragement or approbation of the mob. But no matter how popular he was, the consensus was usually that he was getting what he deserved and that he owed his audience a good show. The mob was very drunk and disorderly, and pickpockets made excellent hauls.[2] Young apprentices especially were cau-

[2] The mob riots which took place on Execution Days and the clear encouragement to crime which these spectacles provided caused the abolition in 1783 of the Procession to Tyburn. Thereafter, executions, although still performed in public, were held in front of the Old Bailey.

tioned by their masters to attend these spectacles of justice—the condemned must have seemed particularly glamorous to these overworked children. As the prisoner's cart was pulled beneath the gallows, the rope was placed around his neck; the Ordinary then listened to his last words and commended his soul to the mercy of God. Then, at the prisoner's own signal, the hangman pushed the cart from under him.

Until the "drop," an apparatus which caused the rope to break the neck of the prisoner instantly, was introduced in 1770, those hanged always strangled to death. Strangulation is a long and agonizing process, and the friends and relatives of the prisoner would frequently pull on his legs to hasten his death. After he was pronounced dead, attempts were sometimes made to revive him, which were, on rare occasions, successful. If they were not, however, his body was surrendered to his relatives —unless it was considered that his crime was of a nature serious enough to demand that his example to the public not end with his execution. If this was the case, his body was chained and locked into a small iron cage and suspended from a gallows-like pole—the gibbet—at a place appropriate to the crime for which he had been executed. Highway robbers were displayed at crossroads, pirates near docks, and traitors' heads were stuck on spikes at city gates or near public buildings.[3]

[3] Hanging was not the only means of execution; until 1790 many women capital offenders were burned at the stake. "Pressing"—placing weights of ever-increasing heaviness on the chained body of the prisoner—was practiced until late in the century for the crime of refusing to give evidence or to plead at his trial. Although stoning was not an official method of execution, a prisoner unpopular with the mob confined in the stocks as punishment stood little chance of survival.

II

The great number of crimes punishable by death
is an evidence not only of the severity of the law,
but of its lack of logic and consistency and, therefore, of its lack of justice. There were only two
legal categories to cover every variety of crime:
the felony and the misdemeanor. The felony was
punishable by death, and the misdemeanor by imprisonment or transportation to the colonies and a
number of years at hard labor. Before the Great
Revolution of 1688, there were approximately fifty
clases of felonies. During the reign of George II
(1727-1760), sixty-two are known to have been
added. The estimated total of capital offences is
one hundred and sixty by the year 1770. At the
close of the eighteenth century, there were over two
hundred.[4]

The law of England was not deliberately formu-
lated with conscious social purpose. It accumulated
capriciously, and the only object of the members
of Parliament was to serve particular and often
conflicting interests. The law tried to make up in
quantity what it lacked in system. This was particularly true of criminal law: one of the least con-
troversial issues in Parliament was the approval of
a new addition to the list of capital offences, and
was often the soap used when one hand washed the
other.

[4] The number of capital offenses is poorly documented until
the nineteenth century, and the above figures are conservative estimates.

A system of cumulative law is adequate, perhaps, in a relatively stable agricultural society. But once the authority of feudal traditions has been undermined, and many royal prerogatives pass to a parliament, the laws lose their coherence and unity, and become both inefficient and open to every kind of abuse. Urban society made new demands upon the laws of England and complicated its enforcement. The rate of crime increased as the urban population exploded. For many, crime was the only means of survival, and new crimes were invented and old ones streamlined to exploit the changing and complex conditions of life. In the absence of rationally conceived categories of crime, and standard, proportionate punishments, Parliament had only one weapon against lawlessness: the death penalty. The death penalty has never been able to discourage crime; applied as inhumanly and indiscriminately as it was by eighteenth century lawmakers, it had the effect of encouraging it. Capricious and oppressive law inspires disrespect and cynicism, especially when it is in the hands of a bureaucracy which is more interested in exploiting the weaknesses of the law for its own gain than it is in enforcing it. And since trivial and major crimes alike were often capital offences, it might well be worth the while of a miscreant to risk hanging for a sheep rather than for a lamb.

The penal system was as antiquated and inadequate as the penal code, and the increase of the number of capital offences was encouraged by the fact that the jails simply could not accommodate the great number of convicted criminals. The prisons were widely acknowledged as some of the best crime schools in the country—and this was used as an argument for the physical and social utility of executions. There was not even the most primitive notion of the possibility of reform of the criminal; physical annihilation was the only cure for his condition. Just as the chronically poor and diseased lower classes were viewed by their superiors, and by Puritan middle-class opinion in general, as lazy wretches responsible for their own condition, so the criminal was an idle, unregenerate, evil creature, who could hope for mercy from God, but certainly could not expect it from his injured countrymen.

Unfortunately for many petty crooks, the distinction between a felony and a misdemeanor was, except for the punishment, rather ambiguous. Laws were passed to meet specific incidents, and there were no constant categories distinguishing minor from major crimes. Here is a sampling of felonies and misdemeanors:

FELONY	MISDEMEANOR
To steal a sheep or a horse	To attempt the life of one's father
To consort with gypsies	
To *be* a gypsy	Premeditated perjury
Fish-pond breaking	To assault and stab a man, if without fatal result
Pocket-picking of more than 12 pence	
Cutting down trees in a garden or orchard	To commit arson on a property on which arsonist holds lease
To steal forty shillings from a house, or five shillings in a shop, "privately" (i.e., without being seen)	To steal from a shop "publically" (i.e., observed by someone)
To steal 40 shillings worth of goods on a navigable river	To steal 40 shillings worth of goods on a navigable canal

To steal fruit already gathered	To gather fruit and steal it
Breaking a pane of glass at or after 5 PM with the purpose of stealing	To break into a house at or after 4:00 AM in summer

It is hardly necessary to say that these laws, and the hundreds of others like them, were not enforced in full; had this been the case England would have suffered the longest and bloodiest reign of terror in the history of Europe. Many law-breakers went unapprehended, and judges and juries were occasionally known to perjure themselves rather than condemn obviously guilty parties for the smaller felonies. Also, more than a third of the condemned either died in prison or obtained reprieves. But the statistics which are available are quite sufficiently shocking. Although the numbers of men and women killed by their governments in the twentieth century is incomparably greater, the eighteenth century was a period of peace and internal stability, and it would be difficult, if possible to find as many people executed in any other time or place simply in the course of everyday legal proceedings, and for nonpolitical offences. Between 1749 and 1772, 1,121 people were condemned to death at the Old Bailey, and 678 were executed. Between 1771 and 1783, 467 men and women were executed in London and Middlesex. In the year 1785, 96 were executed in London alone. These figures do not, of course, include the toll for the rest of England.

The behavior of judges and juries was as irresponsible as the laws were senseless; there was a great deal of drunkenness in court, and there was unlimited and unchecked corruption. The amount of bribery was an open secret, which was condemned by some but tolerated by most. To make matters worse, a prisoner accused of any capital offence with the exception of treason was deprived of counsel, and was totally at the mercy of the court. (This was the practice until 1836.) Most criminal trials, since they were not particularly lucrative to anyone, were usually completed in a day or less. The two factors during a trial were the mood of the judge and jury, (as affected by gin and/or bribes), and the temper of the public, whose outbursts in court carried more than a little influence.

Law enforcement was implemented primarily through the informer, or "thief-taker." There was no police force, and only a few sheriffs and watchmen; these were either unequal to their tasks or unwilling to perform them, and again, more often than not, easily bribed. Informing did not carry quite the stigma it does today; it was no less dishonest than many other acceptable ways of earning a living, and often quite profitable. Jonathan Wild, who managed to advance the interests of both the law and the underworld, was highly respected—and feared—by both, and operated as both a receiver of stolen goods and a thief-taker in comfort and success for a long time. Every "wanted" criminal had a price on his head, and it is not surprising that, given the state of law-enforcement, informing became a regular business enterprise.

III

Newgate was considered to be one of the worst prisons in England, but it was substantially the same as the others, only somewhat more crowded, dirty and disease-ridden. Since it did not specialize in long-term prisoners, but only in prisoners waiting trial or execution, it tended to enforce the usual practices more quickly and extremely than other prisons. But its conditions and organization can be considered typical of the eighteenth-century prison.

The turn-key paid 1000 pounds or more annually for his office. The investment was returned many times over in profits made from the prisoners. The sale of gin was the largest single enterprise. Second was "rent," and then followed a number of fees covering every aspect of prison life.

Officially, there was some division of the prison according to the seriousness of the offence: sections for large debtors, for small debtors, for major felons and for minor felons. But Newgate was actually operated as a bizarre, hellish hotel, and the only significant distinction made among prisoners was determined by their ability to pay.

Upon entering Newgate, a "garnish" was demanded of the prisoner by his fellows, which would buy a round of drinks in the prison taproom, where gin flowed as freely and almost as cheaply as it did outside. Then, depending upon his resources, he would be assigned to a cell. The best and most expensive rooms were in "The Castle." After the failure of the Jacobite rebellion of 1715, cells in "The

Castle" were in great demand by the defeated aristocrats, and the jail keeper cleared close to 4000 pounds in less than four months. Most prisoners could not, of course, afford the high rates of "The Castle," but every kind of accommodation, down to the worst, cost something. (The cheapest bed in Newgate cost 2 shillings a week.) If the prisoner had no money at all, he was simply stripped of his clothes, deposited in the darkest, foulest hole in the establishment, heavily chained, and fed and treated in such a way as to hasten his death. But the conditions suffered by those who could pay were not very much better. The regular fare was bread and water, most prisoners were heavily chained, there were no sanitary facilities, Newgate was very overcrowded, and all suffered constant exposure to a virulent form of typhus known as "jail fever," which killed far more people than did the hangman.

The fees paid to the jailers did not end with room and board. Other sources of profit derived from the sale of candles, water, food (other than stale bread), a blanket, the privilege of approaching the sea-coal fire (if there was one), the privilege of not being whipped or tortured, and the "easement of irons." Henry Fielding, who was a magistrate as well as a novelist, characterized Newgate as a "prototype of hell" and as one of the most expensive places on earth.

IV

Eighteenth-century England was a country both conservative and violent, proud of its political liberties and its adherence to tradition. Yet it engendered corruption in its public life, luxury and profligacy among its upper classes, and squalor and crime in its lower classes.

The Glorious Revolution of 1688 succeeded in finally establishing legislative power and privilege of royalty strictly subservient to law. The liberties of which Englishmen are traditionally jealous were reserved for the propertied class, and government was managed accordingly. The great and confusing body of law which now became the standard for political and juridical action was confused, self-contradictory and, to a large extent, antiquated. A precedent could be found for almost anything, or could, given the proper influence in the right places, be established without too much trouble. The power of executive now belonged, in effect, to the Prime Minister—and the eighteenth century witnessed very strong and efficient, if somewhat ruthless, Prime Ministers in Walpole and the elder Pitt. But their function was not like that which Royalty's had been; they had to administrate, to compromise between parties, to further selected interests, and never to overstep Parliament. Old sanctioned systems of preference inherited from Tudor and Stuart England, and the body of law which was still largely feudal, provided the perfect conditions for thorough-going corruption on every level of public life. Precedence and the law provided for offices and the forms of corporate life for the various institutions, but for no limitations of power within office or safeguards against abuse of delegated power. Thus the institutions—ecclesiastic, academic, municipal—operated autonomously and for the personal aggrandizement of those who held office in them. The 'rights' of Englishmen, provided for by the absence of centralized royal control, were exercised primarily for the personal gain of those who were wealthy enough to possess them. Conservatism and propriety were to a large extent the mask and rationalization for every possible abuse. Thus the relative political stability of the period was part and parcel of its social chaos and its extremes of wealth and poverty. Resistance to change and reform did not halt the evolution of democratic and parliamentary forms and procedures; this was the time of the political ascendence of the bourgeoisie. And although corruption was not invented by the men of the eighteenth century, bureaucracy in its modern sense was, and therefore the types of corruption have a certain modern, professional touch; and crime, too, made great advances in organization and professionalism in the eighteenth century.

Laissez-faire was practiced both in politics and economics, and many merchants and landowners employed their freedom from limitation to acquire the great fortunes which later provided the capital for the Industrial Revolution. The merchants enjoyed free trade, no tariffs, and a minimum of taxation. Thousands of small freeholders were forced off their land by the enclosure movement, and emigrated to the cities, where poverty and unemployment were extreme and chronic, and the risks of crime often no greater than those of an honest living. The misery and exploitation suffered by the greater part of the English population was not without precedent at the time of the Industrial Revolution. Disease, long hours, low pay, corporal punishment, child labor—all these and more were constant conditions of eighteenth-century labor. Advances in technology were not accompanied by improvements in the overall condition of the working class; but the point to be emphasized here is that the industrial revolution did not cause these conditions; manufacturers simply took advantage of those already in existence, and changed them in degree rather than in quality. Although the early nineteenth century is famous for the injustices of its treatment of the working class, the same conditions had, for all practical purposes, existed a hundred years earlier: no reform movement emerged to dramatize the situation until that time.

The lower urban class was a potential, but not yet an actual, proletariat. They were a large group of people with poverty and discontent in common, but without any productive economic function and positive unity of interest. Rebellions occurred, but they were passionate and disorganized, and led only to bloodshed and repression. For the greater part of the time, dissatisfaction could only take the form of crime or disorderly conduct. The pursuance of pleasure and excitement became of major importance, partly in emulation of the luxury and self-indulgence of the upper classes, partly as an escape valve, and generally took the form of gambling, whoring, drinking and associated pastimes. This course often led to Newgate, and thus to the stories of crime and punishment herein chronicled.

—SANDRA LEE KERMAN

CAPTAIN JOHN KIDD,

EXECUTED FOR PIRACY.

PIRACY is an offence committed on the high seas, by villains who man and arm a vessel for the purpose of robbing fair traders. It is also piracy to rob a vessel lying in shore at anchor, or at a wharf. The river Thames, until the excellent establishment of a marine police, was infested by gangs of fresh-water pirates, who were continually rowing about, watching the homeward-bound vessels; which, whenever an opportunity offered, they boarded, and stole whatever part of their cargo they could hoist into their boats. But, of late years, the shipping there, collected from every part of the habitable globe, have lain in tolerable security against such disgraceful depredations, and the introduction of the dock system has further increased this security.

Captain John Kidd was born in the town of Greenock, in Scotland, and bred to the sea. Having quitted his native country, he resided at New York, where he became owner of a small vessel, with which he traded among the pirates, obtained a thorough knowledge of their haunts, and could give a better account of them than any other person whatever. He was neither remarkable for the excess of his courage nor for the want of it. In a word, his ruling passion appeared to be avarice; and to this was owing his connexion with the pirates. While in their company he used to converse and act as they did; yet, at other times, he would make singular professions of honesty, and intimate how easy a matter it would be to extirpate these abandoned people, and prevent their future depredations.

His frequent remarks of this kind engaged the notice of several considerable planters, who, forming a more favourable idea of him than his true character would warrant, procured him the patronage with which he was afterwards honoured. For a series of years great complaints had been made of the piracies committed in the West Indies, which had been greatly encouraged by some of the inhabitants of North America, on account of the advantage they derived from purchasing effects thus fraudulently obtained. This coming to the knowledge of King William III. he, in the year 1695, bestowed the government of New England and New York on the Earl of Bellamont, an Irish nobleman, of distinguished character and abilities, who immediately began to consider of the most effectual method to redress the evils complained of, and consulted with Colonel Levingston, a gentleman who had great property in New York, on the most feasible steps to obviate the evils so long complained of. At this juncture Captain Kidd was arrived from New York in a sloop of his own: him, therefore, the colonel mentioned to Lord Bellamont as a bold and daring man, who was very fit to be employed against the pirates, as he was perfectly well acquainted with the places which they resorted to. This plan met with the fullest approbation of his lordship, who mentioned the affair to his Majesty, and recommended it to the Board of Admiralty: but such were then the hurry and confusion of public affairs, that, though the design was approved, no steps were taken towards carrying it into execution.

Accordingly Colonel Levingstone made application to Lord Bellamont, that, as the affair would not well admit of delay, it was worthy of being undertaken by some private persons of rank and distinction, and carried into execution at their own expense, notwithstanding public encouragement was denied it. His lordship approved of this project, but it was attended with considerable difficulty: at length, however, the Lord-Chancellor Somers, the Duke of Shrewsbury, the Earl of Romney, the Earl of Oxford, and some other persons, with Colonel Levingston, and Captain Kidd, agreed to raise 6000l. for the expense of the voyage;

2

and the colonel and captain were to have a fifth of the profits of the whole undertaking.

Matters being thus far adjusted, a commission, in the usual form, was granted to Captain Kidd, to take and seize pirates, and bring them to justice; but there was no special clause or proviso to restrain his conduct or regulate the mode of his proceeding. Kidd was known to Lord Bellamont, and another gentleman presented him to Lord Romney. With regard to the other parties concerned, he was wholly unacquainted with them; and, so ill was this affair conducted, that he had no private instructions how to act, but received his sailing orders from Lord Bellamont, the purport of which was, that he should act agreeably to the letter of his commission.

Accordingly a vessel was purchased and manned, and received the name of the Adventure Galley; and in this Captain Kidd sailed for New York towards the close of the year 1695, and in his passage made prize of a French ship. From New York he sailed to the Madeira Islands, thence to Bonavista and St. Jago, and from this last place to Madagascar. He now began to cruise at the entrance of the Red Sea; but, not being successful in those latitudes, he sailed to Calicut, and there took a ship of one hundred and fifty tons' burden, which he carried to Madagascar, and disposed of there. Having sold this prize he again put to sea, and, at the expiration of five weeks, took the Quedah Merchant, a ship of above four hundred tons' burden, the master of which was an Englishman, named Wright, who had two Dutch mates on board, and a French gunner; but the crew consisted of Moors, natives of Africa, and were about ninety in number. He carried the ship to St. Mary's, near Madagascar, where he burnt the Adventure Galley, belonging to his owners, and divided the lading of the Quedah Merchant with his crew, taking forty shares to himself.

They then went on board the last-mentioned ship,

and sailed for the West Indies. It is uncertain whether the inhabitants of the West India Islands knew that Kidd was a pirate, but he was refused refreshments at Anguilla and St. Thomas's, and therefore sailed to Mona, between Porto Rico and Hispaniola, where, through the management of an Englishman, named Bolton, he obtained a supply of provisions from Curaçoa. He now bought a sloop of Bolton, in which he stowed great part of his ill-gotten effects, and left the Quedah Merchant, with eighteen of the ship's company, in Bolton's care. While at St. Mary's, ninety men of Kidd's crew left him, and went on board the Mocha Merchant, an East India ship, which had just then commenced pirate.

Kidd now sailed in the sloop, and touched at several places, where he disposed of a great part of his cargo, and then steered for Boston, in New England. In the interim Bolton sold the Quedah Merchant to the Spaniards, and immediately sailed as a passenger in a ship for Boston, where he arrived a considerable time before Kidd, and gave information of what had happened to Lord Bellamont. Kidd, therefore, on his arrival, was seized by order of his lordship, when all he had to urge in his defence was, that he thought the Quedah Merchant was a lawful prize, as she was manned with Moors, though there was no kind of proof that this vessel had committed any act of piracy.

Upon this the Earl of Bellamont immediately dispatched an account to England of the circumstances that had arisen, and requested that a ship might be sent for Kidd, who had committed several other notorious acts of piracy. The ship Rochester was accordingly sent to bring him to England; but this vessel, happening to be disabled, was obliged to return : a circumstance which greatly increased a public clamour which had for a time subsisted respecting this affair, and which, no doubt, took its rise from party prejudice. It was carried to such a height, that the

4

members of parliament for several places were instructed to move the House for an inquiry into the affair; and accordingly it was moved, in the House of Commons, that ' The letters-patent granted to the Earl of Bellamont and others, respecting the goods taken from pirates, were dishonourable to the king, against the law of nations, contrary to the laws and statutes of this realm, an invasion of property, and destructive to commerce.' Though a negative was put on this motion, yet the enemies of Lord Somers and the Earl of Oxford continued to charge those noblemen with giving countenance to pirates; and it was even insinuated that the Earl of Bellamont was not less culpable than the actual offenders. Another motion was accordingly made in the House of Commons, to address his majesty that ' Kidd might not be tried till the next session of parliament; and that the Earl of Bellamont might be directed to send home all examinations and other papers relative to the affair.' This motion was carried, and the King complied with the request which was made.

As soon as Kidd arrived in England, he was sent for, and examined at the bar of the House of Commons, with a view to fix part of his guilt on the parties who had been concerned in sending him on the expedition; but nothing arose to criminate any of those distinguished persons. Kidd, who was in some degree intoxicated, made a very contemptible appearance at the bar of the House; on which a member, who had been one of the most earnest to have him examined, violently exclaimed, ' This fellow! I thought he had been only a knave, but unfortunately he happens to be a fool likewise.' Kidd was at length tried at the Old Bailey, and was convicted on the clearest evidence; but neither at that time nor afterwards charged any of his employers with being privy to his infamous proceedings.

He suffered, with one of his companions (Darby Mullins), at Execution Dock, on the 23d of May, 1701. After Kidd had been tied up to the gallows, the rope

5

broke,* and he fell to the ground; but being immediately tied up again, the ordinary, who had before exhorted him, desired to speak with him once more; and, on this second application, entreated him to make the most careful use of the few further moments thus providentially allotted him for the final preparation of his soul to meet its important change. These exhortations appeared to have the wished-for effect; and he was left, professing his charity to all the world, and his hopes of salvation through the merits of his Redeemer.

Thus ended the life of Captain Kidd, a man who, if he had entertained a proper regard to the welfare of the public, or even to his own advantage, might have become an useful member of society, instead of a disgrace to it. The opportunities he had obtained of acquiring a complete knowledge of the haunts of the pirates rendered him one of the most proper men in the world to have extirpated this nest of villains; but his own avarice defeated the generous views of some of the greatest and most distinguished men of the age in which he lived. Hence we may learn the destructive nature of avarice, which generally counteracts all its own purposes. Captain Kidd might have acquired a fortune, and rendered a capital service to his country, in a point the most essential to its interests; but he appeared to be dead to all those generous sensations which do honour to humanity, and materially injured his country, while he was bringing final disgrace on himself.

The story of this wretched malefactor will effectually impress on the mind of the reader the truth of the old observation, that ' Honesty is the best policy.'

* In cases of this distressing nature, and which hath often happened to the miserable sufferer, the sheriff ought to be punished. It is his duty to carry the sentence of the law into execution, and there can be no plea for not providing a rope of sufficient strength. In such a case as the last, it is in fact a double execution, inflicting unnecessary torments, both of body and mind, on the already too-wretched culprit.

MARY YOUNG, *alias* JENNY DIVER,

WE cannot expect to present to our readers a character more skilled in the various arts of imposition and robbery than that of Mary Young. Her depredations, executed with the courage of a man and the softer deceptions of an artful female, surpass any thing which we have as yet come to, in our researches into crimes and punishments.

Mary Young was born in the north of Ireland: her parents were in indigent circumstances; and they dying while she was in a state of infancy, she had no recollection of them.

At about ten years of age she was taken into the family of an ancient gentlewoman, who had known her father and mother, and who caused her to be instructed in reading, writing, and needle-work; and in the latter she attained to a proficiency unusual to girls of her age.

Soon after she had arrived at her fifteenth year, a young man, servant to a gentleman who lived in the same neighbourhood, made pretensions of love to her; but the old lady, being apprized of his views, declared that she would not consent to their marriage, and positively forbade him to repeat his visits at her house.

Notwithstanding the great care and tenderness with which she was treated, Mary formed the resolution of deserting her generous benefactor, and of directing her course towards the metropolis of England; and the only obstacle to this design was the want of money for her support till she could follow some honest means of earning a subsistence.

She had no strong prepossession in favour of the young man who had made a declaration of love to

7

her; but, determining to make his passion subservient to the purpose she had conceived, promised to marry him on condition of his taking her to London. He joyfully embraced this proposal, and immediately engaged for a passage in a vessel bound for Liverpool.

A short time before the vessel was to sail the young man robbed his master of a gold watch and eighty guineas, and then joined the companion of his flight, who was already on board the ship, vainly imagining that his infamously acquired booty would contribute to the happiness he should enjoy with his expected bride. The ship arrived at the destined port in two days; and Mary being indisposed in consequence of her voyage, her companion hired a lodging in the least frequented part of the town, where they lived a short time in the character of man and wife, but avoiding all intercourse with their neighbours, the man being apprehensive that measures would be pursued for rendering him amenable to justice.

Mary being restored to health, they agreed for a passage in a waggon that was to set out for London in a few days. On the day preceding that fixed for their departure they accidentally called at a public house, and the man being observed by a messenger dispatched in pursuit of him from Ireland, he was immediately taken into custody. Mary, who, a few hours before his apprehension, had received ten guineas from him, voluntarily accompanied him to the mayor's house, where he acknowledged himself guilty of the crime alleged against him, but without giving the least intimation that she was an accessary in his guilt. He being committed to prison, Mary sent him all his clothes, and part of the money she had received from him, and the next day took her place in the waggon for London. In a short time her companion was sent to Ireland, where he was tried, and condemned to suffer death; but his sentence was changed to that of transportation.

Soon after her arrival in London Mary contracted an acquaintance with one of her countrywomen, named Anne Murphy, by whom she was invited to partake of a lodging in Long Acre. Here she endeavoured to obtain a livelihood by her needle; but, not being able to procure sufficient employment, in a little time her situation became truly deplorable.

Murphy intimated to her that she could introduce her to a mode of life that would prove exceedingly lucrative; adding, that the most profound secrecy was required. The other expressed an anxious desire of learning the means of extricating herself from the difficulties under which she laboured, and made a solemn declaration that she would never divulge what Murphy should communicate. In the evening, Murphy introduced her to a number of men and women, assembled in a kind of club, near St. Giles's. These people gained their living by cutting off women's pockets, and stealing watches, &c. from men, in the avenues of the theatres, and at other places of public resort; and, on the recommendation of Murphy, they admitted Mary a member of the society.

After Mary's admission they dispersed, in order to pursue their illegal occupation; and the booty obtained that night consisted of eighty pounds in cash, and a valuable gold watch. As Mary was not yet acquainted with the art of thieving, she was not admitted to an equal share of the night's produce; but it was agreed that she should have ten guineas. She now regularly applied two hours every day in qualifying herself for an expert thief, by attending to the instructions of experienced practitioners; and, in a short time, she was distinguished as the most ingenious and successful adventurer of the whole gang.

A young fellow of genteel appearance, who was a member of the club, was singled out by Mary as the partner of her bed; and they cohabited for a considerable time as husband and wife.

9

In a few months our heroine became so expert in her profession as to acquire great consequence among her associates, who, as we conceive, distinguished her by the appellation of Jenny Diver on account of her remarkable dexterity; and by that name we shall call her in the succeeding pages of this narrative.

Jenny, accompanied by one of her female accomplices, joined the crowd at the entrance of a place of worship in the Old Jewry, where a popular divine was to preach, and, observing a young gentleman with a diamond ring on his finger, she held out her hand, which he kindly received in order to assist her: at this juncture she contrived to get possession of the ring without the knowledge of the owner; after which she slipped behind her companion, and heard the gentleman say, that, as there was no probability of gaining admittance, he would return. Upon his leaving the meeting he missed his ring, and mentioned his loss to the persons who were near him, adding that he suspected it to be stolen by a woman whom he had endeavoured to assist in the crowd; but, as the thief was unknown, she escaped.

The above robbery was considered as such an extraordinary proof of Jenny's superior address, that her associates determined to allow her an equal share of all their booties, even though she was not present when they were obtained.

In a short time after the above exploit she procured a pair of false hands and arms to be made, and concealed her real ones under her clothes; she then, putting something beneath her stays to make herself appear as if in a state of pregnancy, repaired on a Sunday evening to the place of worship above mentioned in a sedan chair, one of the gang going before to procure a seat among the genteeler part of the congregation, and another attending in the character of a footman.

Jenny being seated between two elderly ladies, each

of whom had a gold watch by her side, she conducted herself with great seeming devotion; but, the service being nearly concluded, she seized the opportunity, when the ladies were standing up, of stealing their watches, which she delivered to an accomplice in an adjoining pew. The devotions being ended, the congregation were preparing to depart, when the ladies discovered their loss, and a violent clamour ensued. One of the injured parties exclaimed ' That her watch must have been taken either by the devil or the pregnant woman! ' on which the other said, ' She could vindicate the pregnant lady, whose hands she was sure had not been removed from her lap during the whole time of her being in the pew.'

Flushed with the success of the above adventure, our heroine determined to pursue her good fortune; and, as another sermon was to be preached the same evening, she adjourned to an adjacent public house, where, without either pain or difficulty, she soon reduced the protuberance of her waist, and, having entirely changed her dress, she returned to the meeting, where she had not remained long before she picked a gentleman's pocket of a gold watch, with which she escaped unsuspected.

Her accomplices also were industrious and successful; for, on a division of the booty obtained this evening, they each received thirty guineas. Jenny had now obtained an ascendency over the whole gang, who, conscious of her superior skill in the arts of thieving, came to a resolution of yielding an exact obedience to her directions.

Jenny again assumed the appearance of a pregnant woman, and, attended by an accomplice as a footman, went towards St. James's Park on a day when the king was going to the House of Lords; and, there being a great number of persons between the Park and Spring Gardens, she purposely slipped down, and was instantly surrounded by many of both sexes, who were

11

emulous to afford her assistance; but, affecting to be in violent pain, she intimated to them that she was desirous of remaining on the ground till she should be somewhat recovered. As she expected, the crowd increased, and her pretended footman, and a female accomplice, were so industrious as to obtain two diamond girdle-buckles, a gold watch, a gold snuff-box, and two purses, containing together upwards of forty guineas.

The girdle-buckles, watch, and snuff-box, were the following day advertised, a considerable reward was offered, and a promise given that no questions should be asked the party who should restore the property. Anne Murphy offered to carry the things to the place mentioned in the advertisement, saying the reward offered exceeded what they would produce by sale: but to this Jenny objected, observing that she might be traced, and the association utterly ruined. She called a meeting of the whole gang, and informed them that she was of opinion that it would be more prudent to sell the things, even at one half of their real value, than to return them to the owners for the sake of the reward; as, if they pursued the latter measure, they would subject themselves to great hazard of being apprehended. Her associates coincided entirely in Jenny's sentiments, and the property was taken to Duke's Place, and there sold to a Jew.

Two of the gang being confined to their lodgings by illness, Jenny, and the man with whom she cohabited, generally went in company in search of adventures. They went together to Burr Street, Wapping, and, observing a genteel house, the man, who acted as Jenny's footman, knocked at the door, and, saying that his mistress was on a sudden taken extremely ill, begged she might be admitted: this was readily complied with, and, while the mistress of the house and her maid-servant were gone up stairs for such things as they imagined would afford relief to the supposed sick woman, she opened a drawer, and stole sixty guineas; and after this, while the mistress was holding a smelling-bottle to her nose, she picked her pocket of a purse, which, however, did not contain money to any considerable amount. In the mean time the pretended footman, who had been ordered into the kitchen, stole six silver table-spoons, a pepper-box, and a salt-cellar. Jenny, pretending to be somewhat recovered, expressed the most grateful acknowledgments to the lady, and, saying she was the wife of a capital merchant in Thames Street, invited her in the most pressing terms to dinner on an appointed day, and then went away in a hackney-coach, which, by her order, had been called to the door by her pretended servant.

She practised a variety of felonies of a similar nature in different parts of the metropolis and its environs; but the particulars of the above transaction being inserted in the newspapers, people were so effectually cautioned, that our adventurer was under the necessity of employing her invention upon the discovery of other methods of committing depredations on the public.

The parties whose illness we have mentioned being recovered, it was resolved that the whole gang should go to Bristol, in search of adventures, during the fair which is held in that city every summer; but, being unacquainted with the place, they deemed it good policy to admit into their society a man who had long subsisted there by villainous practices.

Being arrived at the place of destination, Jenny and Murphy assumed the characters of merchants' wives, the new member and another of the gang appeared as country traders, and our heroine's favourite retained his former character of footman. They took lodgings at different inns, and agreed that, if any one of them should be apprehended, the others should endeavour to procure their release by appearing to their characters, and representing them as people of reputation in London. They had arrived at such a proficiency in their illegal occupation, that they were almost certain of accomplishing every scheme they suggested; and, when it was inconvenient to make use of words, they were able to convey their meaning to each other by winks, nods, and other intimations.

Being one day in the fair, they observed a west-country clothier giving a sum of money to his servant, and heard him direct the man to deposit it in a bureau. They followed the servant, and one of them fell down before him, expecting that he would also fall, and that, as there was a great crowd, the money might be easily secured. Though the man fell into the snare, they were not able to obtain their expected booty, and therefore had recourse to the following stratagem: one of the gang asked whether his master had not lately ordered him to carry home a sum of money; to which the other replied in the affirmative: the sharper then told him he must return to his master, who had purchased some goods, and waited to pay for them.

The countryman followed him to Jenny's lodging, and, being introduced to her, she desired him to be seated, saying his master was gone on some business in the neighbourhood, but had left orders for him to wait till his return. She urged him to drink a glass of wine, but the poor fellow repeatedly declined her offers with awkward simplicity, the pretended foot-man having taught him to believe her a woman of great wealth and consequence. However, her encouraging solicitations conquered his bashfulness, and he drank till he became intoxicated. Being conducted into another apartment, he was soon fast locked in the arms of sleep, and, while in that situation, he was robbed of the money he had received from his master, which proved to be a hundred pounds.

14

They were no sooner in possession of the cash, than they discharged the demand of the innkeeper, and set out in the first stage for London.

Soon after their return to town Jenny and her associates went to London Bridge in the dusk of the evening, and, observing a lady standing at a door to avoid the carriages, a number of which were passing, one of the men went up to her, and, under pretence of giving her assistance, seized both her hands, which he held till her accomplices had rifled her pockets of a gold snuff-box, a silver case containing a set of instruments, and thirty guineas in cash.

On the following day, as Jenny, and an accomplice, in the character of a footman, were walking through Change Alley, she picked a gentleman's pocket of a bank-note for two hundred pounds, for which she received one hundred and thirty from a Jew, with whom the gang had very extensive connexions.

Our heroine now hired a real footman; and her favourite, who had long acted in that character, assumed the appearance of a gentleman. She hired lodgings in the neighbourhood of Covent Garden, that she might more conveniently attend the theatres. She proposed to her associates to reserve a tenth part of the general produce for the support of such of the gang as might, through illness, be rendered incapable of following their iniquitous occupations; and to this they readily assented.

Jenny dressed herself in an elegant manner, and went to the theatre one evening when the king was to be present; and, during the performance, she attracted the particular attention of a young gentleman of fortune from Yorkshire, who declared, in the most passionate terms, that she had made an absolute conquest of his heart, and earnestly solicited the favour of attending her home. She at first declined a compliance, saying she was newly married, and that the appearance of a stranger might alarm her husband.

15

At length she yielded to his entreaty, and they went together in a hackney-coach, which set the young gentleman down in the neighbourhood where Jenny lodged, after he had obtained an appointment to visit her in a few days, when she said her husband would be out of town.

Upon Jenny's joining her companions, she informed them that while she remained at the playhouse she was only able to steal a gold snuff-box, and they appeared to be much dissatisfied on account of her ill success; but their good humour returned upon learning the circumstances of the adventure with the young gentleman, which they had no doubt would prove exceedingly profitable.

The day of appointment being arrived, two of the gang appeared equipped in elegant liveries, and Anne Murphy acted as waiting-maid. The gentleman came in the evening, having a gold-headed cane in his hand, a sword with a gold hilt by his side, and wearing a gold watch in his pocket, and a diamond ring on his finger.

Being introduced to her bed-chamber, she contrived to steal her lover's ring; and he had not been many minutes undressed before Anne Murphy rapped at the door, which being opened, she said, with an appearance of the utmost consternation, that her master was returned from the country. Jenny, affecting to be under a violent agitation of spirits, desired the gentleman to cover himself entirely with the bed-clothes, saying she would convey his apparel into another room, so that, if her husband came there, nothing would appear to awaken his suspicion; adding, that under pretence of indisposition she would prevail upon her husband to sleep in another bed, and then return to the arms of her lover.

The clothes being removed, a consultation was held, when it was agreed by the gang that they should immediately pack up all their moveables, and decamp

16

with their booty, which, exclusive of the cane, watch, sword, and ring, amounted to a hundred guineas.

The amorous youth waited in a state of the utmost impatience till morning, when he rang the bell, which brought the people of the house to the chamber-door; but they could not gain admittance, the fair fugitive having turned the lock, and taken away the key; but, the door being forced open, an eclaircissement ensued. The gentleman represented in what manner he had been treated; but the people of the house were deaf to his expostulations, and threatened to circulate the adventure throughout the town unless he would indemnify them for the loss they had sustained. Rather than hazard the exposure of his character he agreed to discharge the debt Jenny had contracted; and dispatched a messenger for clothes and money, that he might take leave of a house of which he had sufficient reason to regret having been a temporary inhabitant.

Our heroine's share of the produce of the above adventure amounted to seventy pounds. This infamous association was now become so notorious a pest to society, that they judged it necessary to leave the metropolis, where they were apprehensive they could not long remain concealed from justice. They practised a variety of stratagems with great success in different parts of the country; but, upon re-visiting London, Jenny was committed to Newgate on a charge of having picked a gentleman's pocket; for which she was sentenced to transportation.

She remained in the above prison nearly four months, during which time she employed a considerable sum in the purchase of stolen effects. When she went on board the transport-vessel, she shipped a quantity of goods nearly sufficient to load a waggon. The property she possessed ensured her great respect, and every possible convenience and accommodation during the voyage; and, on her arrival in Virginia, she disposed of her goods, and for some time lived in great splendour and elegance.

She soon found that America was a country where she could expect but little emolument from the practices she had so successfully followed in England; and therefore she employed every art she was mistress of to ingratiate herself into the esteem of a young gentleman who was preparing to embark on board a vessel bound for the port of London. He became much enamoured of her, and brought her to England; but, while the ship lay at Gravesend, she robbed him of all the property she could get into her possession, and, pretending indisposition, intimated a desire of going on shore, in which her admirer acquiesced; but she was no sooner on land than she made a precipitate retreat.

She now travelled through several parts of the country, and by her usual wicked practices obtained many considerable sums. At length she returned to London, but was not able to find her former accomplices.

She now frequented the Royal Exchange, the theatres, London Bridge, and other places of public resort, and committed innumerable depredations on the public. Being detected in picking a gentleman's pocket on London Bridge, she was taken before a magistrate, to whom she declared that her name was Jane Webb, and by that appellation she was committed to Newgate.

On her trial, a gentleman, who had detected her in the very act of picking the prosecutor's pocket, deposed that a person had applied to him, offering fifty pounds, on condition that he should not appear in support of the prosecution: and a lady swore that, on the day she committed the offence for which she stood indicted, she saw her pick the pockets of more than twenty different people. The record of her former conviction was not produced in Court; and, therefore, she was arraigned for privately stealing;

and, on the clearest evidence, the jury pronounced her guilty. The property being valued at less than one shilling, she was sentenced to transportation.

A twelvemonth had not elapsed before she returned from transportation a second time; and, on her arrival in London, renewed her former practices.

A lady going from Sherborne Lane to Walbrook was accosted by a man, who took her hand, seemingly as if to assist her in crossing some planks that were placed over the gutter for the convenience of passengers; but he squeezed her fingers with so much force as to give her great pain, and in the mean time Jenny picked her pocket of thirteen shillings and a penny. The gentlewoman, conscious of being robbed, seized the thief by the gown, and she was immediately conducted to the Compter. She was examined the next day by the lord mayor, who committed her to Newgate in order for trial.

At the ensuing sessions at the Old Bailey she was tried on an indictment for privately stealing, and the jury brought in the verdict ' Guilty; ' in consequence of which she received sentence of death.

After conviction Jenny seemed sincerely to repent of the course of iniquity in which she had so long persisted, punctually attending prayers in the chapel, and employing great part of her time in private devotions. The day preceding that on which she was executed she sent for the woman who nursed her child, then about three years old, and, after informing her that there was a person who would pay for the infant's maintenance, earnestly entreated that it might be carefully instructed in the duties of religion, and guarded from all temptations to wickedness; and then, acknowledging that she had long been a daring offender against the laws both of God and man, and entreating the woman to pray for the salvation of her soul, she bade her farewell, apparently deeply impressed with the sentiments of contrition.

On the following morning she appeared to be in a serene state of mind; but, being brought into the press-yard, the executioner approached to put the halter about her, when her fortitude abated: in a short time, however, her spirits became again tolerably composed.

She was conveyed to Tyburn in a mourning-coach on the 18th of March, 1740, being attended by a clergyman, to whom she declared her firm belief in all the principles of the Protestant religion.

At the place of execution, having employed a considerable time in fervent prayer, her life was resigned a sacrifice to those laws which she had most daringly violated; and her remains were, by her own particular desire, interred in St. Pancras churchyard.

We may, perhaps, fix the most dangerous period of life to be between the years of sixteen and twenty. As we approach towards maturity we grow impatient of control, regardless of all advice that does not flatter the prevailing humour, and direct all our attention to a state of independence, which youthful imagination represents as the summit of human felicity, where no inconvenience can obtrude but such as may, without difficulty, be repelled by the mere efforts of our own resolution.

The advice of a parent sinks into the mind with double weight; but we should allow the due force to such as is offered by those who are unconnected with us in the ties of blood. If the conduct that is recommended to us points to the happiness of life, what folly is it to submit to the suggestions of idle inclination, the indulgence of which can yield but a slight and temporary gratification, and may, perhaps, prove the source of severe and lasting regret!

There are those who censure the laws of these kingdoms as being of too sanguinary a complexion. Be it admitted that there is something extremely dreadful in the idea of depriving a fellow-creature of existence at a time when the weight of his sins is sufficient, without the Divine assistance, to sink him into everlasting perdition: but, as partial favour must always give way to considerations for the public good, it should be remembered that the lives of individuals are not sacrificed so much for the sake of punishing them for the offences of which they have been guilty, as with a view of making them examples for the discontinuance of vice. Justice may for a time be eluded, and no inconvenience may have been sustained by the injured party, who, though entertaining no private animosity, nay, even tenderly compassionating the offender, will be induced, by his regard to the public, to enforce the law. How dangerous, then, must be the situation of those who have been guilty of acts of delinquency! The dread of a violent and disgraceful death, together with all the horrors of conscious guilt, must continually rush upon their minds, and render them miserable beyond the power of expression.

Persons who, having infringed the laws of their country, are committed to prison, too frequently are known to employ their time in a very unprofitable manner. How can this conduct be accounted for but by supposing that they cherish the expectation of an acquittal? No circumstances in life are so desperate as to exclude the hope of a favourable change of fortune. In support of this assertion it need only be said, that scarce an instance can be produced where the most notorious offender has, even at the place of execution, declined all thoughts of a reprieve.

To consider the terrible situation of a condemned prisoner must unquestionably prove distressing, in a peculiar degree, to a humane mind. The unhappy object stands tottering on the verge of eternity, and the dreadful prospect wholly incapacitates him for making that preparation which is necessary to so important a change; for it is a reasonable supposition that, under such alarming circumstances, the mind must be so violently agitated as to be deprived of the power of exerting its usual functions; and there is too much cause to apprehend that, when repentance is thus long delayed, there will be but a feeble support for the hope of its efficacy.

Spurling, a Turnkey, shot by Johnson, in the Old Bailey.

WILLIAM JOHNSON AND JANE HOUSDEN,

EXECUTED FOR THE MURDER OF MR. SPURLING.

THROUGHOUT the whole annals of our Criminal Chronology, though the denial of culprits condemned on the clearest evidence of their guilt is by far too frequently recorded, we cannot adduce an instance similar to the following dying declarations of innocence:

William Johnson, one of these unrelenting sinners, was a native of Northamptonshire, where he served his time to a butcher, and, removing to London, opened a shop in Newport Market; but, business not succeeding to his expectation, he took a house in Long Acre, and commenced corn-chandler: in this business he was likewise unsuccessful, on which he sold his stock in trade, and took a public house near Christ Church, in Surrey. Being equally unsuccessful as a victualler, he sailed to Gibraltar, where he was appointed a mate to

23

one of the surgeons of the garrison; in short, he appears to have possessed a genius suited to a variety of employments. Having saved some money at Gibraltar, he came back to his native country, where he soon spent it, and then had recourse to the highway for a supply. Being apprehended in consequence of one of his robberies, he was convicted, but received a pardon. Previous to this he had been acquainted with one Jane Housden, the other hardened wretch, who had been tried and convicted of coining, but also obtained a pardon. It was not long after this pardon (which was procured by great interest) before Housden was again in custody for a similar offence. On the day that she was to be tried, and just as she was brought down to the bar of the Old Bailey, Johnson called to see her; but Mr. Spurling, the head turnkey, telling him that he could not speak to her till her trial was ended, he instantly drew a pistol, and shot Spurling dead on the spot, in the presence of the court, and all the persons attending to hear the trials; Mrs. Housden at the same time encouraging him in the perpetration of this singular murder. The event had no sooner happened than the judges, thinking it unnecessary to proceed on the trial of the woman for coining, ordered both the parties to be tried for the murder; and there being such a number of witnesses to the deed, they were almost immediately convicted, and received sentence of death. From this time to that of their execution, which took place September 19th, 1712, and even at the place of their death, they behaved as if they were wholly insensible of the enormity of the crime which they had committed; and, notwithstanding the publicity of their offence, to which there were so many witnesses, they had the confidence to deny it to the last moment of their lives: nor did they show any signs of compunction for their former sins.—After hanging the usual time, Johnson was hung in chains near Holloway, between Islington and Highgate.

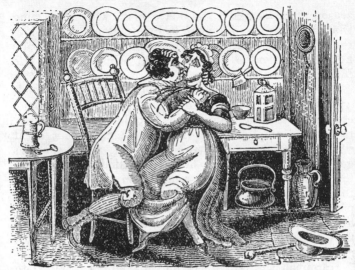

Clarke, whilst in the act of embracing a young Woman, cuts her Throat.

MATTHEW CLARKE,

EXECUTED FOR MURDER.

THIS offender was the son of poor persons at St. Albans, and brought up as a plough-boy; but, being too idle to follow his business, he sauntered about the country, and committed frequent robberies, spending among women the money he obtained in this illegal manner.

Clarke had art enough to engage the affections of a number of young women, to some of whom he promised marriage; and he seems to have intended to have kept his word with one of them, and went with her to London to tie the nuptial knot; but, going into a goldsmith's shop to buy the ring, he said he had forgot to supply himself with money, but would go into the country and fetch it.

The young woman staid in town while he went to Wilsden Green, with a view to commit a robbery, that he might replenish his pocket. As it was now the season of hay-making, he met a man, who, wondering that he should be idle, gave him employment. Besides the business of farming, his employer kept a public house, and had a servant maid, whom Clarke had formerly courted.

The villain, leaving his fellow-labourers in the field, went to the house, and, finding only the girl at home, conversed with her some time; but, having determined to rob his employer, he thought he could not do it securely without murdering her; and, while she was gone to draw him some beer, he pulled out his knife for this horrid purpose; and, when she entered the room, he got up to kiss her, thinking to have then perpetrated the deed, but his conscience prevented him: on this he sat down, and talked with her some time longer; when he got up, and, again kissing her, cut her throat in the same instant.

Hereupon she fell down, and attempted to crawl to the door, while the blood streamed from her throat; on which the villain cut her neck to the bone, and, robbing the house of a small sum, ran off towards London, under all the agonizing tortures of a wounded conscience.

Tyburn being in his way to town, he was so terrified at the sight of the gallows, that he went back a considerable distance, till, meeting a waggon, he offered his service in driving, thinking that his being in employment might prevent his being suspected in case of a pursuit. But he had not gone far before some persons rode up, and asked him if he had seen a man who might be suspected of a murder. He seemed so terrified by the question that the parties could not help noticing his agitation, and, on a close inspection, they found some congealed blood on his clothes, to account for which he said he had quarrelled and fought with a soldier on the road.

Being taken into custody, he soon acknowledged his crime, and, being carried before a magistrate, he was committed to Newgate; and, when brought to trial, he pleaded guilty: in consequence of which he was executed at Tyburn on the 28th of July, 1721, and then hung in chains near the spot where he committed the murder.

There is something dreadfully enormous in the crime for which this man suffered. When under sentence of death he was one of the most miserable wretches that ever endured a situation so calamitous. Nor is this to be wondered at; for the murder he committed was one of the most unprovoked imaginable. It is probable, from the affection the poor girl had for him, that she would have lent him a greater sum than he obtained by cutting her throat.

His terrors at the sight of the gallows should teach those who are prompted to iniquity to avoid all crimes that may lead to a fatal end. The wicked can never be happy; and it is only by a life of integrity, virtue, and piety, that we can hope for the blessing of God, the applause of a good conscience, and ' that peace of mind which passeth all understanding.'

Sheppard, after escaping from Newgate, persuades a Shoemaker to knock his Irons off

JOHN SHEPPARD,

EXECUTED FOR HIGHWAY ROBBERY.

JOHN SHEPPARD was born in Spitalfields, in the year
1702. His father, who was a carpenter, bore the
character of an honest man; yet he had another son,
named Thomas, who, as well as Jack, turned out a
thief.

The father dying while the boys were very young,
they were left to the care of the mother, who placed
Jack at a school in Bishopsgate Street, where he
remained two years, and was then put apprentice to a
carpenter. He behaved with decency in this place for
about four years, when, frequenting the Black Lion
alehouse, in Drury Lane, he became acquainted with
some abandoned women, among whom the principal

was Elizabeth Lyon, otherwise called Edgworth Bess, from the town of Edgworth, where she was born.

While he continued to work as a carpenter, he often committed robberies in the houses where he was employed, stealing tankards, spoons, and other articles, which he carried to Edgworth Bess; but, not being suspected of having committed these robberies, he at length resolved to commence housebreaker.

Exclusive of Edgworth Bess, he was acquainted with a woman named Maggot, who persuaded him to rob the house of Mr. Bains, a piece broker, in White Horse Yard; and Jack, having brought away a piece of fustian from thence, which he deposited in his trunk, went afterwards at midnight, and, taking the bars out of the cellar-window, entered, and stole goods and money to the amount of 22l. which he carried to Maggot.

As Sheppard did not go home that night, nor the following day, his master suspected that he had made bad connexions, and, searching his trunk, found the piece of fustian that had been stolen; but Sheppard, hearing of this, broke open his master's house in the night, and carried off the fustian, lest it should be brought in evidence against him.

Sheppard's master sending intelligence to Mr. Bains of what had happened, the latter looked over his goods, and, missing such a piece of fustian as had been described to him, suspected that Sheppard must have been the robber, and determined to have him taken into custody; but Jack, hearing of the affair, went to him, and threatened a prosecution for scandal, alleging that he had received the piece of fustian from his mother, who bought it for him in Spitalfields. The mother, with a view to screen her son, declared that what he had asserted was true, though she could not point out the place where she had made the purchase. Though this story was not credited, Mr. Bains did not take any farther steps in the affair.

Sheppard's master seemed willing to think well of him, and he remained some time longer in the family; but, after associating himself with the worst of company, and frequently staying out the whole night, his master and he quarrelled, and the headstrong youth totally absconded in the last year of his apprenticeship, and became connected with a set of villains of Jonathan Wild's gang.

Jack now worked as a journeyman carpenter, with a view to the easier commission of robbery; and, being employed to assist in repairing the house of a gentleman in May Fair, he took an opportunity of carrying off a sum of money, a quantity of plate, some gold rings, and four suits of clothes.

Not long after this Edgworth Bess was apprehended, and lodged in the round-house of the parish of St. Giles's, where Sheppard went to visit her, and the beadle refusing to admit him, he knocked him down, broke open the door, and carried her off in triumph; an exploit which acquired him a high degree of credit with the women of abandoned character.

In the month of August, 1723, Thomas Sheppard, the brother of Jack, was indicted at the Old Bailey for two petty offences, and, being convicted, was burnt in the hand. Soon after his discharge, he prevailed on Jack to lend him forty shillings, and take him as a partner in his robberies. The first act they committed in concert was the robbing of a public house in Southwark, whence they carried off some money and wearing apparel; but Jack permitted his brother to reap the whole advantage of this booty.

Not long after this, the brothers, in conjunction with Edgworth Bess, broke open the shop of Mrs. Cook, a linen-draper in Clare Market, and carried off goods to the value of 55*l*.; and in less than a fortnight afterwards stole some articles from the house of Mr. Phillips, in Drury Lane.

Tom Sheppard, going to sell some of the goods stolen

at Mrs. Cook's, was apprehended, and committed to Newgate; when, in the hope of being admitted an evidence, he impeached his brother and Edgworth Bess; but they were sought for in vain.

At length James Sykes, otherwise called Hell and Fury, one of Sheppard's companions, meeting with him in St. Giles's, enticed him into a public house, in the hope of receiving a reward for apprehending him; and, while they were drinking, Sykes sent for a constable, who took Jack into custody, and carried him before a magistrate, who, after a short examination, sent him into St. Giles's round-house; but he broke through the roof of that place, and made his escape in the night.

Within a short time after this, as Sheppard and an associate, named Benson, were crossing Leicester Fields, the latter endeavoured to pick a gentleman's pocket of his watch; but, failing in the attempt, the gentleman called out 'A pickpocket!' on which Sheppard was taken, and lodged in St. Ann's round-house, where he was visited by Edgworth Bess, who was detained on suspicion of being one of his accomplices.

On the following day they were carried before a magistrate; and some persons appearing who charged them with felonies, they were committed to the new prison; and, as they passed for husband and wife, they were permitted to lodge together in a room known by the name of Newgate ward.

Sheppard being visited by several of his acquaintance, some of them furnished him with implements to make his escape; and, early in the morning, a few days after his commitment, he filed off his fetters, and, having made a hole in the wall, he took an iron bar and a wooden one out of the window; but, as the height from which he was to descend was twenty-five feet, he tied a blanket and sheet together, and, making one of them fast to a bar in the window, Edgworth Bess first descended, and Jack followed her.

Having reached the yard, they had still a wall of twenty-two feet high to scale; but, climbing up by the locks and bolts of the great gate, they got quite out of the prison, and effected a perfect escape.

Sheppard's fame was greatly celebrated among the lower order of people by this exploit; and the thieves of St. Giles's courted his company. Among the rest, one Charles Grace, a cooper, begged that he would take him as an associate in his robberies, alleging, as a reason for this request, that the girl he kept was so extravagant, that he could not support her on the profits of his own thefts. Sheppard did not hesitate to make this new connexion; but, at the same time, said that he did not admit of the partnership with a view to any advantage to himself, but that Grace might reap the profits of their depredations.

Sheppard and Grace making acquaintance with Anthony Lamb, an apprentice to a mathematical instrument maker, near St. Clement's Church, it was agreed to rob a gentleman who lodged with Lamb's master, and, at two o'clock in the morning, Lamb let in the other villains, who stole money and effects to a large amount. They put the door open, and Lamb went to bed, to prevent suspicion; but, notwithstanding this, his master did suspect him, and, having him taken into custody, he confessed the whole affair before a magistrate; and, being committed to Newgate, he was tried, convicted, and received sentence to be transported.

On the same day Thomas Sheppard, the brother of Jack, was indicted for breaking open the dwelling-house of Mary Cook, and stealing her goods; and, being convicted, was sentenced to transportation.

Jack Sheppard not being in custody, he and Blueskin committed a number of daring robberies, and sometimes disposed of the stolen goods to William Field. Jack used to say that Field wanted courage to commit a robbery, though he was as great a villain as ever existed.

Sheppard seems to have thought that courage consisted in villainy; and, if this were the case, Field had an undoubted claim to the character of a man of courage; for in October, 1721, he was tried upon four indictments for felony and burglary; and he was an accomplice in a variety of robberies. He was likewise an evidence against one of his associates on another occasion.

Sheppard and Blueskin hired a stable near the Horse Ferry, Westminster, in which they deposited their stolen goods, till they could dispose of them to the best advantage; and in this place they put the woollen cloth which was stolen from Mr. Kneebone; for Sheppard was concerned in this robbery, and at the sessions held at the Old Bailey, in August, 1724, he was indicted for several offences; and, among the rest, for breaking and entering the house of William Kneebone, and stealing 108 yards of woollen cloth, and other articles; and, being capitally convicted, received sentence of death.

We must now go back to observe, that Sheppard and Blueskin, having applied to Field to look at these goods, and procure a customer for them, he promised to do so; nor was he worse than his word, for in the night he broke open their warehouse, and stole the ill-gotten property, and then gave information against them to Jonathan Wild, in consequence of which they were apprehended.

On Monday, the 30th of August, 1724, a warrant was sent to Newgate for the execution of Sheppard, with other convicts under sentence of death.

It is proper to observe, that in the old gaol of Newgate, there was, within the lodge, a hatch, with large iron spikes, which hatch opened into a dark passage, whence there were a few steps into the condemned hold. The prisoners being permitted to come down to the hatch to speak with their friends, Sheppard, having been supplied with instruments, took an opportunity of cutting one of the spikes in such a manner that it might be easily broken off.

On the evening of the above-mentioned 30th of August, two women of Sheppard's acquaintance going to visit him, he broke off the spike, and, thrusting his head and shoulders through the space, the women pulled him down, and he effected his escape, notwithstanding some of the keepers were at that time drinking at the other end of the lodge.

On the day after his escape he went to a public house in Spitalfields, whence he sent for an old acquaintance, one Page, a butcher in Clare Market, and advised with him how to render his escape effectual for his future preservation. After deliberating on the matter, they agreed to go to Warnden, in Northamptonshire, where Page had some relations; and they had no sooner resolved than they made the journey; but Page's relations treating him with indifference, they returned to London, after being absent only about a week.

On the night after their return, as they were walking up Fleet Street together, they saw a watchmaker's shop open, and only a boy attending: having passed the shop, they turned back, and Sheppard, driving his hand through the window, stole three watches, with which they made their escape.

Some of Sheppard's old acquaintance informing him that strict search was making after him, he and Page retired to Finchley, in hope of lying there concealed till the diligence of the gaol-keepers should relax: but the keepers of Newgate, having intelligence of their retreat, took Sheppard into custody, and conveyed him to his old lodgings.

Such steps were now taken as were thought would be effectual to prevent his future escape. He was put into a strong room called the Castle, handcuffed, loaded with a heavy pair of irons, and chained to a staple fixed in the floor.

The curiosity of the public being greatly excited by his former escape, he was visited by great numbers of people of all ranks, and scarce any one left him without making him a present in money; though he would have more gladly received a file, a hammer, or a chisel; but the utmost care was taken that none of his visitors should furnish him with such implements.

Sheppard, nevertheless, was continually employing his thoughts on the means of another escape. On the 14th of October the sessions began at the Old Bailey, and the keepers being much engaged in attending the Court, he thought they would have little time to visit him; and, therefore, the present juncture would be the most favourable to carry his plan into execution.

About two o'clock in the afternoon of the following day one of the keepers carried him his dinner, and having carefully examined his irons, and finding them fast, he left him for the day.

Some days before this Jack had found a small nail in the room, with which he could, at pleasure, unlock the padlock that went from the chain to the staple in the floor; and, in his own account of this transaction, he says, ' that he was frequently about the room, and had several times slept on the barracks, when the keepers imagined he had not been out of his chair.'

The keeper had not left him more than an hour when he began his operations. He first took off his handcuffs, and then opened the padlock that fastened the chain to the staple. He next, by mere strength, twisted asunder a small link of the chain between his legs, and then, drawing up his fetters as high as he could, he made them fast with his garters.

He then attempted to get up the chimney; but had not advanced far before he was stopped by an iron bar that went across it; on which he descended, and with a piece of his broken chain picked out the mortar, and moving a small stone or two, about six feet from the floor, he got out the iron bar, which was three feet long, and an inch square, and proved very serviceable to him in his future proceedings.

He in a short time made such a breach as to enable him to get into the red room over the castle; and here he found a large nail, which he made use of in his farther operations. It was seven years since the door of this red room had been opened; but Sheppard wrenched off the lock in less than seven minutes, and got into the passage leading to the chapel. In this place he found a door which was bolted on the opposite side; but, making a hole through the wall, he pushed the bolt back, and opened it.

Arriving at the door of the chapel, he broke off one of the iron spikes, which keeping for his farther use, he got into an entry between the chapel and the lower leads. The door of this entry was remarkably strong, and fastened with a large lock; and night now coming on, Sheppard was obliged to work in the dark. Notwithstanding this disadvantage, he in half an hour forced open the box of the lock, and opened the door; but this led him to another room still more difficult, for it was barred and bolted as well as locked; however, he wrenched the fillet from the main post of the door, and the box and staples came off with it.

It was now eight o'clock, and Sheppard found no farther obstruction to his proceedings; for he had only one other door to open, which, being bolted on the inside, was opened without difficulty, and he got over a wall to the upper leads.

His next consideration was how he should descend with the greatest safety; accordingly he found that the most convenient place for him to alight on would be the turner's house adjoining to Newgate; but, as it would have been dangerous to have jumped to such a depth, he went back for a blanket with which he used to cover himself when he slept in the castle, and endeavoured to fasten his stocking to the blanket to ease his descent; but, not being able to do so, he was compelled to use the blanket alone : wherefore he made it fast to the wall of Newgate with the spike that he took out of the chapel; and, sliding down, dropped on the turner's leads just as the clock was striking nine. It happened that the door of the garret next the turner's leads was open, on which he stole softly down two pair of stairs, and heard some company talking in a room. His irons clinking, a woman cried, 'What noise is that?' and a man answered, 'Perhaps the dog or cat.'

Sheppard, who was exceedingly fatigued, returned to the garret, and laid down for more than two hours; after which he crept down once more as far as the room where the company were, when he heard a gentleman taking leave of the family, and saw the maid light him down the stairs. As soon as the maid returned, he resolved to venture all hazards; but, in stealing down the stairs, he stumbled against a chamber door; but, instantly recovering himself, he got into the street.

By this time it was after twelve o'clock, and, passing by the watch-house of St. Sepulchre, he bid the watchman good morrow, and, going up Holborn, he turned down Gray's Lane, and about two in the morning got into the fields near Tottenham Court, where he took shelter in a place that had been a cow-house, and slept soundly about three hours. His fetters being still on, his legs were greatly bruised and swelled, and he dreaded the approach of daylight, lest he should be discovered. He had now above forty shillings in his possession, but was afraid to send to any person for assistance.

At seven in the morning it began to rain hard, and continued to do so all day, so that no person appeared in the fields; and during this melancholy day he would, to use his own expression, have given his right hand for 'a hammer, a chisel, and a punch.' Night coming on, and being pressed by hunger, he ventured to a little chandler's shop in Tottenham Court Road, where he got a supply of bread and cheese, small beer, and some other necessaries, hiding his irons with a long great coat. He asked the woman of the house for a hammer; but she had no such utensil; on which he retired to the cow-house, where he slept that night, and remained all the next day.

At night he went again to the chandler's shop, supplied himself with provisions, and returned to his hiding-place. At six the next morning, which was Sunday, he began to beat the basils of his fetters with a stone, in order to bring them to an oval form, to slip his heels through. In the afternoon, the master of the cow-house coming thither, and seeing his irons, said, 'For God's sake, who are you?' Sheppard said he was an unfortunate young fellow, who having had a bastard child sworn to him, and not being able to give security to the parish for its support, he had been sent to Bridewell, from whence he had made his escape. The man said that if that was all it did not much signify; but he did not care how soon he was gone, for he did not like his looks.

Soon after he was gone Sheppard saw a journeyman shoemaker, to whom he told the same story of the bastard child, and offered him twenty shillings if he would procure him a smith's hammer and a punch. The poor man, tempted by the reward, procured them accordingly, and assisted him in getting rid of his irons, which work was completed by five o'clock in the evening.

When night came on, our adventurer tied a handkerchief about his head, tore his woollen cap in several places, and likewise tore his coat and stockings, so as to have the appearance of a beggar; and in this condition he went to a cellar near Charing Cross, where he supped on roasted veal, and listened to the conversation of the company, all of whom were talking of the escape of Sheppard.

On the Monday he sheltered himself at a public

38

house of little trade in Rupert Street, and, conversing with the landlady about Sheppard, he told her it was impossible for him to get out of the kingdom, and the keepers would certainly have him again in a few days; on which the woman wished that a curse might fall on those who should betray him. Remaining in this place till evening, he went into the Haymarket, where a crowd of people were surrounding two ballad-singers, and listening to a song made on his adventures and escape.

On the next day he hired a garret in Newport Market, and soon afterwards, dressing himself like a porter, he went to Blackfriars, to the house of Mr. Applebee, printer of the dying speeches, and delivered a letter, 'in which he ridiculed the printer and the Ordinary of Newgate, and enclosed a letter for one of the keepers of Newgate.

Some nights after this he broke open the shop of Mr. Rawlins, a pawnbroker, in Drury Lane, where he stole a sword, a suit of wearing apparel, some snuff-boxes, rings, watches, and other effects to a considerable amount. Determining to make the appearance of a gentleman among his old acquaintance in Drury Lane and Clare Market, he dressed himself in a suit of black and a tie-wig, wore a ruffled shirt, a silver-hilted sword, a diamond ring, and a gold watch, though he knew that diligent search was making after him at that very time.

On the 31st of October he dined with two women at a public house in Newgate Street, and about four in the afternoon they all passed under Newgate in a hackney-coach, having first drawn up the blinds. Going in the evening to a public house in Maypole Alley, Clare Market, Sheppard sent for his mother, and treated her with brandy, when the poor woman dropped on her knees, and begged he would immediately quit the kingdom, which he promised to do, but had no intention of keeping his word.

Being now grown valiant through an excess of

liquor, he wandered from alehouses to gin-shops in the neighbourhood till near twelve o'clock at night, when he was apprehended in consequence of the information of an alehouse boy, who knew him. When taken into custody he was quite senseless, from the quantity and variety of liquors he had drank, and was conveyed to Newgate in a coach, without being capable of making the least resistance, though he had then two pistols in his possession.

His fame was now so much increased by his exploits that he was visited by great numbers of people, and some of them of the highest quality. He endeavoured to divert them by a recital of the particulars of many robberies in which he had been concerned; and when any nobleman came to see him, he never failed to beg that he would intercede with the king for a pardon, to which he thought that his singular dexterity gave him some pretensions.

Having been already convicted, he was carried to the bar of the Court of King's Bench on the 10th of November; and the record of his conviction being read, and an affidavit being made that he was the same John Sheppard mentioned in the record, sentence of death was passed on him by Mr. Justice Powis, and a rule of Court was made for his execution on the Monday following.

He regularly attended the prayers in the chapel; but, though he behaved with decency there, he affected mirth before he went thither, and endeavoured to prevent any degree of seriousness among the other prisoners on their return.

Even when the day of execution arrived, Sheppard did not appear to have given over all expectations of eluding justice; for, having been furnished with a penknife, he put it in his pocket, with a view, when the melancholy procession came opposite Little Turnstile, to have cut the cord that bound his arms, and, throwing himself out of the cart among the crowd, to have run through the narrow passage, where the sheriff's officers could not follow on horseback; and he had no doubt but he should make his escape by the assistance of the mob.

It is not impossible but this scheme might have succeeded; but, before Sheppard left the press-yard, one Watson, an officer, searching his pockets, found the knife, and was cut with it so as to occasion a great effusion of blood.

Sheppard had yet a farther view to his preservation even after execution; for he desired his acquaintance to put him into a warm bed as soon as he should be cut down, and to try to open a vein, which he had been told would restore him to life.

He behaved with great decency at the place of execution, and confessed the having committed two robberies, for which he had been tried and acquitted. He suffered in the 23d year of his age, on the 16th of November, 1724. He died with difficulty, and was much pitied by the surrounding multitude. When he was cut down, his body was delivered to his friends, who carried him to a public house in Long Acre, whence he was removed in the evening, and buried in the churchyard of St. Martin in the Fields.

No public robber ever obtained more notoriety; no violator of the law had more hair-breadth escapes than Jack Sheppard. He found employment for the bar, the pulpit, and the stage. The arts, too, were busied in handing to posterity a memoranda for us never to follow the example of Jack Sheppard.

Sir James Thornhill,* the first painter of the day,

* This celebrated painter, whilst decorating the dome of St. Paul's Cathedral, nearly fell a victim to his zeal in that undertaking. One day, when pursuing his task on the scaffold erected round the dome for that purpose, he kept walking backwards, surveying the effect of his work, until he had nearly approached the edge, from which another step would have precipitated him. At this instant his servant, who perceived the danger his master was in,

41

painted his portrait, from which engravings in mezzotinto were made, and the few still in preservation are
objects of curiosity. On this subject the following
lines were written at the time:

> ' Thornhill, 'tis thine to gild with fame
> Th' obscure, and raise the humble name;
> To make the form elude the grave,
> And Sheppard from oblivion save.
>
> Tho' life in vain the wretch implores,
> An exile on the farthest shores,
> Thy pencil brings a kind reprieve,
> And bids the dying robber live.

---

with a wonderful presence of mind seized a pot of colour,
and threw it over the painting. This caused Sir James to
rush forward for the preservation of his work, and he was
thus saved from being dashed to pieces, which, but for this
timely intervention, must have been his fate. This eminent
man painted the whole of the cupola of St. Paul's, and
also the halls of Greenwich Hospital and Blenheim. He
was born in 1675, and was originally a house-painter, but
afterwards applied himself to historical subjects, and
equalled the best painters of his time. In 1719 he was
appointed Historical Painter to George I. and, shortly
afterwards, was created a Knight. He was employed in
several extensive works, for which he was in general very
inadequately paid; and, at times, even found it difficult
to obtain the stipulated price. His demands were contested at Greenwich Hospital, although he only received
25s. a square yard; about the same time a foreigner, for
doing less work at Montague House, received 2000l. for his
work, besides 500l. for his diet. For St. Paul's he received
40s. a square yard. He also decorated More Park, but was
obliged to sue Mr. Styles for it; he, however, not only
recovered 3,500l. the sum agreed to be paid him, but 500l.
more for decorations about the house. Notwithstanding
these difficulties, he acquired a considerable fortune, and
was several years in Parliament; he was also a Fellow of
the Royal Society. His genius was equally happy in
history, allegory, landscape, and architecture; he even
practised the last science as a man of business, and built
several houses. He died in 1734, in the same place where
he was born. He left a son, who followed his father's
profession; and a daughter, who married the celebrated
Hogarth.

This piece to latest time shall stand,
And show the wonders of thy hand.
Thus former masters grac'd their name,
And gave egregious robbers fame.

Appelles Alexander drew,
Cæsar is to Aurelius due;
Cromwell in Lily's works doth shine,
And Sheppard, Thornhill, lives in thine.'

He was, for a considerable time, the principal subject of conversation in all ranks of society. Histories of his life issued from the press in a variety of forms. A pantomime entertainment was brought forward at the royal theatre of Drury Lane, called 'Harlequin Sheppard,' wherein his adventures, prison-breakings, and other extraordinary escapes, were represented. Another dramatic work was published, as a farce of three acts, called 'The Prison Breaker; or, The Adventures of John Sheppard;' and a part of it, with songs, catches, and glees added, was performed at Bartholomew Fair, under the title of 'The Quaker's Opera.' The clergy also preached his adventures; and the following is part of a sermon preached on the occasion, warning people against following the steps of this notorious character:

'Now, my beloved, what a melancholy consideration it is that men should show so much regard for the preservation of a poor perishing body, that can remain at most but a few years, and at the same time be so unaccountably negligent of a precious soul, which must continue to the age of eternity! O, what care, what pains, what diligence, and what contrivances, are made use of for, and laid out upon, these frail and tottering tabernacles of clay: when, alas! the nobler part of us is allowed so very small a share of our concern, that we scarce will give ourselves the trouble of bestowing a thought upon it!

'We have a remarkable instance of this in a notorious malefactor, well known by the name of Jack

Sheppard! What amazing difficulties has he over-come, what astonishing things has he performed, for the sake of a stinking miserable carcass, hardly worth hanging! How dexterously did he pick the padlock of his chain with a crooked nail! how manfully did he burst his fetters asunder, climb up the chimney, wrench out an iron bar, break his way through a stone wall, and make the strong doors of a dark entry fly before him, till he got upon the leads of the prison; and then, fixing a blanket to the wall with a spike he stole out of the chapel, how intrepidly did he descend to the top of the turner's house, and how cautiously pass down the stair, and make his escape at the street-door!'

JONATHAN WILD,

EXECUTED FOR FELONIOUSLY CONNIVING WITH THIEVES.

OF all the thieves that ever infested London, this man was the most notorious. That eminent vagabond, Bamfylde Moore Carew, was recognized as 'King of the Beggars:'—in like manner may the name and memory of Jonathan Wild be ever held in abhorrence as 'The Prince of Robbers.'

The history of the arts, deceptions, cruelty, and perfidy of this man, have alone filled a volume; and, should he occupy more room in our epitome than may be deemed necessary, we have only to observe, that the whole catalogue of other crimes exposed in this Chronology, centred in one individual, would scarcely produce a parallel with this thief-taker, and most finished thief.

Jonathan Wild was born at Wolverhampton, in Staffordshire, about the year 1682. He was the eldest son of his parents, who, at a proper age, put him to a day-school, which he continued to attend till he had gained a sufficient knowledge in reading, writing, and accounts, to qualify him for business. His father had intended to bring him up to his own trade; but changed that design, and, at about the age of fifteen, apprenticed him for seven years to a buckle-maker in Birmingham. Upon the expiration of this term he returned to Wolverhampton, married a young woman of good character, and gained a tolerable livelihood by working at his business.

Butler, a Thief, discovered under a tub by Jonathan Wild

About two years after, in the course of which time his wife gave birth to a son, he formed the resolution of visiting London, deserted his wife and child, and set out for the metropolis, where he got into employment, and maintained himself by his trade: being, however, of an extravagant disposition, many months had not elapsed after his arrival before he was arrested for debt, and thrown into Wood Street Compter, where he remained upwards of four years. In a pamphlet which he published, and which we shall more particularly mention hereafter, he says that during his imprisonment ' it was impossible but he must, in some measure, be let into the secrets of the criminals there under confinement, and particularly Mr. Hitchin's management.'

Whilst in the Compter, Wild assiduously cultivated the acquaintance of his fellow-captives, and attended to their accounts of the exploits in which they had been engaged with singular satisfaction. In this prison was a woman named Mary Milliner, who had long been considered as one of the most abandoned prostitutes and pickpockets in the town. After having escaped the punishment due to the variety of felonies of which she had been guilty, she was put under confinement for debt. An intimacy soon commenced between this woman and Wild, and they had no sooner obtained their freedom than they lived under the denomination of man and wife. By their iniquitous practices they quickly obtained a sum of money, which enabled them to open a little public house in Cock Alley, facing Cripplegate church.

Milliner being personally acquainted with most of the depraved characters by whom London and its environs were infested, and perfectly conversant as to the manner of their proceedings, she was considered by Wild as a most useful companion; and indeed very materially contributed towards rendering him one of the most accomplished proficients in the arts of villainy. He industriously penetrated into the secrets of felons of every description, who resorted in great numbers to his house, in order to dispose of their booties; and they looked upon him with a kind of awe, arising from the consciousness that their lives were at all times in his power.

Wild was at little trouble to dispose of the articles brought to him by thieves at something less than their real value, no law existing at this period for the punishment of the receivers of stolen goods; but the evil increased at length to so enormous a degree, that it was deemed expedient by the legislature to frame a law for its suppression. An act was passed, therefore, consigning such as should be convicted of receiving goods, knowing them to have been stolen, to transportation for the space of fourteen years.

Wild's practices were considerably interrupted by the above-mentioned law; to elude the operation of which, however, he adopted the following plan:—he called a meeting of all the thieves known to him, and observed that, if they carried their booties to such of the pawnbrokers as were known to be not much affected by scruples of conscience, they would scarcely receive on the property one-fourth of the real value; and that if they were offered to strangers, either for sale, or by way of deposit, it was a chance of ten to one but the parties offering were rendered amenable to the laws. The most industrious thieves, he said, were now scarcely able to obtain a livelihood, and must either submit to be half starved, or live in great and continual danger of Tyburn. He informed them that he had devised a plan for removing the inconveniences under which they laboured, recommended them to follow his advice, and to behave towards him with honour; and concluded by proposing that, when they made prize of any thing, they should deliver it to him, instead of carrying it to the pawnbroker, saying he would *restore the goods to the owners*, by which means greater sums might be raised, while the thieves would remain perfectly secure from detection.

This proposal was received with general approbation, and it was resolved to carry it into immediate execution. All the stolen effects were to be given into the possession of Wild, who soon appointed convenient places wherein they were to be deposited, rightly judging that it would not be prudent to have them left at his own house.

47

The infamous plan being thus concerted, it became the business of Wild to apply to persons who had been robbed, pretending to be greatly concerned at their misfortunes, saying that some suspected property had been stopped by a very honest man, a broker, with whom he was acquainted, and that, if their goods happened to be in the hands of his friend, restitution should be made. But he failed not to suggest that the broker ought to be rewarded for his trouble and disinterestedness; and to use every argument in his power towards exacting a promise that no disagreeable consequences should ensue to his friend, who had imprudently neglected to apprehend the supposed thieves.

Happy in the prospect of regaining their property, without the trouble and expense necessarily attending prosecutions, people generally approved of the conduct of Wild, and sometimes rewarded him even with one half of the real value of the goods restored. It was not, however, uniformly so; and sundry pertinacious individuals, not satisfied with Wild's superficial statement, questioned him particularly as to the *manner* of their goods being discovered. On these occasions he pretended to feel hurt that his honour should be disputed, alleging that his motive was to afford all the service in his power to the injured party, whose goods he imagined might possibly be those stopped by his friend; but since his honest intentions had been received in so ungracious a manner, and himself interrogated respecting the robbers, he had nothing further to say on the subject, but must take his leave; adding, that his name was Jonathan Wild, and that he was every day to be found at his house in Cock Alley, Cripplegate. This affectation of resentment seldom failed to answer the purposes proposed by it; and a more favourable estimate of his principles and character thus formed, he had an opportunity of advancing his demands.

Wild received in his own name no gratuity from the

owners of stolen goods, but deducted his profit from the money which was to be paid *the broker* : thus did he amass considerable sums without danger of prosecution, his offences coming under the operation of no law then in existence. For several years indeed he preserved a tolerably fair character, so consummate was the art employed in the management of his schemes.

Our hero's business greatly increasing, and his name becoming well known, he altered his mode of action. Instead of applying directly to parties who had been plundered, he opened an office, to which great numbers resorted, in hopes of recovering their effects. He made a great parade in his business, and assumed a consequence which enabled him more effectually to impose upon the public. When persons came to his office, they were informed that they must each pay a crown in consideration of receiving his advice. This ceremony being dispatched, he entered in his book the name and address of the applicants, with all the particulars they could communicate respecting the robberies, and the rewards that would be given provided the goods were recovered : they were then desired to call again in a few days, when he hoped he should be able to give them some agreeable intelligence. Upon returning to know the success of his inquiries, he told them that he had received some information concerning their goods, but that the agent he had employed to trace them had apprised him that the robbers pretended they could raise more money by pawning the property than by restoring it for the promised reward; saying, however, that, if he could by any means procure an interview with the villains, he doubted not of being able to settle matters agreeably to the terms already stipulated; but, at the same time, artfully insinuating that the safest and most expeditious method would be to make some addition to the reward.

Wild, at length, became eminent in his profession, which proved highly lucrative. When he had discovered the utmost sum that it was likely would be given for the recovery of any property, he requested its owner to apply at a particular time, and, mean while, caused the goods to be ready for delivery.

Considerable advantages were derived from examining the person who had been robbed; as he thence became acquainted with particulars which the thieves might omit to communicate, and was enabled to detect them if they concealed any part of their booties. Being in possession of the secrets of every notorious thief, they were under the necessity of complying with whatever terms he thought proper to exact, being aware that, by opposing his inclination, they should involve themselves in the most imminent danger of being sacrificed to the injured laws of their country.

Through the infamous practices of this man, articles which had been before considered as of little use but to the owners now became matters claiming particular attention from the thieves, by whom the metropolis and its environs were haunted. Pocket-books, books of accounts, watches, rings, trinkets, and a variety of articles of but small intrinsic worth, were at once esteemed very profitable plunder. Books of accounts, and other writings, being of great importance to the owners, produced very handsome rewards; and the same may be said of pocket-books, which generally contained curious memorandums, and sometimes banknotes and other articles on which money could be readily procured.

Wild accumulated cash so fast, that he considered himself a man of consequence; and, to support his imaginary dignity, dressed in laced clothes and wore a sword, which martial instrument he first exercised on the person of his accomplice and reputed wife, Mary Milliner, who having on some occasion provoked him, he instantly struck at her with it and cut off one of her ears. This event was the cause of a separation; but, in acknowledgment of the great services she had rendered him, by introducing him to so advantageous a *profession*, he allowed her a weekly stipend till her decease.

Before Wild had brought the plan of his office to perfection, he for some time acted as an assistant to Charles Hitchin, once city-marshal, a man as wicked as himself. These celebrated copartners in villainy, under the pretext of controlling the enormities of the dissolute, paraded the streets from Temple-bar to the Minories, searching houses of ill fame, and apprehending disorderly and suspected persons; but those who complimented these *public* reformers with *private* douceurs were allowed to practise every species of wickedness with impunity. Hitchin and Wild, however, grew jealous of each other, and, an open rupture taking place, they parted, each pursuing the business of thief-taking on his own account.

In the year 1715 Wild removed from his house in Cock Alley to a Mrs. Seagoe's, in the Old Bailey, where he pursued his business with the usual success, notwithstanding the efforts of Hitchin, his rival in iniquity, to suppress his proceedings.

The reader's astonishment will increase when we state that these two abandoned miscreants had the daring effrontery to appeal to the public, and attacked each other with all possible scurrility in pamphlets and advertisements. Never, surely, was the press so debased as in disgorging the filth of their pens. Hitchin published what he called ' The Regulator; or a Discovery of Thieves and Thief-takers.' It is an ignorant and impudent insult to the reader, and replete with abuse of Wild, whom he brands, in his capacity of thief-taker, with being worse than the thief. Wild retorts with great bitterness; and his pamphlet containing much curious information, we shall incorporate a part of it, requesting the reader to

51

bear in mind that it refers to a previous part of our hero's career.

Hitchin having greatly debased the respectable post of city marshal, the lord mayor suspended him from that office. In order to repair his loss, he determined, as the most prudent step, to strive to bury his aversion, and confederate with Wild. To effect this, he wrote as follows:

' I am very sensible that you are let into the know-ledge of the secrets of the Compter, particularly with relation to the securing of pocket-books; but your experience is inferior to mine: I can put you in a far better method than you are acquainted with, and which may be done with safety; for, though I am suspended, I still retain the power of acting as con-stable, and, notwithstanding I cannot be heard before my lord mayor as formerly, I have interest among the aldermen upon any complaint.

' But I must first tell you that you spoil the trade of thief-taking, in advancing greater rewards than are necessary. I give but half-a-crown a book, and, when the thieves and pickpockets see you and I confederate, they will submit to our terms, and likewise continue their thefts, for fear of coming to the gallows by our means. You shall take a turn with me, as my servant or assistant, and we'll commence our rambles this night.'

Wild, it appears, readily accepted the ex-marshal's proposals: towards dark they proceeded to Temple-bar, and called in at several brandy-shops and ale-houses between that and Fleet Ditch; some of the masters of these houses complimented the marshal with punch, others with brandy, and some presented him with fine ale, offering their service to their worthy protector. Hitchin made them little answer; but gave them to understand all the service he expected from them was, to give information of pocket-books, or any goods stolen, as a pay-back: ' For you women

52

of the town,' addressing himself to some females in one of the shops, ' make it a common practice to resign things of this nature to the bullies and rogues of your retinue; but this shall no longer be borne with. I'll give you my word both they and you shall be detected, unless you deliver all the pocket-books you meet with to me. What do you think I bought my place for, but to make the most of it? and you are to understand this is my man (pointing to our buckle-maker) to assist me. And if you at any time, for the future, refuse to yield up the watches or books you take, either to me or my servant, you may be assured of being all sent to Bridewell, and not one of you shall be permitted to walk the streets longer. For, notwithstanding I am under suspension (chiefly for not suppressing the practices of such vermin as you), I have still a power of punishing, and you shall dearly pay for not observing deference to me.' Strutting along a little farther, he on a sudden seized two or three dexterous pickpockets, reprimanding them for not paying their respects, asking to what part of the town they were rambling, and whether they did not see him? They answered that they saw him at a distance, but he caught hold of them so hastily that they had no time to address him. ' We have been strolling,' said they, ' over Moorfields, and from thence to the Blue Boar, in pursuit of you; but not finding you, as usual, were under some fears that you were indisposed.' The marshal replied, he should have given them a meeting there, but had been employed the whole day with his new man. ' You are to be very careful,' said he, ' not to oblige any person but myself, or servant, with pocket-books; if you presume to do otherwise you shall swing for it, and we are out in the city every night to observe your motions.' These instructions given, the pickpockets left, making their master a low congee, and promising obedience. Such was the progress of the first night with the buckle-maker, whom he told that his staff of authority terrified the ignorant to the extent of his wishes.

Some nights afterwards, walking towards the back part of St. Paul's, the ex-marshal thus addressed Jonathan:—' I will now show you a brandy-shop that entertains no company but whores and thieves. This is a house for our purpose, and I am informed that a woman of the town who frequents it has lately robbed a gentleman of his watch and pocket-book: this advice I received from her companion, with whom I have a good understanding. We will go into this house, and, if we can find this woman, I will assume a sterner countenance (though at best I look like an infernal), by continued threats extort a confession, and by that means get possession of the watch and pocket-book; in order to which, do you slily accost her companion.'—Here he described her.—' Call to her, and say that your master is in a damned ill humour, and swears if she does not instantly make a discovery where the watch and pocket-book may be found, at farthest by to-morrow, he will certainly send her to the Compter, and thence to the workhouse.'

The means being thus concerted to obtain the valuable goods, both master and man entered the shop in pursuit of the game, and, according to expectation, found the person wanted, with several others; whereupon the marshal, showing an enraged countenance becoming the design, and Wild being obliged to follow his example, the company said that the master and man looked as sour as two devils. ' Devils!' said the marshal; ' I'll make some of you devils, if you do not immediately discover the watch and pocket-book I am employed to procure.' ' We do not know your meaning, Sir,' answered some.—' Who do you discourse to?' said others; ' we know nothing of it.' The marshal replied in a softer tone, ' You are ungrateful to the last degree to deny me this small request, when I was never let into the secret of any thing to be taken from a gentleman but I communicated it to you, describing the person so exactly that you could not mistake your man; and there is so little got at this rate, that the devil may trade with you for me!'

This speech being made, the marshal gave a nod to his man, who called one of the women to the door, and, telling the story above directed, the female answered, 'Unconscionable devil! when he gets five or ten guineas, not to bestow above as many shillings upon us unfortunate wretches! but, however, rather than go to the Compter, I'll try what is to be done.'

The woman, returning to Hitchin, asked him what he would give for the delivery of the watch, being seven or eight pounds in value, and the pocket-book, having in it various notes and goldsmiths' bills: to whom the marshal answered, a guinea; and told her it was much better to comply than to go to Newgate, which she must certainly expect upon her refusal. The woman replied that the watch was in pawn for forty shillings, and if he did not advance that sum she should be obliged to strip herself for its redemption; though, when her furbelowed scarf was laid aside, she had nothing underneath but furniture for a paper-mill. After abundance of words, he allowed her thirty shillings for the watch and book, which she accepted, and the watch was never returned to the owner!

Some little time after this, a gentleman in liquor going into the Blue Boar, near Moorfields, with a woman of the town, immediately lost his watch. H applied to the ex-marshal, desiring his assistance; but the buckle-maker, being well acquainted with the walk between Cripplegate and Moorfields, had the fortune to find the woman. The master immediately seized her, on notice given, and by vehement threatenings obliged her to a confession She declared that she had stolen the watch, and carried it to a woman that kept a brandy-shop near, desiring her to assist in the sale of it. The mistress of the brandy-shop readily answered that she had it from an honest young woman who frequented her house, whose husband was gone to sea; whereupon she pawned the watch for its value, and ordered the sale.

This story seeming reasonable, a watchmaker had purchased the watch, and gave the money agreed for it, which was fifty shillings. Thus the sale of the watch being discovered, the marshal, with his staff and assistants, immediately repaired to the watchmaker's house, and, seizing the watchmaker in the same manner as a person would do the greatest criminal, carried him to a public house, telling him that if he did not forthwith send for the watch he should be committed to Newgate.

The watchmaker, not being any ways accustomed to unfair dealings, directly answered that he bought the watch, and the person he had it of would produce the woman that stole it, if it were stolen, the woman being then present. The marshal replied he had no business with the persons that stole the property, but with him in whose possession it was found; and that, if he did not instantly send for the watch, and deliver it without insisting upon any money, but on the contrary return him thanks for his civility, which deserved five or ten pieces, he would without delay send him to Newgate.

Hereupon the innocent artisan, being much surprised, sent for the watch, and surrendered it; and since that it has sufficiently appeared that the owner made a present to Hitchin of three guineas for his trouble, whilst the poor watchmaker underwent a dead loss of his fifty shillings. This story and the following afford a pretty good example of the honesty of this city-marshal:

A biscuit-baker near Wapping having lost a pocket-book, wherein was, among other papers, an exchequer-bill for 100*l.* applied himself to the marshal's man, the buckle-maker, for the recovery thereof : the buckle-maker advised him to advertise it, and stop the payment of the bill, which he did accordingly; but having no account of his property, he came to Wild several times about it; and, at length, told him that he had received a visit from a tall man, with a long peruke and sword, calling himself the city-marshal, who asked him if he had lost his pocket-book. The biscuit-baker answered yes; and desiring to know his reasons for putting such a question, or whether he could give him any intelligence; he replied, no, he could not give him any intelligence of it as yet, but wished to be informed whether he had employed any person to search after it. To which the biscuit-baker answered, he had employed one Wild. Hereupon the marshal told him he was under a mistake; that he should have applied to him, who was the only person in England that could serve him, being well assured it was entirely out of the power of Wild, or any of those fellows, to know where the pocket-book was (this, says the pamphlet, was very certain, he having it at that time in his custody); and begged to know the reward that would be given. The biscuit-baker replied he would give 10*l*. The marshal said that a greater reward should be offered, for that exchequer-bills and those things were ready money, and could immediately be sold; and that, if he had employed him in the beginning, and offered 40*l*. or 50*l*. he would have served him.

The biscuit-baker having acquainted Wild with this story, the latter gave it as his opinion that the pocket-book was in the marshal's possession, and that it would be to no purpose to continue advertising it, he being well assured that the marshal would not have taken the pains to find out the biscuit-baker, unless he knew how to get at it.

Upon the whole, therefore, he advised the owner rather to advance his bidding, considering what hands the note was in, especially as the marshal had often told his servant how easily he could dispose of bank-notes and exchequer-bills at gaming-houses, which he very much frequented.

Pursuant to this advice, the losing party went a second time to the marshal, and bid 40l. for his pocket-book and bill. ' Zounds, sir,' said the marshal, ' you are too late ! ' which was all the satisfaction he gave him. Thus was the poor biscuit-baker tricked out of his exchequer-bill, which was paid to another person, though it could never be traced back; but it happened, a short time after, that some of the young fry of pick-pockets under the tuition of the marshal fell out in sharing the money given them for this very pocket-book; whereupon one of them came to Wild, and dis-covered the whole matter, viz. that he had sold the pocket-book, with the 100l. exchequer-note in it, and other bills, to the city-marshal, at a tavern in Alders-gate Street, for four or five guineas.

A person standing in the pillory, near Charing Cross, a gentleman in the crowd was deprived of a pocket-book, which had in it bills and lottery-tickets to the value of several hundred pounds; and a handsome reward (30l.) was at first offered for it in a public advertisement. The marshal, having a suspicion that a famous pickpocket, known by his lame hand, had taken the book, he applied to him; and, to enforce a confession and delivery, told him, with a great deal of assurance, that he must be the person, such a man, with a lame hand, having been described by the gentle-man to have been near him, and whom he was certain had stolen his book. ' In short,' says he, ' you had the book, and you must bring it to me, and you shall share the reward; but, if you refuse to comply with such advantageous terms, you must never expect to come within the city gates; for, if you do, Bridewell, at least, if not Newgate, shall be your residence.'

After several meetings, the marshal's old friend

could not deny that he had the pocket-book: but he said to the marshal, ' I did not expect this rigorous treatment from you, after the services I have done you, in concealing you several times, and by that means keeping you out of a gaol. It is not the way to expect any future service, when all my former good offices are forgotten.' Notwithstanding these reasons, Hitchin still insisted upon what he had at first proposed; and at length the pickpocket, considering that he could not repair to the Exchange, or elsewhere, to follow his pilfering employment, without the marshal's consent, and fearing to be made a mark of his revenge, condescended to part with the pocket-book upon terms reasonable between buyer and seller. Whereupon says the marshal, ' I lost all my money last night at gaming, except a gold watch in my pocket, which I believe there will be no inquiry after, it coming to hand by an intrigue with a woman of the town, whom the gentleman will be ashamed to prosecute for fear of exposing himself. I'll exchange goods for goods with you.' So the pickpocket, rather than he would risk the consequence of disobliging his master, concluded the bargain.

One night, not far from St. Paul's, the marshal and his man met with a detachment of pickpocket boys, who instantly, at the sight of their master, took to their heels and ran away. The buckle-maker asked the meaning of their surprise. To which the marshal answered, ' I know their meaning, a pack of rogues! they were to have met me in the fields, this morning, with a book I am informed they have taken from a gentleman, and they are afraid of being secured for their disobedience. There is Jack Jones among them. —We'll catch the whore's bird.' Jack Jones, running behind a coach to make his escape, was taken by the marshal and his man. The master carried him to a tavern, and threatened him severely, telling him he believed they were turned housebreakers, and that they were concerned in a burglary lately committed by four young criminals. This happened to be the fact, and the boy fearing the marshal had been informed of it, he, for his own security, confessed, and the marshal promised to save his life on his becoming evidence: whereupon the marshal committed the boy to the Compter till the next morning, when he carried him before a justice of the peace, who took his information, and issued a warrant for the apprehension of his companions.

Notice being given where the criminals were to be found, viz. at a house in Beech Lane, Hitchin and Wild went privately in the night thither, and, listening at the door, they overheard the boys, with several others, in a mixed company. Entering the house, they met ten or twelve persons, who were in a great rage, inquiring what business the marshal had there, and saluting him with a few oaths, which occasioned the marshal to make a prudent retreat, pulling the door after him, and leaving his little man to the mercy of the savage company.

In a short time the marshal returned with eight or ten watchmen and a constable; and, at the door, out of his dastardly disposition, though his pretence was a ceremonious respect, obliged the constable to go in first; but the constable and marshal were both so long with their compliments that the man thought neither of them would enter in: at last the constable appearing, with his long staff extended before him, the marshal manfully followed, crying out, ' Where are the rebel villains? Why don't ye secure them? ' Wild answered that they were under the table; upon which the constable pulled out the juvenile offenders, neither of whom were above twelve years of age. The two boys now taken were committed to Newgate; but the fact having been perpetrated in the county of Surrey, they were afterwards removed to the Marshalsea prison. The assizes coming on at Kingston, and

Jones giving his evidence against his companions before the grand jury, a true bill was found, and the marshal indorsed his name on the back of it, to have the honour of being an evidence against these monstrous housebreakers. On the trial, the nature of the fact was declared; but the parents of the offenders appeared, and satisfied the Court that the marshal was the occasion of the ruin of these boys, by taking them into the fields, and encouraging them in the stealing of pocket-books; and told him, on his affirming they were thieves, that he had made them such. The judge, observing the marshal's views were more to get the reward than to do justice, summed up the charge to the jury in favour of the boys, who were thereupon acquitted, and the marshal reprimanded. He was so enraged at this, and so angry with himself for not accusing them of other crimes, that he immediately returned to London, leaving his man to discharge the whole reckoning at Kingston.

A gentleman, who had lost his watch when in company with a woman of the town, applied to a person belonging to the Compter, who recommended him to the buckle-maker, to procure the same; and the gentleman applying accordingly to him, and giving him a description of the woman, the buckle-maker, a few days after, traversing Fleet Street with his master in an evening, happened to meet with the female (as he apprehended by the description of the gentleman) who had stolen the watch, and, coming nearer, was satisfied therein.

He told his master that she was the very person described: to which the master answered, with an air of pleasure, ' I am glad to find we have a prospect of something to-night to defray our expenses,' and immediately, with the assistance of Wild, seized the female and carried her to a public house, where, upon examination, she confessed it was in her power to serve the marshal in it; telling him that if he would please to go with her home, or send his man, the watch would be returned, with a suitable reward for his trouble. The man asked his master his opinion, whether he thought he might pursue the woman with safety? To which the other replied, Yes, for that he knew her, at the same time giving hints of his following at a reasonable distance, for his security, which he did with a great deal of precaution, as will appear; for, proceeding with the female, she informed him that her husband, who had the watch about him, was at a tavern near Whitefriars, and, if he would condescend to go thither, he might be furnished with it without giving himself any farther trouble, together with the reward he deserved.—To which Wild consenting, they came to the tavern, where she made inquiry for the company she had been with but a short space before; and, being informed they were still in the house, she sent in word by the drawer that the gentlewoman who had been with them that evening desired the favour to speak with them. The drawer going in, and delivering the message, immediately three or four men came from the room to the female: she gave them to understand that the marshal's man had accused her of stealing a watch, telling them she supposed it must be some other woman who had assumed her name, and desired their protection: upon this the whole company sallied out, and attacked the marshal's man in a very violent manner, to make a rescue of the female, upbraiding him for degrading a gentlewoman of her reputation.

The marshal having followed at a little distance, and observed the ill success of his man, fearing the like discipline, made off, hugging himself that he had escaped the severe treatment he had equally deserved. Jonathan in the struggle showed his resentment chiefly against the female; who, after a long contest, was thrust out at the back door; and immediately the watch being called, he and the rest of the party were seized.

As they were going to the Compter, the marshal overtook them near Bow church, and, coming up to Wild in great haste, asked him the occasion of his long absence: the man said, that he had been at a tavern with the woman, where he thought he saw him: the master answered, that indeed he was there; but seeing the confusion so great, he went off to call the watch and constables. The marshal used his interest to get his servant off, but to no purpose, he being carried to the Compter with the rest of the company, in order to make an agreement there.

The next morning the woman sent to her companions in the Compter, letting them know that, if they could be released, the watch should be returned without any consideration, which was accordingly done, and a small present made to the marshal's man for smart-money. They were now all discharged, paying their fees.

The watch being thus ready to be produced to the owner, the marshal insisted upon the greatest part of the reward, as being the highest person in authority: the man declared this unreasonable, he himself having received the largest share of the bastinado. ' But, however,' says the marshal, ' I have now an opportunity of playing my old game; I'll oblige the gentleman to give me ten guineas to save his reputation, which is so nearly concerned with a common prostitute.' But the gentleman knew too much of his character to be thus imposed upon, and would give him no more than what he promised, which was three guineas. Hitchin at first refused; but his man (who had the most right to make a new contract) advising him to act cautiously, he at last agreed to accept the reward first offered, giving Jonathan only one guinea for his services and the cure of his wounds. The above is a farther instance of the marshal's cowardice and inhumanity.

The marshal, going one night up Ludgate Hill,

observed a well-dressed woman walking before, whom he told Wild was a lewd woman, for that he saw her talking with a man. This was no sooner spoke but he seized her, and asked who she was. She made answer that she was a bailiff's wife. ' You are more likely to be a whore,' said the marshal, ' and as such you shall go to the Compter.'

Taking the woman through St. Paul's Church-yard, she desired liberty to send for some friends; but he would not comply with her request. He forced her into the Nag's Head tavern in Cheapside, where he presently ordered a hot supper and plenty of wine to be brought in; commanding the female to keep at a distance from him, and telling her that he did not permit such vermin to sit in his company, though he intended to make her pay the reckoning.

When the supper was brought to the table, he fell to it lustily, and would not allow the woman to eat any part of the supper with him, or to come near the fire, though it was extreme cold weather. When he had supped, he stared round, and, applying himself to her, told her that if he had been an informer, or such a fellow, she would have called for eatables and wine herself, and not have given him the trouble of direction, or else would have slipped a piece into his hand; adding, ' You may do what you please : but I can assure you it is in my power, if I see a woman in the hands of informers, to discharge her, and commit them. You are not so ignorant but you must guess my meaning.' She replied, that she had money enough to pay for the supper, and about three half-crowns more. This desirable answer being given, he ordered his attendant to withdraw, while he compounded the matter with her.

When Wild returned, the gentlewoman was civilly asked to sit by the fire, and eat the remainder of the supper, and in all respects treated very kindly, only with a pretended reprimand to give him better language whenever he should speak to her for the future; and, after another bottle drank at her expense, she was discharged. This is an excellent method to get a good supper gratis, and to fill an empty pocket.

The marshal, previous to his suspension, had daily meetings with the pickpocket boys in Moorfields, and treated them there plentifully with cakes and ale; offering them sufficient encouragement to continue their thefts: and at a certain time it happened that one of the boys, more cunning than his companions, having stolen an alderman's pocket-book, and finding, on opening it, several bank bills, he gave the marshal to understand that it was worth a great deal beyond the usual price; and, the notes being of considerable value, insisted upon five pieces. The marshal told the boy that five pieces were enough to break him at once; that if he gave him two guineas he would be sufficiently paid; but assured him that, if he had the good luck to obtain a handsome reward, he would then make it up five pieces. Upon this present encouragement and future expectation the boy delivered up the pocket-book, and a few days afterwards, being informed that a very large reward had been given for the notes, he applied to the marshal for the remaining three guineas, according to promise; but all the satisfaction he got was, that he should be sent to the house of correction if he continued to demand it; the marshal telling him that such rascals as he were ignorant how to dispose of their money.

This conniving at the intrigues of the pickpockets, taking the stolen pocket-books, and sending threatening letters to the persons that lost them, under pretence that they had been in company with lewd women; extorting money also from persons in various other ways; were the causes of the marshal's being suspended; and this most detestable villain having subsequently been fined twenty pounds, and pilloried, for a crime too loathsome to be named in these pages, left Wild at length alone to execute his plans of depredation on the public.

We shall now, quitting Mr. Wild's recriminating pamphlet, proceed in our regular account of the hero of this narrative.—When the vagabonds with whom he was in league faithfully related to him the particulars of the robberies they had committed, and intrusted to him the disposal of their booties, he assured them that they might safely rely on him for protection against the vengeance of the law; and indeed it must be acknowledged that in cases of this nature he would persevere in his utmost endeavours to surmount very great difficulties rather than wilfully falsify his word.

Wild's artful behaviour, and the punctuality with which he discharged his engagements, obtained him a great share of confidence among thieves of every denomination; insomuch, that if he caused it to be intimated to them that he was desirous of seeing them, and that they should not be molested, they would attend him with the utmost willingness, without entertaining the most distant apprehension of danger, although conscious that he had informations against them, and that their lives were absolutely in his power; but if they presumed to reject his proposals, or proved otherwise refractory, he would address them to the following effect: ' I have given you my word that you should come and go in safety, and so you shall; but take care of yourself, for, if ever you see me again, you see an enemy.'

The great influence that Wild obtained over the thieves will not be thought a very extraordinary matter, if it is considered that, when he promised to use his endeavours for rescuing them from impending fate, he was always desirous, and generally able, to succeed. Such as complied with his measures he would never interrupt; but, on the contrary, afford them every encouragement for prosecuting their iniquitous practices; and, if apprehended by any other person, he seldom failed of procuring their discharge. His most usual method (in desperate cases, and when matters could not be managed with more ease and expedition) was to procure them to be admitted evidences, under pretext that it was in their power to make discoveries of high importance to the public. When they were in prison he frequently attended them, and communicated to them from his own memorandums such particulars as he judged it would be prudent for them to relate to the Court. When his accomplices were apprehended, and he was not able to prevent their being brought to trial, he contrived stratagems (in which his invention was amazingly fertile) for keeping the principal witnesses out of Court; so that the delinquents were generally dismissed in defect of evidence.

Jonathan was ever a most implacable enemy to those who were hardy enough to reject his terms, and dispose of their stolen effects for their own separate advantage. He was industrious to an extreme in his efforts to surrender them into the hands of justice; and, being acquainted with all their usual places of resort, it was scarcely possible for them to escape his vigilance.

By his subjecting such as incurred his displeasure to the punishment of the law, he obtained the rewards offered for pursuing them to conviction; greatly extended his ascendancy over the other thieves, who considered him with a kind of awe; and, at the same time, established his character as being a man of great public utility.

It was the practice of Wild to give instructions to the thieves whom he employed as to the manner in which they should conduct themselves; and, if they followed his directions, it was seldom that they failed of success. But if they neglected a strict observance of his rules, or were, through inadvertency or ignorance, guilty of any kind of mismanagement or error in the prosecution of the schemes he had suggested, it was to be understood almost as an absolute certainty that he would procure them to be convicted at the next sessions, deeming them to be unqualified for the profession of roguery.

He was frequently asked how it was possible that he could carry on the business of restoring stolen effects, and yet not be in league with the robbers; and his replies were always to this purpose:—' My acquaintance among thieves is very extensive, and, when I receive information of a robbery, I make inquiry after the suspected parties, and leave word at proper places that, if the goods are left where I appoint, the reward shall be paid, and no questions asked. Surely no imputation of guilt can fall upon me; for I hold no interviews with the robbers, nor are the goods given into my possession.'

We will now give a relation of the most remarkable exploits of the hero of these pages; and our detail must necessarily include many particulars relating to other notorious characters of the same period.

A lady of fortune being on a visit in Piccadilly, her servants, leaving her sedan at the door, went to refresh themselves at a neighbouring public house. Upon their return the vehicle was not to be found; in consequence of which the men immediately went to Wild, and having informed him of their loss, and complimented him with the usual fee, they were desired to call upon him again in a few days. Upon their second application, Wild extorted from them a considerable reward, and then directed them to attend the chapel in Lincoln's Inn Fields on the following morning, during the time of prayers. The men went according to the appointment, and under the piazzas of the chapel perceived the chair, which upon examination they found to contain the velvet seat, curtains, and other furniture, and that it had received no kind of damage.

A young gentleman, named Knap, accompanied his mother to Sadler's Wells, on Saturday, March 31, 1716. On their return they were attacked, about ten at night, near the wall of Gray's Inn Gardens, by five villains. The young gentleman was knocked down, and his mother, being exceedingly alarmed, called for assistance; upon which a pistol was discharged at her, and she instantly fell down dead. A considerable reward was offered by proclamation in the Gazette for the discovery of the perpetrator of this horrid crime; and Wild was remarkably assiduous in his endeavours to apprehend the offenders. From a description given of some of the villains, Wild immediately judged the gang to be composed of William White, Thomas Thurland, John Chapman, alias Edward Darvel, Timothy Dun, and Isaac Rag.

On the evening of Sunday, April 8, Wild received intelligence that some of the above-named men were drinking with their prostitutes at a house kept by John Weatherly, in Newtoner's Lane. He went to Weatherly's, accompanied by his man Abraham, and seized White, whom he brought away about midnight, in a hackney-coach, and lodged him in the round-house.

White being secured, information was given to Wild that a man named James Aires was then at the Bell Inn, Smithfield, in company with a woman of the town. Having an information against Aires, Wild, accompanied by his assistants, repaired to the inn, under the gateway of which they met Thurland, whose person had been mistaken for that of Aires. Thurland was provided with two brace of pistols; but, being suddenly seized, he was deprived of all opportunity of making use of those weapons, and taken into custody.

They went on the following night to a house in

White Horse Alley, Drury Lane, where they apprehended Chapman, alias Darvel. Soon after the murder of Mrs. Knap, Chapman and others stopped the coach of Thomas Middlethwaite, Esq., but that gentleman escaped being robbed by discharging a blunderbuss, and wounding Chapman in the arm, on which the villains retired.

In a short time after, Wild apprehended Isaac Rag at a house which he frequented in St. Giles's, in consequence of an information charging him with a burglary. Being taken before a magistrate, in the course of his examination Rag impeached twenty-two accomplices, charging them with being housebreakers, footpads, and receivers of stolen effects; and, in consequence thereof, was admitted an evidence for the crown. This man had been convicted of a misdemeanour in January, 1714-15, and sentenced to stand three times in the pillory. He had concealed himself in the dust-hole belonging to the house of Thomas Powell, where being discovered, he was searched, and a pistol, some matches, and a number of pick-lock keys, were found in his possession. His intention was evidently to commit a burglary; but, as he did not enter the house, he was indicted for a misdemeanour in entering the yard with intent to steal. He was indicted in October, 1715, for a burglary, in the house of Elizabeth Stanwell, on the 24th of August; but he was acquitted of this charge.

White, Thurland, and Chapman, were arraigned on the 18th of May, 1716, at the sessions-house in the Old Bailey, on an indictment for assaulting John Knap, Gent. putting him in fear, and taking from him a hat and wig, on the 31st of March, 1716. They were also indicted for the murder of Mary Knap, widow: White by discharging a pistol loaded with powder and bullets, and thereby giving her a wound, of which she immediately died, March 31, 1716. They were a second time indicted for assaulting and robbing John Gough. White was a fourth time indicted with James Russel for a burglary in the house of George Barklay. And Chapman was a fourth time indicted for a burglary in the house of Henry Cross. These three offenders were executed at Tyburn on the 8th of June, 1716.

Wild was indefatigable in his endeavours to apprehend Timothy Dun, who had hitherto escaped the hands of justice by removing to a new lodging, where he concealed himself in the most cautious manner. Wild, however, did not despair of discovering this offender, whom he supposed must either perish through want of the necessaries of life, or obtain the means of subsistence by returning to his felonious practices; and so confident was he of success, that he made a wager of ten guineas that he would have him in custody before the expiration of an appointed time.

Dun's confinement, at length, became exceedingly irksome to him; and he sent his wife to make inquiries respecting him of Wild, in order to discover whether he was still in danger of being apprehended. Upon her return Wild ordered one of his people to follow her home. She took water at Blackfriars, and landed at the Falcon; but suspecting the man was employed to trace her, she again took water, and crossed to Whitefriars: observing that she was still followed, she ordered the waterman to proceed to Lambeth, and having landed there, it being nearly dark, imagined she had escaped the observation of Wild's man, and therefore walked immediately home. The man traced her to Maid Lane, near the Bankside, Southwark, and perceiving her enter a house, he marked the wall with chalk, and then returned to his employer, with an account of the discovery he had made.

Wild, accompanied by a fellow named Abraham, a Jew, who acted the part himself had formerly done to the worthless marshal, one Riddlesden, and another man, went on the following morning to the house where the woman had been seen to enter. Dun, hearing a noise, and thence suspecting that he was discovered, got through a back-window on the second floor upon the roof of the pantry, the bottom of which was about eight feet from the ground. Abraham discharged a pistol, and wounded Dun in the arm; in consequence of which he fell from the pantry into the yard; after his fall Riddlesden fired also, and wounded him in the face with small-shot. Dun was secured and carried to Newgate, and being tried at the ensuing sessions, was soon after executed at Tyburn.

Riddlesden was bred to the law, but he entirely neglected that business, and abandoned himself to every species of wickedness. His irregular course of life having greatly embarrassed his circumstances, he broke into the chapel of Whitehall, and stole the communion-plate. He was convicted of this offence, and received sentence of death; but, through the exertion of powerful interest, a pardon was obtained, on condition of transporting himself for the term of seven years. He went to America, but soon returned to England, and had the address to ingratiate himself into the favour of a young lady, daughter to an opulent merchant at Newcastle-upon-Tyne. Before he could get his wife's fortune, which was considerable, into his hands, he was discovered and committed to Newgate. She followed him, and was brought to bed in the prison. Her friends, however, being apprized of her unhappy situation, caused her to return home. He contracted an intimacy with the widow of Richard Revel, one of the turnkeys of Newgate; and, being permitted to transport himself again, that woman went with him to Philadelphia, under the character of his wife. In consequence, however, of a disagreement between them, Mrs. Revel returned, and took a public house in Golden Lane; but what became of Riddlesden does not appear.

One night, during the connexion of Wild with

Hitchin the city marshal, being abroad in their walks, not far from the Temple, they discovered a clergyman standing against the wall in an alley, to which he had retired, as persons frequently do, on account of modesty and decency. Immediately a woman of the town, lying in wait for prey, brushing by, the clergyman exclaimed aloud, 'What does the woman want?' The marshal instantly rushed in upon them, and seized the clergyman, bidding his man secure the

woman. The clergyman resisted, protesting his innocence which his language to the woman confirmed; but, finding it to no purpose, he at last desired that he might be permitted to go into an ironmonger's house near. This the marshal refused, and dragged the clergyman to the end of Salisbury Court, in Fleet Street, where he raised a mob about him; and two or three gentlemen, who knew the parson, happening to come by, asked the mob what they were doing with him, telling them he was chaplain to a noble lord. The rough gentry answered, ' Damn him, we believe he's chaplain to the devil, for we caught him with a whore.'

Hereupon the gentlemen desired the marshal to go to a tavern, that they might talk with him without noise and tumult, which he consented to. When they came into the tavern, the clergyman asked the marshal by what authority he thus abused him. The marshal replied he was a city officer (pulling out his staff), and would have him to the Compter, unless he gave very good security for his appearance next morning, when he would swear that he caught him with a whore.

The clergyman seeing him so bent upon perjury, which would very much expose him, sent for other persons to vindicate his reputation, who, putting a purse of gold into the marshal's hand (which they found was the only way to deal with such a monster in iniquity), the clergyman was permitted to depart.

A thief of most infamous character, named Arnold Powel, being confined in Newgate, on a charge of having robbed a house in the neighbourhood of Golden Square of property to a great amount, was visited by Jonathan, who informed him that, in consideration of a sum of money, he would save his life; adding that, if the proposal was rejected, he should inevitably die at Tyburn for the offence on account of which he was then imprisoned. The prisoner, however, not believing that it was in Wild's power to do him any injury, bade him defiance. Powel was brought to trial; but, through a defect of evidence, he was acquitted. Having gained intelligence that Powel had committed a burglary in the house of Mr. Eastlick, near Fleet Ditch, Wild caused that gentleman to prosecute the robber. Upon receiving information that a bill was found for the burglary, Powel sent for Wild, and a compromise was effected according to the terms which Wild himself had proposed, in consequence of which

Powel was assured that his life should be preserved. Upon the approach of the sessions, Wild informed the prosecutor that the first and second days would be employed in other trials, and, as he was willing Mr. Eastlick should avoid attending with his witnesses longer than was necessary, he would give timely notice when Powel would be arraigned. But he contrived to have the prisoner put to the bar; and, no persons appearing to prosecute, he was ordered to be taken away; but after some time he was again set to the bar, then ordered away, and afterwards put up a third time, proclamation being made each time for the prosecutor to appear. At length the jury were charged with the prisoner, and, as no accusation was adduced against him, he was necessarily dismissed; and the Court ordered Mr. Eastlick's recognisances to be estreated.

Powel was ordered to remain in custody till the next sessions, there being another indictment against him; and Mr. Eastlick represented the behaviour of Wild to the Court, who justly reprimanded him with great severity.

Powel put himself into a salivation, in order to avoid being brought to trial the next sessions; but, notwithstanding this stratagem, he was arraigned and convicted, and executed on the 20th of March, 1716-7.

At this time Wild had quitted his apartments at Mrs. Seagoe's, and hired a house adjoining to the Coopers' Arms, on the opposite side of the Old Bailey. The unexampled villainies of this man were now become an object of so much consequence, as to excite the particular attention of the legislature. In the year 1718 an act was passed, deeming every person guilty of a capital offence who should accept a reward in consequence of restoring stolen effects without prosecuting the thief. It was the general opinion that this law would effectually suppress the iniquitous practices of Wild; but, after some interruption to his proceedings, he devised means for evading it, which were for several years attended with success.

He now declined the custom of receiving money from the persons who applied to him; but, upon the second or third time of calling, informed them that all he had been able to learn respecting their business was, that, if a sum of money was left at an appointed place, their property would be restored the same day.

Sometimes, as the person robbed was returning from Wild's house, he was accosted in the street by a man who delivered the stolen effects, at the same time producing a note, expressing the sum that was to be paid for them.

In cases wherein he supposed danger was to be apprehended, he advised people to advertise that whoever would bring the stolen goods to Jonathan Wild should be rewarded, and no questions asked.

In the two first instances it could not be proved that he either saw the thief, received the goods, or accepted of a reward; and in the latter case he acted agreeably to the directions of the injured party, and there appeared no reason to criminate him as being in confederacy with the felons.

When he was asked what would satisfy him for his trouble, he told the persons who had recovered their property that what he had done was without any interested view, and merely from a principle of doing good; that therefore he made no claim; but, if he accepted a present, he should not consider it as being his due, but as an instance of generosity, which he should acknowledge accordingly.

Our adventurer's business increased exceedingly, and he opened an office in Newtoner's Lane, to the management of which he appointed his man Abraham. This Israelite proved a remarkably industrious and faithful servant to Jonathan, who intrusted him with matters of the greatest importance.

By too strict an application to business Wild much

impaired his health, so that he judged it prudent to retire into the country for a short time. He hired a lodging at Dulwich, leaving both offices under the direction of Abraham.

A lady had her pocket picked of bank-notes to the amount of seven thousand pounds. She related the particulars of her robbery to Abraham, who in a few days apprehended three pickpockets, and conducted them to Jonathan's lodgings at Dulwich. Upon their delivering up all the notes, Wild dismissed them. When the lady applied to Abraham, he restored her property, and she generously made him a present of four hundred pounds, which he delivered to his employer. These three pickpockets were afterwards apprehended for some other offences, and transported. One of them carefully concealed a bank-note for a thousand pounds in the lining of his coat. On his arrival at Maryland, he procured cash for the note, and, having purchased his freedom, went to New York, where he assumed the character of a gentleman.

Wild's business would not permit him to remain long at Dulwich; and being under great inconvenience from the want of Abraham's immediate assistance, he did not keep open his office in Newtoner's Lane for more than three months.

About a week after the return of Jonathan from Dulwich, a mercer in Lombard Street ordered a porter to carry to a particular inn a box containing goods to the amount of two hundred pounds. In his way the porter was observed by three thieves, one of whom, being more genteelly dressed than his companions, accosted the man in the following manner: ' If you are willing to earn sixpence, my friend, step to the tavern at the end of the street, and ask for the roque-laure I left at the bar; but, lest the waiter should scruple giving it to you, take my gold watch as a token. Pitch your burden upon this bulk, and I will take care of it till you return; but be sure you make

77

haste.' The man went to the tavern, and, having delivered his message, was informed that the thing he inquired for had not been left there; upon which the porter said, ' Since you scruple to trust me, look at this gold watch, which the gentleman gave me to produce as a token.' What was called a gold watch, being examined, proved to be only pewter lacquered. In consequence of this discovery, the porter hastened back to where he had left the box; but neither that nor the sharpers were to be found.

The porter was, with reason, apprehensive that he should incur his master's displeasure if he related what had happened; and, in order to excuse his folly, he determined upon the following stratagem:—he rolled himself in the mud, and then went home, saying he had been knocked down, and robbed of the goods.

The proprietor of the goods applied to Wild, and related to him the story he had been told by his servant. Wild told him he had been deceived as to the manner in which the trunk was lost, and that he should be convinced of it if he would send for the porter. A messenger was accordingly dispatched for him, and, upon his arrival, Abraham conducted him into a room separated from the office only by a slight partition. ' Your master,' said Abraham, ' has just been here concerning the box you lost; and he desired that you might be sent for, in order to communicate the particulars of the robbery.—What kind of people were the thieves, and in what manner did they take the box away? ' In reply the man said, ' Why, two or three fellows knocked me down, and then carried off the box.' Hereupon Abraham told him, that, ' if they knocked him down, there was but little chance of the property being recovered, since that offence rendered them liable to be hanged. But,' continued he, ' let me prevail upon you to speak the truth; for, if you persist in a refusal, be assured we shall discover it by some other means. Pray, do you recollect nothing about a token? Were you not to fetch a roquelaure from a tavern? and did you not produce a gold watch as a token to induce the waiter to deliver it?'—Astonished at Abraham's words, the porter declared 'he believed he was a witch,' and immediately acknowledged in what manner he had lost the box.

One of the villains concerned in the above transaction lived in the house formerly inhabited by Wild, in Cock Alley, near Cripplegate. To this place Jonathan and Abraham repaired, and, when they were at the door, they overheard a dispute between the man and his wife, during which the former declared that he would set out for Holland the next day. Upon this they forced open the door; and Wild, saying he was under the necessity of preventing his intended voyage, took him into custody, and conducted him to the Compter. On the following day, the goods being returned to the owner, Wild received a handsome reward; and he contrived to procure the discharge of the thief.

On the 23d or 24th of January, 1718-19, Margaret Dodwell and Alice Wright went to Wild's house, and desired to have a private interview with him. Observing one of these women to be with child, he imagined she might want a father to her expected issue; for it was a part of his business to procure persons to stand in the place of the real fathers of children born in consequence of illicit commerce. Being shown into another room, Dodwell spoke in the following manner:—' I do not come, Mr. Wild, to inform you that I have met with any loss, but that I wish to find something. If you will follow my advice, you may acquire a thousand pounds, or perhaps many thousands.' Jonathan here expressed the utmost willingness to engage in an enterprise so highly lucrative, and the woman proceeded thus: ' My plan is this: you must procure two or three stout resolute fellows who will undertake to rob a house in Wormwood Street, near Bishopsgate. This house is kept by a cane chair maker, named John Cooke, who has a lodger, an ancient maiden lady, immensely rich; and she keeps her money in a box in her apartment; she is now gone into the country to fetch more. One of the men must find an opportunity of getting into the shop in the evening, and conceal himself in a sawpit there: he may let his companions in when the family are retired to rest. But it will be particularly necessary to secure two stout apprentices, and a boy, who lie in the garret. I wish, however, that no murder may be committed.' Upon this Wright said, ' Phoo! phoo! when people engage in matters of this sort, they must manage as well as they can, and so as to provide for their own safety.' Dodwell now resumed her discourse to Jonathan. ' The boys having been secured, no kind of difficulty will attend getting possession of the old lady's money, she being from home, and her room under that where the boys sleep. In the room facing that of the old lady, Cooke and his wife lie: he is a man of remarkable courage; great caution, therefore, must be observed respecting him; and indeed I think it would be as well to knock him on the head; for then his drawers may be rifled, and he is never without money. A woman and a child lie under the room belonging to the old lady, but I hope no violence will be offered to them.'

Having heard the above proposal, Wild took the women into custody, and lodged them in Newgate. It is not to be supposed that his conduct in this affair proceeded from a principle of virtue or justice, but that he declined engaging in the iniquitous scheme from an apprehension that their design was to draw him into a snare.

Dodwell had lived five months in Mr. Cooke's house, and, though she paid no rent, he was too generous to turn her out, or in any manner to oppress her. Wild prosecuted Dodwell and Wright for a misdemeanour, and, being found guilty, they were sentenced each to six months' imprisonment.

Wild had inserted in his book a gold watch, a quantity of fine lace, and other property of considerable value, which one John Butler had stolen from a house at Newington Green; but Butler, instead of coming to account as usual, had declined his felonious practices, and lived on the produce of his booty. Wild, highly enraged at being excluded his share, determined to pursue every possible means for subjecting him to the power of justice.

Being informed that he lodged at a public house in Bishopsgate Street, Wild went to the house early one morning, when Butler, hearing him ascending the stairs, jumped out of the window of his room, and, climbing over the wall of the yard, got into the street. Wild broke open the door of the room; but was exceedingly disappointed and mortified to find that the man of whom he was in pursuit had escaped. In the mean time Butler ran into a house, the door of which stood open, and, descending to the kitchen, where some women were washing, told them he was pursued by a bailiff, and they advised him to conceal himself in the coalhole.

Jonathan, coming out of the ale-house, and seeing a shop on the opposite side of the way open, he inquired of the master, who was a dyer, whether a man had not taken refuge in his house. The dyer answered in the negative, saying he had not left his shop more than a minute since it had been opened. Wild requested to search the house, and the dyer readily complied. Wild asked the women if they knew whether a man had taken shelter in the house, which they denied; but, informing them that the man he sought was a thief, they said he would find him in the coalhole.

Having procured a candle, Wild and his attendants searched the place without effect, and they examined every part of the house with no better success. He observed that the villain must have escaped into the street; on which the dyer said that could not be the case; that if he had entered, he must still be in the house, for he had not quitted the shop, and it was impossible that a man could pass to the street without his knowledge; advising Wild to search the cellar again. They now all went into the cellar, and, after some time spent in searching, the dyer turned up a large vessel, used in his business, and Butler appeared. Wild asked him in what manner he had disposed of the goods he stole from Newington Green, upbraided him as being guilty of ingratitude, and declared that he should certainly be hanged.

Butler, however, knowing the means by which an accommodation might be effected, directed our hero to go to his lodging, and look behind the head of the bed, where he would find what would recompense him for his time and trouble. Wild went to the place, and found what perfectly satisfied him; but, as Butler had been apprehended in a public manner, the other was under the necessity of taking him before a magistrate, who committed him for trial. He was tried the ensuing sessions at the Old Bailey; but, by the artful management of Wild, instead of being condemned to die, he was only sentenced to transportation.

Being at an inn in Smithfield, Wild observed a large trunk in the yard, and, imagining that it contained property of value, he hastened home, and instructed one of the thieves he employed to carry it off. The man he used in this matter was named Jeremiah Rann, and he was reckoned one of the most dexterous thieves in London. Having dressed himself so as exactly to resemble a porter, he carried away the trunk without being observed.

Mr. Jarvis, a whipmaker by trade, and the proprietor of the trunk, had no sooner discovered his loss than he applied to Wild, who returned him the goods, in consideration of receiving ten guineas. Some time after, a disagreement taking place between Jonathan and Rann, the former apprehended the latter, who was tried and condemned to die. The day preceding that on which Rann was executed he sent for Mr. Jarvis, and related to him all the particulars of the trunk. Wild was threatened with a prosecution by Mr. Jarvis; but all apprehensions arising hence were soon dissipated by the decease of that gentleman.

Wild, being much embarrassed in endeavouring to find out some method by which he might safely dispose of the property that was not claimed by the respective proprietors, revolved in his mind a variety of schemes; but at length he adopted that which follows: he purchased a sloop, in order to transport the goods to Holland and Flanders, and gave the command of the vessel to a notorious thief, named Roger Johnson.

Ostend was the port where this vessel principally traded; but, when the goods were not disposed of there, Johnson navigated her to Bruges, Ghent, Brussels, and other places. He brought home lace, wine, brandy, etc., and these commodities were landed in the night, without making any increase to the business of the revenue officers. This trade was continued about two years, when, five pieces of lace being lost, Johnson deducted the value of them from the mate's pay. Violently irritated by this conduct, the mate lodged an information against Johnson for running a great quantity of various kinds of goods.

In consequence of this the vessel was exchequered, Johnson cast in damages to the amount of 700l. and the commercial proceedings were entirely ruined.

A disagreement had for some time subsisted between Johnson and Thomas Edwards, who kept a house of resort for thieves in Long Lane, concerning the division of some booty. Meeting one day in the Strand, they charged each other with felony, and were both taken into custody. Wild bailed Johnson, and Edwards was not prosecuted. The latter had no sooner recovered his liberty than he gave information against Wild, whose private warehouses being searched, a great quantity of stolen goods were there found. Wild now arrested Edwards in the name of Johnson, to whom he pretended the goods belonged, and he was taken to the Marshalsea, but the next day procured bail. Edwards determined to wreak his revenge upon Johnson, and for some time industriously sought him in vain; but, meeting him accidentally in Whitechapel Road, he gave him into the custody of a peace-officer, who conducted him to an adjacent alehouse. Johnson sent for Wild, who immediately attended, accompanied by his man, Quilt Arnold. Wild promoted a riot, during which Johnson availed himself of an opportunity of effecting an escape.

Information being made against Wild for the rescue of Johnson, he judged it prudent to abscond, and he remained concealed for three weeks; at the end of which time, supposing all danger to be over, he returned to his house. Being apprized of this, Mr. Jones, high-constable of Holborn division, went to Jonathan's house in the Old Bailey, on the 15th of February, 1725, apprehended him and Quilt Arnold, and took them before Sir John Fryer, who committed them to Newgate on a charge of having assisted in the escape of Johnson.

On Wednesday, the 24th of the same month, Wild moved to be either admitted to bail or discharged, or brought to trial that sessions. On the following Friday a warrant of detainer was produced against him in Court, and to it was affixed the following articles of information:

I. That for many years past he had been a confederate with great numbers of highwaymen, pick-pockets, housebreakers, shop-lifters, and other thieves.

II. That he had formed a kind of corporation of thieves, of which he was the head or director; and that notwithstanding his pretended services, in detecting and prosecuting offenders, he procured such only to be hanged as concealed their booty, or refused to share it with him.

III. That he had divided the town and country into so many districts, and appointed distinct gangs for each, who regularly accounted with him for their robberies. That he had also a particular set to steal at churches in time of divine service: and likewise other moving detachments to attend at Court on birth-days, balls, &c. and at both houses of parliament, circuits, and country fairs.

IV. That the persons employed by him were for the most part felon convicts, who had returned from transportation before the time for which they were transported was expired; and that he made choice of them to be his agents, because they could not be legal evidences against him, and because he had it in his power to take from them what part of the stolen goods he thought fit, and otherwise use them ill, or hang them, as he pleased.

V. That he had from time to time supplied such convicted felons with money and clothes, and lodged them in his own house, the better to conceal them: particularly some against whom there are now informations for counterfeiting and diminishing broad pieces and guineas.

VI. That he had not only been a receiver of stolen goods, as well as of writings of all kinds, for near fifteen years past, but had frequently been a con-federate, and robbed along with the above-mentioned convicted felons.

VII. That in order to carry on these vile practices, and to gain some credit with the ignorant multitude, he usually carried a short silver staff, as a badge of authority from the government, which he used to produce when he himself was concerned in robbing.

VIII. That he had, under his care and direction, several warehouses for receiving and concealing stolen goods; and also a ship for carrying off jewels, watches, and other valuable goods, to Holland, where he had a superannuated thief for his factor.

IX. That he kept in pay several artists to make alterations, and transform watches, seals, snuff-boxes, rings, and other valuable things, that they might not be known, several of which he used to present to such persons as he thought might be of service to him.

X. That he seldom or never helped the owners to the notes and papers they had lost unless he found them able exactly to specify and describe them, and then often insisted on more than half the value.

XI. And, lastly, it appears that he has often sold human blood, by procuring false evidence to swear persons into facts they were not guilty of; sometimes to prevent them from being evidences against himself, and at other times for the sake of the great reward given by the government.

The information of Mr. Jones was also read in Court, setting forth that two persons would be produced to accuse the prisoner of capital offences. The men alluded to in the above affidavit were John Follard and Thomas Butler, who had been convicted; but, it being deemed expedient to grant them a pardon on condition of their appearing in support of a prosecution against Wild, they pleaded to the same, and were remanded to Newgate till the next sessions.

Saturday, the 12th of April, Wild, by counsel, moved that his trial might be postponed till the ensuing sessions; and an affidavit made by the prisoner was read in Court, purporting that till the preceding evening he was entirely ignorant of a bill having been found against him; that he knew not what offence he was charged with, and was unable to procure two material witnesses, one of them living near Brentford, and the other in Somersetshire. This was opposed by the counsel for the crown, who urged that it would be improper to defer the trial on so frivolous a pretext as that made by the prisoner; that the affidavit expressed an ignorance of what offence he was charged with, and yet declared that two nameless persons were material witnesses.

The prisoner informed the Court that his witnesses were —— Hays, at the Pack Horse, on Turnham Green, and —— Wilson, a clothier, at Frome; adding that he had heard it slightly intimated that he was indicted for a felony upon a person named Stretham. Wild's counsel moved that the names of Hays and Wilson might be inserted in the affidavit, and that it should be again sworn to by the prisoner. The counsel for the prosecution observed that justice would not be denied the prisoner, though it could not be reasonably expected that he would be allowed any extraordinary favours or indulgences. Follard and Butler were, at length, bound each in the penalty of 500l. to appear at the ensuing sessions, when it was agreed that Wild's fate should be determined.

Saturday, May 15, 1725, Jonathan Wild was indicted for privately stealing in the house of Catherine Stretham, in the parish of St. Andrew, Holborn, fifty yards of lace, the property of the said Catherine, on the 22d of January, 1724-5. He was a second time indicted for feloniously receiving from the said Catherine, on the 10th of March, ten guineas, on account, and under pretence, of restoring the said lace, without apprehending and prosecuting the felon who stole the property.

Previous to his trial Wild distributed among the jurymen, and other persons who were walking on the leads before the Court, a great number of printed papers, under the title of ' A List of Persons discovered, apprehended, and convicted of several Robberies on the Highway; and also for Burglary and Housebreaking; and also for returning from Transportation: by Jonathan Wild.' This list contained the names of thirty-five for robbing on the highway, twenty-two for housebreaking, and ten for returning from transportation. To the list was annexed the following *Nota Bene:*—

' Several others have been also convicted for the like crimes, but, remembering not the persons' names who had been robbed, I omit the criminals' names.

' Please to observe that several others have been also convicted for shop-lifting, picking of pockets, &c., by the female sex, which are capital crimes, and which are too tedious to be inserted here, and the prosecutors not willing of being exposed.

' In regard, therefore, of the numbers above convicted, some, that have yet escaped justice, are endeavouring to take away the life of the said

' JONATHAN WILD.'

The prisoner, being put to the bar, requested that the witnesses might be examined apart, which was complied with. Henry Kelly deposed that by the prisoner's direction he went, in company with Margaret Murphy, to the prosecutor's shop, under pretence of buying some lace; that he stole a tin box, and gave it to Murphy in order to deliver to Wild, who waited in the street for the purpose of receiving their booty, and rescuing them if they should be taken into custody; that they returned together to Wild's house, where the box, being opened, was found to contain eleven pieces of lace; that Wild said he could afford to give no more than five guineas, as he should not be able to get more than ten guineas for returning the goods to the owner; that he received, as his share, three guineas and a crown, and that Murphy had what remained of the five guineas.

Margaret Murphy was next sworn, and her evidence

corresponded in every particular with that of the former witness.*

Catherine Stretham, the elder, deposed that, between three and four in the afternoon of the 22d of January, a man and woman came to her house, pretending that they wanted to purchase some lace; that she showed them two or three parcels, to the quality and price of which they objected; and that in about three minutes after they had left the shop she missed a tin box, containing a quantity of lace, the value of which she estimated at 50*l.*

The prisoner's counsel observed that it was their opinion he could not be legally convicted, because the indictment positively expressed that *he stole* the lace *in* the house, whereas it had been proved in evidence that he was at a considerable distance when the fact was committed. They allowed that he might be liable to conviction as an accessory before the fact, or guilty of receiving the property, knowing it to be stolen; but conceived that he could not be deemed guilty of a capital felony unless the indictment declared (as the act directs) that he did *assist, command,* or *hire.*

Lord Raymond presided when Wild was tried, and, in summing up the evidence, his lordship observed that the guilt of the prisoner was a point beyond all dispute; but that, as a similar case was not to be found in the law-books, it became his duty to act with great caution: he was not perfectly satisfied that the construction urged by the counsel for the crown could be put upon the indictment; and, as the life of a fellow-creature was at stake, recommended the prisoner to the mercy of the jury, who brought in their verdict Not Guilty.

Wild was indicted a second time for an offence committed during his confinement in Newgate. The indictment being opened by the counsel for the crown,

* Margaret Murphy was executed March 27, 1728, for stealing plate.

the following clause in an act passed in the 4th year of Geo. I. was ordered to be read:

' And whereas there are divers persons who have secret acquaintance with felons, and who make it their business to help persons to their stolen goods, and by that means gain money from them, which is divided between them and the felons, whereby they greatly encourage such offenders:—Be it enacted, by the authority aforesaid, that whenever any person taketh money or reward, directly or indirectly, under pretence, or upon account, of helping any person or persons to any stolen goods or chattels, every such person so taking money or reward as aforesaid (unless such person do apprehend, or cause to be apprehended, such felon who stole the same, and give evidence against him) shall be guilty of felony, according to the nature of the felony committed in stealing such goods, and in such and the same manner as if such offender had stolen such goods and chattels in the manner, and with such circumstances, as the same were stolen.'

Catherine Stretham deposed to the following effect: ' A box of lace being stolen out of my shop on the 22d of January, I went in the evening of the same day to the prisoner's house, in order to employ him in recovering my goods; but, not finding him at home, I advertised them, offering a reward of fifteen guineas, and saying no questions should be asked. The advertisement proved ineffectual: I therefore went again to the prisoner's house, and by his desire gave the best description that I was able of the persons I suspected to be the robbers; and, promising to make inquiry after my property, he desired me to call again in two or three days. I attended him a second time, when he informed me that he had learnt something concerning my goods, and expected more particular information in a short time. During this conversation we were joined by a man who said he had reason to suspect that one Kelly, who had been tried for circulating plated shillings, was concerned in stealing the lace. I went to the prisoner again on the day he was apprehended, and informed him that, though I had advertised a reward of no more than fifteen, I would give twenty or twenty-five guineas, rather than not recover my property; upon which he desired me not to be in too great a hurry, and said the people who had the lace were gone out of town, but that he would contrive to foment a disagreement between them, by which means he should be enabled to recover the goods on more easy terms. He sent me word, on the 10th of March, that if I would attend him in Newgate, and bring ten guineas with me, the goods should be returned. I went to the prisoner, who desired a person to call a porter, and then gave me a letter, saying it was the direction he had received where to apply for the lace. I told him I could not read, and gave the letter to the man he had sent for, who appeared to be a ticket-porter. The prisoner then told me I must give the porter ten guineas, that he might pay the people who had my goods, otherwise they would not return them. I gave the money, and the man went out of the prison; but in a short time he returned with a box sealed up, though it was not the box I lost. I opened it, and found all my lace, excepting one piece. I asked the prisoner what satisfaction he expected; and he answered, ' Not a farthing; I have no interested views in matters of this kind, but act from a principle of serving people under misfortune. I hope I shall soon be able to recover the other piece of lace, and to return you the ten guineas, and perhaps cause the thief to be apprehended. For the service I can render you I shall only expect your prayers. I have many enemies, and know not what will be the consequence of this imprisonment.'

The prisoner's counsel argued that as Murphy had deposed that Wild, Kelly, and herself, were concerned in the felony, the former could by no means be considered as coming within the description of the act on which the indictment was founded, for the act in question was not meant to operate against the actual perpetrators of felony, but to subject such persons to punishment as held a correspondence with felons.

The counsel for the crown observed that, from the evidence adduced, no doubt could remain of the prisoner's coming under the meaning of the act, since it had been proved that he had engaged in combinations with felons, and had not discovered them.

The judge recapitulated the arguments enforced on each side, and was of opinion that the case of the prisoner was clearly within the meaning of the act; for it was plain that he had maintained a secret correspondence with felons, and received money for restoring stolen goods to the owners, which money was divided between him and the felons, whom he did not prosecute. The jury pronounced him guilty, and he was executed at Tyburn on Monday, the 24th of May, 1725, along with Robert Harpham.

Wild, when he was under sentence of death, frequently declared that he thought the service he had rendered the public in returning the stolen goods to the owners, and apprehending felons, was so great as justly to entitle him to the royal mercy. He said that, had he considered his case as being desperate, he should have taken timely measures for inducing some powerful friend at Wolverhampton to intercede in his favour; and that he thought it not unreasonable to entertain hopes of obtaining a pardon through the interest of some of the dukes, earls, and other persons of high distinction, who had recovered their property through his means. It was observed to him that he had trained up a great number of thieves, and must be conscious that he had not enforced the execution of the law from any principle of virtue, but had sacrificed the lives of a great number of his accomplices, in order to provide for his own safety, and to gratify his desire of revenge against such as had incurred his displeasure.

He was observed to be in an unsettled state of mind, and, being asked whether he knew the cause thereof, he said he attributed his disorder to the many wounds he had received in apprehending felons, and particularly mentioned two fractures of his skull, and his throat being cut by Blueskin.

He declined attending divine service in the chapel, excusing himself on account of his infirmities, and saying that there were many people highly exasperated against him, and therefore he could not expect but that his devotions would be interrupted by their insulting behaviour. He said he had fasted four days, which had greatly increased his weakness. He asked the Ordinary the meaning of the words ' Cursed is every one that hangeth on a tree ; ' and what was the state of the soul immediately after its departure from the body. He was advised to direct his attention to matters of more importance, and sincerely to repent of the crimes he had committed.

By his desire the Ordinary administered the sacrament to him, and during the ceremony he appeared to be somewhat attentive and devout. The evening preceding the day on which he suffered he inquired of the Ordinary whether self-murder could be deemed a crime, since many of the Greeks and Romans, who had put a period to their own lives, were so honourably mentioned by historians. He was informed that the most wise and learned heathens accounted those guilty of the greatest cowardice who had not fortitude sufficient to maintain themselves in the station to which they had been appointed by the providence of Heaven; and that the Christian doctrines condemned the practice of suicide in the most express terms.

He pretended to be convinced that self-murder was a most impious crime; but about two in the morning he endeavoured to put an end to his life by drinking laudanum : however, on account of the largeness of the dose, and his having fasted for a considerable time, no other effect was produced than drowsiness, or a kind of stupefaction. The situation of Wild being observed by two of his fellow-prisoners, they advised him to rouse his spirits, that he might be able to attend to the devotional exercises, and, taking him by the arms, they obliged him to walk, which he could not have done alone, being much afflicted with the gout. The exercise revived him a little, but he presently became exceedingly pale, then grew very faint; a profuse sweating ensued, and soon afterwards his stomach discharged the greatest part of the laudanum. Though he was somewhat recovered, he was nearly in a state of insensibility; and in this situation he was put into the cart and conveyed to Tyburn.

On his way to the place of execution the populace treated this offender with remarkable severity, incessantly pelting him with stones, dirt, &c. and execrating him as the most consummate villain that had ever disgraced human nature.

Upon his arrival at Tyburn he appeared to be much recovered from the effects of the laudanum; and the executioner informed him that a reasonable time would be allowed him for preparing himself for the important change that he must soon experience. He continued sitting some time in the cart; but the populace were at length so enraged at the indulgence shown him, that they outrageously called to the executioner to perform the duties of his office, violently threatening him with instant death if he presumed any longer to delay. He judged it prudent to comply with their demands, and when he began to prepare for the execution the popular clamour ceased.

About two o'clock on the following morning the remains of Wild were interred in St. Pancras Churchyard; but a few nights afterwards the body was taken up (for the use of the surgeons, as it was supposed). At midnight a hearse and six was waiting at the end of Fig Lane, where the coffin was found the next day.

Wild had by the woman he married at Wolverhampton a son about nineteen years old, who came to London a short time before the execution of his father. He was a youth of so violent and ungovernable a disposition, that it was judged prudent to confine him while his father was conveyed to Tyburn, lest he should create a tumult, and prove the cause of mischief among the populace. Soon after the death of his father he accepted a sum of money to become a servant in one of our plantations.

Besides the woman to whom he was married at Wolverhampton, five others lived with him under the pretended sanction of matrimony: the first was Mary Milliner; the second Judith Nun, by whom he had a daughter; the third Sarah Grigson, alias Perrin; the fourth Elizabeth Man, who cohabited with him above five years; the fifth, whose real name is uncertain, married some time after the death of Wild.

History can scarcely furnish an instance of such complicated villainy as was shown in the character of Jonathan Wild, who possessed abilities which, had they been properly cultivated, and directed into a right course, would have rendered him a respectable and useful member of society; but it is to be lamented that the profligate turn of mind which distinguished him in the early part of his life disposed him to adopt the maxims of the abandoned people with whom he became acquainted.

During his apprenticeship Wild was observed to be fond of reading; but, as his finances would not admit of his buying books, his studies were confined to such as casually fell in his way; and they unfortunately happened to contain those abominable doctrines to which thousands have owed the ruin of both their bodies and souls. In short, at an early period of life he imbibed the principles of deism and atheism; and the sentiments he thus early contracted he strictly adhered to nearly till the period of his dissolution.

Voluminous writings were formerly beyond the purchase of persons in the inferior classes of life; but the great encouragement that has of late years been given to the publication of weekly numbers has so liberally diffused the streams of knowledge, that but few even of the lower ranks of society can be sensible of any impediment to the gratification of the desire of literary acquirements.

Wild trained up and instructed his dependents in the practice of roguery; and, when they became the objects of his displeasure, he laboured with unremitting assiduity to procure their deaths. Thus his temporal and private interest sought gratification at the expense of every religious and moral obligation. We must conceive it to be impossible for a man acknowledging the existence of an Almighty Being to expect his favour, while devising the means of corrupting his fellow-creatures, and cutting them off ' even in the blossom of their sins: ' but the atheist, having nothing after this world either to hope or fear, is only careful to secure himself from detection; and the success of one iniquitous scheme naturally induces him to engage in others, and the latter actions are generally attended with circumstances of more aggravated guilt than the former.

There is a principle implanted in our nature, which will exert itself when we are approaching to a state of dissolution, and impress our minds with a full confidence in the existence of an eternal God, who will reward or punish us according to our deserts or demerits. Thus it happened to the miserable subject of these pages, who, when he had relinquished the hope of surviving the sentence of the law, anxiously inquired into the meaning of several texts of scripture, and concerning the intermediate state of the soul.

The horrors of his guilt rushed upon his conscience with such force that reflection became intolerable; and, instead of repenting of his enormous crimes, he employed the last of his moments that were enlightened by reason (the distinguished characteristic of humanity) in meditating the means of self-destruction.

NATHANIEL HAWES,

TORTURED, AND AFTERWARDS EXECUTED, FOR ROBBERY.

At the time of the sufferings of this man, in the year 1721, such prisoners as contumaciously refused to plead to their indictments underwent torture until they complied with the law as it then regarded their case. This punishment is, however, no longer deemed compatible with freedom; and it was therefore abrogated in the year 1772. Yet, as the inhuman practice still prevails in some of the English settlements abroad, and as many nations continue to torture criminals, we shall, previous to entering upon the case of Hawes, offer some observations thereon.

In order to extort confession, torture is not peculiar to Roman Catholic countries, but is even a custom in China. The instrument of barbarity called the rack is composed of a thick strong plank, having a contrivance at one end to secure the hands, and at the other a sort of double wooden vice. The vice is formed of three stout uprights, two of which are moveable, but steadied by a block that is fastened on each side. The ancles of the culprit being placed in the machine, a cord is passed round the uprights, and held fast by two men. The chief tormentor then gradually introduces a wedge into the intervals, alternately changing sides. The method of forcing an expansion at the upper part causes the lower ends to draw towards the central upright, which is fixed unto the plank, and thereby compresses the ancles of the wretched sufferer; who, provided he be fortified by innocence or resolution, endures the advances of the wedge, until his bones are reduced to a jelly.

Stedman, in his account of Surinam, relates the following horrid scene, to which he was an eye-witness:

'There was a negro whose name was Neptune, no slave, but his own master, and a carpenter by trade: he was young and handsome, but, having killed the overseer of the estate of Altona, in the Para Creek, in consequence of some dispute, he justly forfeited his life. The particulars, however, are worth relating:

'This man having stolen a sheep to entertain a favourite young woman, the overseer, who burned with jealousy, had determined to see him hanged; to prevent which, the negro shot him dead among the sugar-canes. For these offences, of course, he was sentenced to be broken alive upon the rack, without the benefit of the *coup de grace*, or mercy-stroke. Informed of the dreadful sentence, he composedly laid himself down upon his back on a strong cross, on which, with his arms and legs extended, he was fastened by ropes. The executioner, also a black man, having now with a hatchet chopped off his left hand, next took up a heavy iron bar, with which, by repeated blows, he broke his bones to shivers, till the marrow, blood, and splinters, flew about the field; but the prisoner never uttered a groan nor a sigh! The ropes being next unlashed, I imagined him dead, and felt happy; till the magistrates stirring to depart, he writhed himself from the cross, when he fell on the grass, and damned them all as a set of barbarous rascals. At the same time, removing his right hand by the help of his teeth, he rested his head on part of the timber, and asked the by-standers for a pipe of tobacco, which was infamously answered by kicking and spitting on him, till I, with some American seamen, thought proper to prevent it. He then begged his head might be chopped off; but to no purpose. At last, seeing no end to his misery, he declared, " that though he had deserved death, he had not expected to die so many deaths; however, (said he,) you *Christians* have missed your aim at last, and I now care not were I to remain thus one month longer." After which he sung two extempore songs with a clear voice; the subjects of which were to bid adieu to his living friends, and to acquaint his deceased relations that in a very little time he should be with them, to enjoy their company for ever in a better place. This done, he calmly entered into conversation with some gentlemen concerning his trial, relating every particular with uncommon tranquillity. "But (said he abruptly), by the sun it must be eight o'clock, and by any longer discourse I should be sorry to be the cause of your losing your breakfast." Then, casting his eyes on a Jew, whose name was De Veries, "Apropos, Sir (said he), won't you please to pay me the ten shillings you owe me?" "For what to do?" "To buy meat and drink, to be sure—don't you perceive I'm to be kept alive?" Which speech, on seeing the Jew stare like a fool, this mangled wretch accompanied with a loud and hearty laugh. Next observing the soldier that stood sentinel over him biting occasionally a piece of dry bread, he asked him how it came to pass that he, a *white man*, should have no meat to eat along with it? "Because I am not so rich," answered the soldier. "Then I will make you a present, Sir (said the negro). First pick my hand that was chopped off, clean to the bones; next begin to devour my body till you are glutted; when you will have both bread and meat, as best becomes you:" which piece of humour was followed by a second laugh. And thus he continued until I left him, which was about three hours after the dreadful execution.

' Wonderful it is, indeed, that human nature should be able to endure so much torture! which assuredly could only be supported by a mixture of rage, contempt, pride, and the glory of braving his tormentors, from whom he was so soon to escape.

' I never recall to my remembrance without the most painful sensation this horrid scene, which must revolt the feelings of all who have one spark of humanity. If the reader, however, should be offended with my dwelling so long on this unpleasant subject, let it be some relief to his reflection to consider this punishment not inflicted as a wanton and unprovoked act of cruelty, but as the extreme severity of the Surinam laws on a desperate wretch, suffering, as an example to others, for complicated crimes; while, at the same time, it cannot but give me, and I hope many others, some consolation to reflect that the above barbarous mode of punishment was hitherto never put in practice in the British colonies. I must now relate an incident which, as it had a momentary effect on my imagination, might have had a lasting one on some who had not investigated the real cause of it, and which it gave me no small satisfaction to discover.

' About three in the afternoon, walking towards the place of execution, with my thoughts full of the affecting scene, and the image of the sufferer fresh in my mind, the first object I saw was his head, at some distance, placed on a stake, *nodding* to me backwards and forwards, as if he had been really alive. I instantly stopped short, and, seeing no person in the Savannah, nor a breath of wind sufficient to move a leaf or a feather, I acknowledge that I was rivetted to the ground where I stood, without having the resolution of advancing one step for some time; till, reflecting that I must be weak indeed not to approach this dead skull, and find out the wonderful phenomenon if possible, I boldly walked up, and instantly discovered the natural case, by the return of a vulture to the gallows, who perched upon it as if he meant to dispute with me this feast of carrion; which bird, having already picked out one of the eyes, had fled at my first approach, and, striking the skull with his talons, as he took his sudden flight, occasioned the motion already

100

described. I shall now only add, that this poor wretch, after living more than six hours, had been knocked on the head by the commiserating sentinel, the marks of whose musket were perfectly visible by a large open fracture in the skull.'

The torture of a criminal during the course of his trial is a cruelty consecrated by custom in most nations. It is used with an intent either to make him confess his crime, or explain some contradictions into which he had been led during his examination; or to discover his accomplices; or for some kind of metaphysical and incomprehensible purgation of infamy; or, finally, in order to discover other crimes, of which he is not accused, but of which he may be guilty.

No man can be judged a criminal until he be found guilty; nor can society take from him the public protection until it have been proved that he has violated the conditions on which it was granted. What right, then, but that of power, can authorize the punishment of a citizen, so long as there remains any doubt of his guilt? This dilemma is frequent. Either he is guilty or not guilty. If guilty, he should only suffer the punishment ordained by the laws, and torture becomes useless, as his confession is unnecessary. If he be not guilty, you torture the innocent; for, in the eye of the law, every man is innocent whose crime has not been proved. Besides, it is confounding all relations to expect that a man should be both the accuser and the accused; and that pain should be the test of truth, as if truth resided in the muscles and fibres of a wretch in torture. By this method the robust will escape and the feeble be condemned. These are the inconveniences of this pretended test of truth, worthy only of a cannibal, and which the Romans, in many respects barbarous, and whose savage virtue has been too much admired, reserved for the slaves alone.

What is the political intention of punishments?— To terrify, and be an example to others. Is this intention answered by thus privately torturing the guilty and the innocent? It is doubtless of importance that no crime should remain unpunished: but it is useless to make a public example of the author of a crime hid in darkness. A crime already committed, and for which there can be no remedy, can only be punished by a political society with an intention that no hopes of impunity should induce others to commit the same. If it be true that the number of those who from fear or virtue respect the laws is greater than of those by whom they are violated, the risk of torturing an innocent person is greater, as there is a greater probability that, *cæteris paribus*, an individual hath observed than he hath infringed the laws.

There is another ridiculous motive for torture—namely, to purge a man from infamy. Ought such an abuse to be tolerated in the nineteenth century? Can pain, which is a sensation, have any connexion with a moral sentiment, a matter of opinion? Perhaps the rack may be considered as the refiner's furnace.

It is not difficult to trace this senseless law to its origin; for an absurdity adopted by a whole nation must have some affinity with other ideas established and respected by the same nation. This custom seems to be the offspring of religion, by which mankind, in all nations, and in all ages, are so generally influenced. We are taught by our infallible Church that those stains of sin contracted through human frailty, and which have not deserved the eternal anger of the Almighty, are to be purged away in another life by an incomprehensible fire. Now infamy is a stain; and, if the punishments and fire of purgatory can take away all spiritual stains, why should not the pain of torture take away those of a civil nature? I imagine that the confession of a criminal, which in some tribunals is required as being essential to his condemnation, has a similar origin, and has been taken from the mysterious tribunal of penitence, where the confession of sins is a necessary part of the sacrament. Thus have men abused the unerring light of revelation; and, in the times of tractable ignorance, having no other, they naturally had recourse to it on every occasion, making the most remote and absurd applications. Moreover, infamy is a sentiment regulated neither by the laws nor by reason, but entirely by opinion; but torture renders the victim infamous, and therefore cannot take infamy away.

Another intention of torture is to oblige the supposed criminal to reconcile the contradictions into which he may have fallen during his examinations; as if the dread of punishment, the uncertainty of his fate, the solemnity of the Court, the majesty of the judge, and the ignorance of the accused, were not abundantly sufficient to account for contradictions, which are so common to men even in a state of tranquillity, and which must necessarily be multiplied by the perturbation of the mind of a man entirely engaged in the thoughts of saving himself from imminent danger.

This infamous test of truth is a remaining monument of that ancient and savage legislation in which trials by fire, by boiling water, or the uncertainty of combats, were called *judgments of God;* as if the links of that eternal chain whose beginning is in the breast of the First Cause of all things could ever be disunited by the institutions of men. The only difference between torture and trials by fire and boiling water is, that the event of the first depends on the will of the accused, and of the second on a fact entirely physical and external; but this difference is apparent only, not real. A man on the rack, in the convulsions of torture, has it as little in his power to declare the truth as, in former times, to prevent, without fraud, the effects of fire or boiling water.

Every act of the will is invariably in proportion to the force of the impression on our senses. The impression of pain, then, may increase to such a degree, that, occupying the mind entirely, it will compel the sufferer to use the shortest method of freeing himself from torment. His answer, therefore, will be an effect as necessary as that of fire or boiling water, and he will accuse himself of crimes of which he is innocent; so that the very means employed to distinguish the innocent from the guilty will most effectually destroy all difference between them.

It would be superfluous to confirm these reflections by examples of innocent persons who, from the agony of torture, have confessed themselves guilty : innumerable instances may be found in all nations and in every age. How amazing that mankind have always neglected to draw the natural conclusion ! Lives there a man who, if he has carried his thoughts ever so little beyond the necessities of life, when he reflects on such cruelty, is not tempted to fly from society, and return to his natural state of independence?

The result of torture, then, is a matter of calculation, and depends on the constitution, which differs in every individual, and is in proportion to his strength and sensibility; so that to discover truth by this method is a problem which may be better resolved by a mathematician than a judge, and may be thus stated. The force of the muscles and the sensibility of the nerves of an innocent person being given, it is required to find the degree of pain necessary to make him confess himself guilty of a given crime.

The examination of the accused is intended to find out the truth; but if this be discovered with so much difficulty in the air, gesture, and countenance of a man at ease, how can it appear in a countenance distorted by the convulsions of torture? Every violent action destroys those small alterations in the features which sometimes disclose the sentiments of the heart.

These truths were known to the Roman legislators, amongst whom slaves only, who were not considered as citizens, were tortured. They are known to the

104

English, a nation in which the progress of science, superiority in commerce, riches, and power, its natural consequences, together with the numerous examples of virtue and courage, leave no doubt of the excellence of its laws. They have been acknowledged in Sweden, where torture has been abolished. They are known to one of the wisest monarchs in Europe, who, having seated philosophy on the throne, by his beneficent legislation has made his subjects free, though dependent on the laws; the only freedom that reasonable men can desire in the present state of things. In short, torture has not been thought necessary in the laws of armies, composed chiefly of the dregs of mankind, where its use should seem most necessary. Strange phenomenon, that a set of men, hardened by slaughter and familiar with blood, should teach humanity to the sons of peace!

A very strange but necessary consequence of the use of torture is, that the case of the innocent is worse than that of the guilty. With regard to the first, either he confesses the crime which he has not committed, and is condemned; or he is acquitted, and has suffered a punishment he did not deserve. On the contrary, the person who is really guilty has the most favourable side of the question; for, if he supports the torture with firmness and resolution, he is acquitted, and has gained, having exchanged a greater punishment for a less.

The law by which torture is authorized says—' Men, be insensible to pain. Nature has indeed given you an irresistible self-love, and an unalienable right of self-preservation; but I create in you a contrary sentiment, an heroical hatred of yourselves. I command you to accuse yourselves, and to declare the truth, amidst the tearing of your flesh and the dislocation of your bones.'

Torture is used to discover whether the criminal be guilty of other crimes besides those of which he is accused, which is equivalent to the following reasoning:—'Thou art guilty of one crime, therefore it is possible that thou mayest have committed a thousand others; but the affair being doubtful, I must try it by my criterion of truth. The laws order thee to be tormented because thou art guilty, because thou mayest be guilty, and because I choose thou shouldest be guilty.'

Torture is used to make the criminal discover his accomplices; but, if it has demonstrated that it is not a proper means of discovering truth, how can it serve to discover the accomplices, which is one of the truths required? Will not the man who accuses himself yet more readily accuse others? Besides, is it just to torment one man for the crime of another? May not the accomplices be found out by the examination of the witnesses, or of the criminal—from the evidence, or from the nature of the crime itself—in short, by all the means that have been used to prove the guilt of the prisoner? The accomplices commonly fly when their comrade is taken.

All mankind, being exposed to the attempts of violence or perfidy, detest the crimes of which they may possibly be the victims; all desire that the principal offender and his accomplices may be punished; nevertheless, there is a natural compassion in the human heart, which makes all men detest the cruelty of torturing the accused, in order to extort confession. The law has not condemned them; and yet, though uncertain of their crime, you inflict a punishment more horrible than that which they are to suffer when their guilt is confirmed. 'Possibly thou mayest be innocent; but I will torture thee that I may be satisfied: not that I intend to make thee any recompense for the thousand deaths which I have made thee suffer, in lieu of that which is preparing for thee.' Who does not shudder at the idea? St. Augustin opposed such cruelty; the Romans tortured their slaves only; and Quintilian, recollecting that they were men, reproved the Romans for such want of humanity.

If there were but one nation in the world which had abolished the use of torture—if in that nation crimes were no more frequent than in others—and if that nation be more enlightened and more flourishing since the abolition—its example surely were sufficient for the rest of the world. England alone might instruct all other nations in this particular, but England is not the only nation. Torture hath been abolished in other countries, and with success; the question, therefore, is decided. Shall not a people who pique themselves on their politeness pride themselves also on their humanity? shall they obstinately persist in their inhumanity, merely because it is an ancient custom? Reserve, at least, such cruelty for the punishment of those hardened wretches who shall have assassinated the father of a family, or the father of his country; but that a young person who commits a fault which leaves no traces behind it should suffer equally with a parricide, is not this an useless piece of barbarity?

Nathaniel Hawes was a native of Norfolk, in which county he was born in the year 1701. His father was a grazier in ample circumstances, but, dying while the son was an infant, a relation in Hertfordshire took care of his education.

At a proper age he was apprenticed to an upholsterer in London; but, becoming connected with people of bad character, and thus acquiring an early habit of vice, he robbed his master when he had served only two years of his time, for which he was tried at the Old Bailey; and, being convicted of stealing to the amount of thirty-nine shillings, was sentenced to seven years' transportation.

This sentence, however, was not carried into execution, owing to the following circumstance:—A man named Phillips had encouraged the unhappy youth in his depredations, by purchasing, at a very low rate, such goods as he stole from his master: but, when Hawes was taken into custody, he gave information of this affair, in consequence of which a search-warrant was procured, and many effects belonging to Hawes's master were found in Phillips's possession.

Hereafter application was made to the king, and a free pardon was granted to Hawes, whereby he was rendered a competent evidence against Phillips, who was tried for receiving stolen goods, and transported for fourteen years.

Hawes, during his confinement in Newgate, had made such connexions as greatly contributed to the contamination of his morals; and, soon after his release, he connected himself with a set of bad fellows who acted under the direction of Jonathan Wild; and, having made a particular acquaintance with one John James, they joined in the commission of a number of robberies.

After an uncommon share of success for some days, they quarrelled on the division of the booty: in consequence each acted on his own account. Some little time after they had thus separated, Hawes, being apprehensive that James would impeach him, applied to Jonathan Wild, and informed against his old acquaintance, on which James was taken into custody, tried, convicted, and executed.

Notwithstanding this conviction, the Court sentenced Hawes to be imprisoned in the New Prison; and that gaol was preferred to Newgate, because the prisoners in the latter threatened to murder Hawes, for being an evidence against James.

Here it should be observed that, by an act of the 4th and 5th of William and Mary, for the more effectual conviction of highwaymen, the evidence of accomplices is allowed; but the evidence cannot claim his liberty unless two or more of his accomplices are convicted; but may be imprisoned during the pleasure of the Court.

Soon after his commitment, Hawes and another fellow made their escape, and, entering into partnership, committed a variety of robberies, particularly on the road between Hackney and Shoreditch.

This connexion, like the former, lasted but a short time: a dispute on dividing their ill-gotten gains occasioned a separation; soon after which Hawes went alone to Finchley Common, where, meeting with a gentleman riding to town, he presented a pistol to his breast, and commanded him instantly to dismount, that he might search him for his money.

The gentleman offered him four shillings, on which Hawes swore the most horrid oaths, and threatened instant death if he did not immediately submit. The gentleman quitted his horse, and in the same moment seized the pistol, which he snatched from the hand of the robber, and, presenting it to him, told him to expect death if he did not surrender himself.

Hawes, who was now as terrified as he had been insolent, made no opposition; and, the driver of a cart coming up just at that juncture, he was easily made prisoner, conveyed to London, and committed to Newgate.

When the sessions came on, and he was brought to the bar, he refused to plead to his indictment, alleging the following reasons for so doing: that he would die, as he had lived, like a gentleman: 'The people (said he), who apprehended me, seized a suit of fine clothes, which I intended to have gone to the gallows in; and, unless they are returned, I will not plead; for no one shall say that I was hanged in a dirty shirt and ragged coat.'

On this he was told what would be the consequence of his contempt of legal authority; but, this making no impression on him, sentence was pronounced that he should be pressed to death; whereupon he was taken from the Court, and, being laid on his back, sustained a load of two hundred and fifty pounds' weight about seven minutes; but, unable any longer to bear the pain, he entreated he might be conducted back to the Court, which being complied with, he pleaded not guilty; but the evidence against him being complete, he was convicted, and sentenced to die.

After conviction his behaviour was very improper. He told the other capital convicts he would die like a hero, and behaved in the same thoughtless way till the arrival of the warrant for his execution : after which his conduct was not altogether so imprudent. He owned to the Ordinary of Newgate that he was induced to refuse to plead to his indictment that the other prisoners might deem him a man of honour, and not from the idle vanity of being hanged in fine clothes.

He acknowledged many robberies which he had committed, but charged Jonathan Wild as being the principal author of his ruin, by purchasing the stolen goods. He likewise owned that he had been base enough to inform against persons who were innocent, particularly a gentleman's servant who was then in custody; but he did not discover many signs of contrition for this or any other of his offences.

He was executed at Tyburn on the 22d of December, 1721.

The inferences to be drawn from the case of this malefactor are obvious. By his informing against James, lest James should impeach him, we see how little confidence thieves can place in each other; and that partnerships in wickedness are sure to end in destruction.

From the resistance made by the gentleman whom Hawes attacked, and the consequent apprehension of the offender, we may fairly conclude that there is a cowardice naturally attached to guilt, which will almost infallibly favour the cause of the honest man.

MARGARET DIXON,

MURDERER.

THE following case is more remarkable for resuscitation after execution than even the flagitious life of the condemned. Though some doubt may arise of her guilt regarding the crime of which she was convicted, none can be entertained of her being restored to existence after having hanged the usual time, and enjoying life more than thirty years afterwards.

This remarkable woman was the daughter of poor parents, who lived at Musselburgh, about five miles from Edinburgh, and who brought up their child in the practice of religious duties, having instructed her in such household business as was likely to suit her future situation in life. The village of Musselburgh is almost entirely inhabited by gardeners, fishermen, and persons employed in making salt. The husbands having prepared the several articles for sale, the wives carry them to Edinburgh, and procure a subsistence by crying them through the streets of that city. When Margaret Dixon had attained years of maturity, she was married to a fisherman, by whom she had several children : but, there being a want of seamen, her husband was impressed into the naval service; and, during his absence from Scotland, his wife had an illicit connexion with a man at Musselburgh, in con-

It has frequently, from some accident happening in strangling the malefactor, produced the horrid effects above related. In the reign of Mary (the cruel) this death was commonly practised upon the objects of her vengeance; and many bishops, rather than deny their religious opinions, were burnt even without previous strangulation. It was high time this part of the sentence, the type of barbarism, should be dispensed with. The punishment now inflicted for this most unnatural and abhorred crime is hanging; but, once convicted, a woman need never look for mercy.

sequence of which she became pregnant. At this time it was the law in Scotland that a woman known to have been unchaste should sit in a distinguished place in the church, on three Sundays, to be publicly rebuked by the minister; and many poor infants have been destroyed because the mother dreaded this public exposure,* particularly as many Scotch ladies went to church to be witnesses of the frailty of a sister, who were never seen there on any other occasion.

The neighbours of Mrs. Dixon averred that she was with child; but this she constantly denied, though there was every appearance that might warrant the discrediting what she said. At length, however, she was delivered of a child; but it is uncertain whether it was born alive or not.

Be this as it may, she was taken into custody, and lodged in the gaol of Edinburgh. When her trial came on, several witnesses deposed that she had been frequently pregnant; others proved that there were signs of her having been delivered, and that a new-born infant had been found dead near the place of her residence.

The jury, giving credit to the evidence against her, brought in a verdict of guilty; in consequence of which she was doomed to suffer.

After her condemnation she behaved in the most penitent manner, confessed that she had been guilty of many sins, and even owned that she had departed from the line of duty to her husband; but she constantly and steadily denied that she had murdered her child, or even formed an idea of so horrid a crime. She owned that the fear of being exposed to the ridicule of her neighbours in the church had tempted her to deny that she was pregnant; and she said that,

* This proves, in a striking manner, the value of our Foundling Hospital in London, which has, doubtless, been the means of saving numbers of infants who would otherwise have been destroyed.

being suddenly seized with the pains of child-birth, she was unable to procure the assistance of her neighbours; and that a state of insensibility ensued, so that it was impossible she should know what became of the infant.

At the place of execution her behaviour was consistent with her former declaration. She avowed her total innocence of the crime of which she was convicted, but confessed the sincerest sorrow for all her other sins.

After execution her body was cut down and delivered to her friends, who put it into a coffin, and sent it in a cart to be buried at her native place; but, the weather being sultry, the persons who had the body in their care stopped to drink at a village called Pepper-Mill, about two miles from Edinburgh. While they were refreshing themselves, one of them perceived the lid of the coffin move, and, uncovering it, the woman immediately sat up, and most of the spectators ran off, with every sign of trepidation.

It happened that a person who was then drinking in the public house had recollection enough to bleed her. In about an hour she was put to bed; and by the following morning she was so far recovered as to be able to walk to her own house.

By the Scottish law, which is in part founded on that of the Romans, a person against whom the judgment of the Court has been executed can suffer no more in future, but is thenceforward totally exculpated; and it is likewise held that the marriage is dissolved by the execution of the convicted party; which indeed is consistent with the ideas that common sense would form on such an occasion.

Mrs. Dixon, then, having been convicted and executed as above mentioned, the king's advocate could prosecute her no farther; but he filed a bill in the High Court of Justiciary against the sheriff, for omitting to fulfil the law. The husband of this revived convict married her publicly a few days after she was hanged! and she constantly denied that she had been guilty of the alleged crime. She was living as late as the year 1753. This singular transaction took place in the year 1728.

FRANCIS CHARTERIS,

CONVICTED OF USING VIOLENCE TO THE PERSON OF ANN BOND.

THE name of Charteris, during life, was a terror to female innocence; may, therefore, his fate, and the exposure of his villainy, act as their shield against the destructive machinations of profligate men, especially such as those upon whom the blind and fickle goddess, Fortune, may have unworthily heaped riches. The wealthy profligate, in order to gratify an inordinate passion, will promise, perjure, and pay, to any length, or to any amount—then, ' like a loathsome weed, cast you away.'

> Be thus advis'd, ye young and fair,
> Let virtuous men engage your care.
> The rake and libertine despise;
> Their breath is poison—O be wise!
> Their arts and wiles turn quick away,
> And from fair Virtue's path ne'er stray.

By the law of Egypt rapes were punished by removal of the offending parts. The Athenian laws compelled the ravisher of a virgin to marry her. It was long before this offence was punished capitally by the Roman law; but at length the Lex Julia inflicted the pains of death on the ravisher. The Jewish law also punished this crime with death; but, if a virgin was deflowered without force, the offender was obliged to pay a fine and marry the woman.

By the 18th of Elizabeth, cap. 7, this offence was made felony without benefit of clergy.

It is certainly of a very heinous nature, and, if tolerated, would be subversive of all order and morality; yet it may still be questioned how far it is either useful or politic to punish it with death; and it is worth considering whether, well knowing that it originates in the irregular and inordinate gratification of unruly appetite, the injury to society may not be repaired without destroying the offender.

In most cases this injury might be repaired by compelling, where it could be done with propriety, the criminal to marry the injured party; and it would be well for society if the same rule extended not only to all forcible violations of chastity, but even to instances of premeditated and systematic seduction.

In cases, however, where marriage could not take place, on account of legal disability or refusal on the part of the woman, the criminal ought to be severely punished by pecuniary damages to the party injured, and by hard labour and confinement, or transportation for life.

The execrable subject of this narrative was born at Amsfield, in Scotland, where he was heir to an estate which his ancestors had possessed above four hundred years; he was also related to some of the first families in the North by intermarriages with the nobility.

Young Charteris, having received a liberal education, made choice of the profession of arms, and served first under the Duke of Marlborough, as an ensign of foot, but was soon advanced to the rank of cornet of dragoons: he appears, however, to have had other views than fighting when he embraced the life of a soldier.

Being a most expert gamester, and of a disposition uncommonly avaricious, he made his knowledge of gambling subservient to his love of money; and, while the army was in winter-quarters, he stripped many of the officers of all their property by his skill at cards and dice. But he was as knavish as he was dexterous;

and, when he had defrauded a brother-officer of all his money, he would lend him a sum at the *moderate* interest of a hundred per cent, taking an assignment of his commission as security for the payment of the debt.

John, Duke of Argyle, and the Earl of Stair, were at this time young men in the army; and, being determined that the inconsiderate officers should not be thus ruined by the artifices of Charteris, they applied to the Earl of Orkney, who was also in the army then quartered at Brussels, representing the destruction that must ensue to young gentlemen in the military line, if Charteris was not stopped in his proceedings.

The Earl of Orkney, anxious for the credit of the army in general, and his countrymen in particular, represented the state of the case to the Duke of Marlborough, who gave orders that Charteris should be put under arrest, and tried by court-martial. The court was composed of an equal number of English and Scotch officers, that Charteris might have no reason to say he was treated with partiality.

After a candid hearing of the case, the proofs of Charteris's villainy were so strong, that he was sentenced to return the money he had obtained by usurious interest, to be deprived of his commission, and to be drummed out of the regiment, his sword being first broken; which sentence was executed in its fullest extent.

Thus disgraced, Charteris quitted Brussels, and, in the road between that place and Mecklin, he threw his breeches into a ditch, and then, buttoning his scarlet cloak below his knees, he went into an inn to take up his lodgings for the night.

It is usual, in places where armies are quartered, for military officers to be treated with all possible respect; and this was the case with Charteris, who had every distinction shown him that the house could afford, and, after an elegant supper, was left to repose.

Early in the morning he rang the bell violently, and, the landlord coming terrified into his room, he swore furiously that he had been robbed of his breeches, containing a diamond ring, a gold watch, and money to a considerable amount; and, having previously broken the window, he intimated that some person must have entered that way, and carried off his property; and he even insinuated that the landlord himself might have been the robber.

It was in vain that the innkeeper solicited mercy in the most humiliating posture. Charteris threatened that he should be sent to Brussels, and suffer death, as an accessory to the felony.

Terrified at the thought of approaching disgrace and danger, the landlord of the house sent for some friars of an adjacent convent, to whom he represented his calamitous situation, and they generously supplied him with a sum sufficient to reimburse Charteris for the loss he pretended to have sustained.

Our unprincipled adventurer now proceeded through Holland, whence he embarked for Scotland, and had not been long in that kingdom before his servile submission, and his money, procured him another commission in a regiment of horse; and he was afterwards advanced to the rank of colonel.

Amidst all his other avocations, the love of money was his ruling passion; for the acquirement whereof there was no crime of which he would not have been guilty.

The Duke of Queensbury was at this time commissioner to the Parliament of Scotland, which was assembled at Edinburgh, to deliberate on the proposed union with England. Charteris having been invited to a party at cards with the Duchess of Queensbury, he contrived that her Grace should be placed in such a manner, near a large glass, that he could see all her cards; and he won three thousand pounds of her in consequence of this stratagem. One good, however, resulted from this circumstance: the Duke of Queensbury, incensed at the imposition, brought a bill into the House to prohibit gaming for above a certain sum; and this bill passed into a law.

Our adventurer continued his depredations on the thoughtless till he had acquired considerable sums. When he had stripped young men of their ready cash at the gaming-tables, it was his practice, as before, to lend them money at an extravagant interest, for which he took their bonds to confess judgment, and the moment the bonds became due he failed not to take every legal advantage.

By a continued rapacity of this kind he acquired several considerable estates in Scotland, and then removed to London, which, as it was the seat of greater dissipation, was a place better adapted to the exertion of his abilities.

He now became a great lender of money on mortgages, always receiving a large premium, by which at length he became so rich as to purchase several estates in England, particularly in the county of Lancaster.

Colonel Charteris was as infamous on account of his amours as for the unfeeling avarice of his disposition: his house was no better than a brothel, and no woman of modesty would live within his walls. He kept in pay some women of abandoned character, who, going to inns where the country waggons put up, used to prevail on harmless young girls to go to the colonel's house as servants; the consequence of which was, that their ruin soon followed, and they were turned out of doors, exposed to all the miseries consequent on poverty and a loss of reputation.

His agents did not confine their operations to inns, but, wherever they found a handsome girl, they endeavoured to decoy her to the colonel's house; and, among the rest, Ann Bond fell a prey to his artifices. This young woman had lived in London, but, having quitted her service on account of illness, took lodgings at a private house, where she recovered her health, and was sitting at the door, when a woman addressed her, saying, she could help her to a place in the family of Colonel Harvey; for the character of Charteris was now become so notorious, that his agents did not venture to make use of his name.

Bond being hired, the woman conducted her to the colonel's house, where she was three days before she was acquainted with his real name. Her master gave her money to redeem some clothes, which she had pledged to support her in her illness; and would have bought other clothes for her, but she refused to accept them.

He now offered her a purse of gold, an annuity for life, and a house, if she would lie with him; but the virtuous girl resisted the temptation; declared she would not be guilty of so base an act; that she would discharge her duty as a servant, and that her master might dismiss her if her conduct did not please him.

On the day following this circumstance she heard a gentleman asking for her master by the name of Charteris, which alarmed her fears still more, as she was not unapprized of his general character; wherefore she told the housekeeper that she must quit her service, as she was very ill.

The housekeeper informing the colonel of this circumstance, he sent for the poor girl, and threatened that he would shoot her if she left his service. He likewise ordered the servants to keep the door fast, to prevent her making her escape; and, when he spoke of her, it was in the most contemptuous terms.

On the following day he directed his clerk of the kitchen to send her into the parlour; and, on her attending him, he bade her stir the fire: while she was thus employed, he suddenly seized and committed violence on her, first stopping her mouth with his night-cap; and afterwards, on her saying that she

119

would prosecute him, he beat her with a horsewhip, and called her by the most opprobrious names.

On his opening the door the clerk of the kitchen appeared, to whom the colonel pretended that she had robbed him of thirty guineas, and directed him to turn her out of the house, which was accordingly done.

Hereupon she went to a gentlewoman named Parsons, and, informing her of what had happened, asked her advice how to proceed. Mrs. Parsons recommended her to exhibit articles against him for the assault; but, when the matter came afterwards to be heard by the grand jury, they held that it was not an attempt, but an actual commission, of the fact; and a bill was found accordingly.

When the colonel was committed to Newgate he was loaded with heavy fetters; but he soon purchased a lighter pair, and paid for the use of a room in the prison, and for a man to attend him.

Colonel Charteris had been married to the daughter of Sir Alexander Swinton, of Scotland, who bore him one daughter, afterwards married to the Earl of Wemys; and the earl, happening to be in London at the time of the above-mentioned transaction, procured a writ of habeas corpus, in consequence of which the colonel was admitted to bail.

When the trial came on every art was used to traduce the character of the prosecutrix, with a view to destroy the force of her evidence; but, happily, her character was so fair, and there was so little reason to think that she had any sinister view in the prosecution, that every artifice failed; and, after a long trial, in which the facts were proved to the satisfaction of the jury, a verdict of guilty was given against the colonel, who received sentence to be executed in the accustomed manner.*

---

* At Exeter, on the 5th of October, 1753, an unworthy minister of the Holy Gospel, the Reverend Peter Vine, was hanged for committing a crime of this nature.

On this occasion Charteris was not a little obliged to his son-in-law, Lord Wemys, who caused the Lord President Forbes to come from Scotland, to plead the cause before the privy council; and an estate of 300*l.* per annum for life was assigned to the president for this service.

At length the king consented to grant the colonel a pardon, on his settling a handsome annuity on the prosecutrix.

Colonel Charteris was tried at the Old Bailey on the 25th of February, 1730.

After his narrow escape from a fate which he had so well deserved he retired to Edinburgh, where he lived about two years, and then died in a miserable manner, a victim to his own irregular course of life.

He was buried in the family vault, in the churchyard of the Grey Friars of Edinburgh; but his vices had rendered him so detestable, that it was with some difficulty he was committed to the grave; for the mob almost tore the coffin in pieces, and committed a variety of irregularities, in honest contempt of such an abandoned character.

Soon after Charteris was convicted a fine mezzotinto print of him was published, representing him standing at the bar of the Old Bailey, with his thumbs tied; and under the print was the following inscription:

Blood !——must a colonel, with a lord's estate,
Be thus obnoxious to a scoundrel's fate ?
Brought to the bar, and sentenc'd from the bench,
Only for ravishing a country wench ?

Captain Porteous put to Death by the Edinburgh Mob.

CAPTAIN JOHN PORTEOUS,

CONVICTED OF MURDER, AND MURDERED BY THE MOB.

JOHN PORTEOUS was born of indigent parents, near the city of Edinburgh, who bound him apprentice to a tailor, with whom, after the expiration of his apprenticeship, he worked as journeyman.

Porteous was soon noticed by several reputable gentlemen as a young man of good address and fine accomplishments, and one whom they entertained a desire to serve.

It happened at this time that a gentleman who had been lord provost of Edinburgh, growing tired of his mistress, wished to disengage himself from her in a genteel manner; and, knowing Porteous to be very poor, he proposed his taking her off his hands by making her his wife.

122

When the proposition was first made to the lady she rejected it with much disdain, thinking it a great degradation to match with a journeyman tailor; but, on the gentleman's promising her a fortune of five hundred pounds, she consented, and they were married accordingly.

Porteous now commenced master, and met with good success for some time; but, being much addicted to company, he neglected his business, by which means he lost many of his customers. His wife, in consequence, was obliged to apply to her old friend the provost, to make some other provision for them.

In Edinburgh there are three companies of men, in number twenty-five each, who are employed to keep the peace, and take up all offenders, whom they keep in custody till examined by a magistrate. An officer is appointed to each of these companies, whom they style Captain, with a salary of eighty pounds a year, and a suit of scarlet uniform, which in that part of the world is reckoned very honourable.

A vacancy happening by the death of one of these captains, the provost immediately appointed his friend Porteous to fill up the place; and the latter, being now advanced to honour, forgot all his former politeness, for which he was so much esteemed when a tradesman, assuming the consequence of a man in authority.

If a riot happened in the city, Porteous was generally made choice of by the magistrates to suppress it, he being a man of resolute spirit, and unacquainted with fear. On these occasions he would generally exceed the bounds of his commission, and would treat the delinquents with the utmost cruelty, by knocking them down with his musket, and frequently breaking legs and arms.

If sent to quell a disturbance in a house of ill fame, notwithstanding he was a most abandoned debauchee himself, he would take pleasure in exposing the characters of all he found there, thus destroying the peace of many families: he would treat the unhappy prostitutes with the greatest inhumanity, and even drag them to a prison, though many of them had been seduced by himself.

Amongst other instances of cruelty he committed we shall mention the following, because it procured him the universal hatred of the people in that city:—

A vacancy happening in the lectureship of a neighbouring church, two young gentlemen were candidates; and, having each an equal number of votes, the dispute was referred to the presbytery, who declared in favour of Mr. Dawson. The other candidate, Mr. Wotherspoon, appealed to the synod, who reversed the order of the presbytery. As the parishioners were much exasperated, and a tumult being apprehended at the church on the day Mr. Wotherspoon was to preach his first sermon, Porteous was ordered there to keep the peace; but finding, on his arrival, Mr. Dawson had got possession of the pulpit, he went up the steps without the least ceremony, seized him by the collar, and dragged him down like a thief. In consequence of the wounds he received at this time, Mr. Dawson died a few weeks after.

Mr. Wotherspoon coming in at the time of the affray, Mr. Dawson's friends were so enraged, that they immediately fell on him, whom they beat in such a terrible manner, that he also died about the same time as Mr. Dawson.

Thus the lives of two amiable men were sacrificed to the brutality of this inhuman monster. Many men, women, and children, were also much wounded in the affray; yet the wretch himself escaped unpunished, no regular notice being taken of the affair.

Nothing gave more pleasure to this fellow than his being employed to quell riots, on which occasions he never wanted an opportunity of exercising his savage disposition.

The condemnation and death of Porteous happened in the following most extraordinary manner:—

Smuggling was so much practised in Scotland at that time that no laws could restrain it. The smugglers assembled in large bodies, so that the revenue-officers could not attack them without endangering their lives.

The most active person in striving to suppress these unlawful practices was Mr. Stark, collector for the county of Fife, who, being informed that one Andrew Wilson had a large quantity of contraband goods at his house, persuaded a number of men to accompany him; and they seized the goods, and safely lodged them (as they thought) in the custom-house: but Wilson being a man of an enterprising spirit, and conceiving himself injured, went, in company with one Robertson, and some more of his gang, to the custom-house, where, breaking open the doors, they recovered their goods, which they brought off in carts, in defiance of all opposition.

Mr. Stark, hearing that such a daring insult had been committed, dispatched an account thereof to the barons of the Exchequer, who immediately applying to the Lord Justice Clerk, his lordship issued his warrant to the sheriff of Fife, commanding him to assemble all the people in his jurisdiction to seize the delinquents, and replace the goods.

In consequence of the above order many were apprehended, but all discharged again for want of evidence, except Wilson and Robertson, who were both found guilty, and sentenced to die.

A custom prevailed in Scotland, at that time, of taking the condemned criminals to church every Sunday, under the care of three or four of the city guards. The above two criminals were accordingly taken to one of the churches on the Sunday before they were to suffer; when, just getting within the door, Wilson, though handcuffed, assisted in his companion's escape, by seizing hold of one soldier with his teeth, and keeping the others from turning upon him, while he cried out to Robertson to run.

Robertson accordingly took to his heels, and, the streets being crowded with people going to church, he passed uninterrupted, and got out at one of the city gates just as they were going to shut it, a custom constantly observed during divine service.

The city being now alarmed, Porteous was immediately dispatched in search of him, but all in vain; Robertson, meeting with a friend who knocked off his handcuffs and procured him a horse, got the same evening on board a vessel at Dunbar, which landed him safely in Holland.

We are informed that, in the year 1756, he was living, and kept a public house with great credit near the bridge at Rotterdam.

On the following Wednesday a temporary gallows was erected in the Grass-market for the execution of Wilson, who was ordered to be conducted there by fifty men, under the command of Porteous.

Porteous, being apprehensive an attempt would be made to rescue the prisoner, represented to the provost the necessity there was for soldiers to be drawn up ready to preserve the peace: on which five companies of the Welsh Fuzileers, commanded by a major, were ordered to be in readiness in the Lawn-market, near the place of execution.

No disturbance arising, the prisoner finished his devotions, ascended the ladder, was turned off, and continued hanging the usual time; at the expiration of which, the hangman going up the ladder to cut him down, a stone struck him on the nose, and caused it to bleed. This stone was immediately followed by many others; at which Porteous was so much exasperated, that he instantly called out to his men, 'Fire, and be damned!' discharging his own piece at the same time, and shooting a young man, who was apprentice to a confectioner, dead on the spot.

Some of the soldiers, more humanely, fired over the heads of the people, but unfortunately killed two or three who were looking out at the windows. Others of the soldiers wantonly fired amongst the feet of the mob, by which many were so disabled as to be afterwards obliged to suffer amputation.

Porteous now endeavoured to draw off his men, as the mob grew exceedingly outrageous, throwing stones, with every thing else they could lay their hands on, and continuing to press on the soldiers; on which Porteous, with two of his men, turned about and fired, killing three more of the people, which amounted to nine in the whole that were left dead on the spot, besides many wounded.

A sergeant was sent by the major of the Welsh Fuzileers to inquire into the cause of the disturbance, but the mob was so outrageous that he could gain no intelligence. Porteous, being assisted by the Fuzileers, at last conducted his men to the guard, when, being sent for by the provost, he passed a long examination, and was committed to prison in order to take his trial for murder.

On the 6th of July, 1736, the trial came on before the lords of justiciary, previously to which Porteous made a judicial confession that the people were killed as mentioned in the indictments; but pleaded self-defence. His counsel then stated the following point of law, to be determined by the judges previously to the jury being charged with the prisoner : —

' Whether a military officer, with soldiers under his command, who, being assaulted by the populace, should fire, or order his men to fire, was not acting consistently with the nature of self-defence, according to the laws of civilized nations? '

The counsel for the prosecution being ordered to plead to the question by the Court, they pronounced, as their opinion, ' That if it was proved that Captain Porteous either fired a gun, or caused one or more to be fired, by which any person or persons was or were killed, and if the said firing happened without orders from a magistrate properly authorized, then it would be murder in the eye of the law.'

Thus the question being decided against him, and the jury empannelled, forty-four witnesses were examined for and against the prosecution.

The prisoner being now called on for his defence, his counsel insisted that the magistrates had ordered him to support the execution of Wilson, and repel force by force, being apprehensive of a rescue; that powder and ball had been given them for the said purpose, with orders to load their pieces.

They insisted, also, that he only meant to intimidate the people by threats, and actually knocked down one of his own men for presenting his piece; that, finding the men would not obey orders, he drew off as many as he could; that he afterwards heard a firing in the rear, contrary to his directions. That, in order to know who had fired, he would not suffer their pieces to be cleaned till properly inspected; and that he never attempted to escape, though he had the greatest opportunity, and might have effected it with the utmost ease.

They farther insisted, that, admitting some excesses had been committed, it could not amount to murder, as he was in the lawful discharge of his duty; neither could it be supposed to be done with premeditated malice.

In answer to this the counsel for the crown argued, that the trust reposed in the prisoner ceased when the execution was over; that he was then no longer an officer employed for that purpose for which the fire-arms had been loaded; and that the reading of the Riot Act only could justify their firing, in case a rescue had been actually attempted.

The prisoner's counsel replied, that the magistrates, whose duty it was to have read the act, had deserted the soldiery, and taken refuge in a house for their own security; and that it was hard for men to suffer themselves to be knocked on the head when they had lawful weapons put into their hands to defend themselves.

The charge being delivered to the jury, they retired for a considerable time, when they brought him in guilty, and he received sentence of death.

The king being then at Hanover, and much interest being made to save the prisoner, the queen, by the advice of her council, granted a respite till his majesty's return to England. The respite was only procured one week before his sentence was to be put in execution, of which when the populace were informed, such a scheme of revenge was meditated as is perhaps unprecedented.

On the 7th of September, between nine and ten in the evening, a large body of men entered the city of Edinburgh, and seized the arms belonging to the guard: they then patrolled the streets, crying out, ' All those who dare avenge innocent blood, let them come here.' They then shut the gates, and placed guards at each.

The main body of the mob, all disguised, marched in the mean time to the prison; when, finding some difficulty in breaking open the door with hammers, they immediately set fire to it, taking great care that the flames should not extend beyond their proper bounds. The outer door was hardly consumed before they rushed in, and, ordering the keeper to open the door of the captain's apartment, cried out, ' Where is the villain, Porteous? ' He replied, ' Here I am; what do you want with me? ' To which they answered, that they meant to hang him in the Grass-market, the place where he had shed so much innocent blood.

His expostulations were all in vain; they seized him by the legs and arms, and dragged him instantly to the place of execution.

On their arrival they broke open a shop, to find a rope suitable to their purpose, which they immediately fixed round his neck; then, throwing the other end over a dyer's pole, hoisted him up; when he, endeavouring to save himself, fixed his hands between the halter and his neck, which being observed by some of the mob, one of them struck him with an axe, and this obliging him to quit his hold, they soon put an end to his life.

When they were satisfied he was dead, they immediately dispersed to their several habitations, unmolested themselves, and without molesting any one else.

Upon this circumstance being made known, a royal proclamation was issued, offering a large reward for the apprehension of the offenders; and the magistrates of Edinburgh, the scene of the murder, were summoned to answer for their neglect in not quelling the riot, fined, and rendered incapable of acting again in any judicial capacity. In such a mob as that which seized Porteous, it was difficult to fix upon individuals; and the deceased having rendered himself very obnoxious to the whole people, the affair there rested.

Thus ended the life of Captain John Porteous, a man possessed of qualifications which, had they been properly applied, would have rendered him an ornament to his country, and made him exceedingly useful in a military capacity. His uncommon spirit and invincible courage would have done honour to the greatest hero of antiquity; but, when advanced to power, he became intoxicated with pride, and, instead of being the admiration of, he became despised and hated by, his fellow-citizens. The fate of this unhappy man, it is hoped, will be a caution to those in power not to abuse it; but, by an impartial distribution of justice, to render themselves worthy members of society.

He was put to death at Edinburgh, September 7, 1736.

JOHN COLLINS,

EXECUTED FOR MURDER.

THIS man of blood lived in a village called Harledown, near Exeter, and was by trade a thatcher. He had kept company with a young woman named Jane Upcot, and who received his addresses, which appeared to be honourably offered. The account of the circumstances which led to the shocking catastrophe we have to relate does not disclose the motive for which the devil worked him up to put to death the object of his love. It was proved that on the 16th of May, 1737, the villain murdered this Jane Upcot. He afterwards, not glutted with shedding her blood, actually cut off the head from the body, tore out the heart, and stuck them on a spar-hook, with which he had killed her; and then, fixing the instrument near the decollated body, left the horrid spectacle to the view of the passing traveller!!!

Nature sickens at the recital—let us therefore pass to some less inhuman malefactor: this man deserved a severer death than the gallows.

He was executed at Exeter, in the year 1737.

JONATHAN BRADFORD,

EXECUTED FOR A SUPPOSED MURDER

JONATHAN BRADFORD kept an inn at the city of Oxford. A gentleman, (Mr. Hayes,) attended by a man-servant, put up one evening at Bradford's house; and in the night, the former being found murdered in his bed, the landlord was apprehended on suspicion of having committed the barbarous and inhospitable crime.

The evidence given against him was to the following effect:—Two gentlemen who had supped with Mr. Hayes, and who retired at the same time to their respective chambers, being alarmed in the night with a noise in his room, and soon hearing groans, as of a wounded man, got up in order to discover the cause, and found their landlord, with a dark lantern, and a knife in his hand, standing, in a state of astonishment and horror, over his dying guest, who almost instantly expired.

On this evidence, apparently conclusive, the jury convicted Bradford, and he was executed; but the fate of this man may serve as an additional lesson to jury-men to be extremely guarded in receiving circum-stantial evidence. On a trial at Nisi Prius, and between personal right and wrong, the jury are often directed by the judge to take into consideration pre-sumptive evidence where positive proof is wanting; but, in criminal charges, it seldom should, unsup-

Bradford, going to murder his Guest, finds the Deed already accomplished.

ported by some oral testimony, or ocular demonstra-tion, be sufficient to find a verdict against the accused.

The facts attending the above dreadful tragedy were not fully brought to light until the death-bed con-fession of the real murderer, a time when we must all endeavour to make our peace with God.

Mr. Hayes was a man of considerable property, and greatly respected. He had about him, when his sad destiny led him under the roof of Bradford, a considerable sum of money; and the landlord, knowing this, determined to murder and rob him. For this horrid purpose, he proceeded with a dark lantern and a carving-knife, intending to cut the throat of his guest while yet sleeping; but what must have been his astonishment and confusion to find his intended victim already murdered, and weltering in his blood?

The wicked and unworthy servant had also determined on the murder of his master; and had just committed the bloody deed, and secured his treasure, a moment before the landlord entered for the same purpose ! ! !

LYDIA ADLER,

CONVICTED OF MANSLAUGHTER.

THIS woman was tried at the Old Bailey, in June, 1744, for the wilful murder of her husband, John Adler, by throwing him on the ground, kicking and stamping on his groin, and giving him thereby a mortal bruise, of which he languished in St. Bartholomew's Hospital from the 11th till the 23d of May, and then died: and she was again indicted on the coroner's inquest for manslaughter.

Hannah Adler, daughter of the deceased, swore that he told her his wife had given him the wounds which afterwards occasioned his death.

Benjamin Barton deposed that the deceased came to him on the 11th of May, with a bloody handkerchief about his head, and asked him for a spare bed, saying, ' This eternal fiend (meaning his wife) will be the death of me; ' but Barton, knowing the woman to be of a very turbulent disposition, refused to lodge the man. After this, he visited him every other day during his illness; and he very often said, ' I wish, Mr. Barton, you would be so good as to get a warrant to secure this woman, for she will be the death of me;' and, two hours before he died, he inquired if such a warrant was procured; and desired that Barton would see her brought to justice, which he promised he would, if it lay in his power.

Hannah Adler, being farther questioned, said that her father died between twelve and one o'clock: that, about two hours and a half before, he said, 'I am a dead man, and this woman (the prisoner) has killed me.' That, after this, he repeatedly declared that his wife was the person that had murdered him, and begged that she might be brought to justice. His last declaration was made only about ten minutes before he died.

Mr. Godman, a surgeon, deposed that the husband died of a mortification, occasioned by a blow; but acknowledged that the deceased had a rupture, and that such a blow as he had received would not have hurt a person in sound health.

The prisoner, in her defence, said that her husband had two wives besides her; and that a quarrel happening between her and one of the others, the husband endeavoured to part them, and, in so doing, fell down, and the other woman fell on him; but that she herself never lifted hand or foot against him.

Joseph Steel deposed that the deceased had had four wives; that he was kind to them all at the first, but afterwards used to beat them severely; and that he had seen the prisoner and her husband frequently fight together.

The jury gave a verdict of manslaughter; in consequence of which she was burnt in the hand.

EUGENE ARAM,

EXECUTED FOR MURDER.

WE are now arrived at that period which brings to our
view, perhaps, the most remarkable and extraordinary
trial in our whole Calendar.

The perpetrator was a man of extraordinary endow-
ments, and of high education; therefore little to be
suspected of committing so very foul a crime. The
discovery of the murder is a striking proof that from
the eye of Providence nothing can be concealed.

This case, once the topic of general conversation,
and the subject of almost every pen, we have carefully
gleaned from the records and prints of the day, and
compiled, perhaps, a more particular account of this
mysterious matter than has yet been presented to the
public.

Mr. Eugene Aram was born in a village called
Netherdale, in Yorkshire, in the year 1704, of an
ancient family, one of his ancestors having served the
office of high sheriff for that county in the reign of
Edward III. The vicissitudes of fortune had, however, reduced them, as we find the father of Eugene,
a poor, but honest man, by profession a gardener; in
which walk of life he was, nevertheless, greatly
respected.

From the high erudition of the unfortunate subject
under consideration he may be truly called a prodigy.
On the very slender stock of learning found in a day-
school he built a fabric which would have been worthy
the shoulders of our literary Atlas, Dr. Johnson. It
may be truly said that, like M'Nally, the celebrated
Irish barrister and admirable dramatist, he was self-
taught. As the one excelled in his profession as usher
to an academy, so did the other as an advocate at the
bar of justice.

In the infancy of Aram his parents removed to

EUGENE ARAM.

another village, called Shelton, near Newby, in the same county; and, when about six years of age, his father, who had laid by a small sum from his weekly labour, made a purchase of a little cottage in Bondgate, near Rippon.

When he was about thirteen or fourteen years of age he went to his father in Newby, and attended him in the family there till the death of Sir Edward Blackett. It was in the house of this gentleman, to whom his father was gardener, that his propensity for literature first appeared. He was, indeed, always of a solitary disposition, and uncommonly fond of retirement and books; and here he enjoyed all the advantages of leisure and privacy. He applied himself at first chiefly to mathematical studies, in which he made a considerable proficiency.

At about sixteen years of age he was sent to London, to the house of Mr. Christopher Blackett, whom he served for some time in the capacity of book-keeper. After continuing here a year or more he was taken with the small pox, and suffered severely under that distemper. He afterwards returned into Yorkshire, in consequence of an invitation from his father, and there continued to prosecute his studies; but found in polite literature much greater charms than in the mathematics, which occasioned him now chiefly to apply himself to poetry, history, and antiquities. After this he was invited to Netherdale, where he engaged in a school, and married. But this marriage proved an unhappy connexion; for to the misconduct of his wife he afterwards attributed the misfortunes that befell him. In the mean while, having perceived his deficiency in the learned languages, he applied himself to the grammatical study of the Latin and Greek tongues; after which he read, with great avidity and diligence, all the Latin classics, historians, and poets. He then went through the Greek Testament; and, lastly, ventured upon Hesiod, Homer, Theocritus, Herodotus, and

Thucydides, together with all the Greek tragedians. In 1734 William Norton, Esq. a gentleman who had a friendship for him, invited him to Knaresborough. Here he acquired the knowledge of the Hebrew, and read the Pentateuch in that language. In 1744 he returned to London, and served the Rev. Mr. Plainblanc, in Piccadilly, as usher in Latin and writing; and, with this gentleman's assistance, he acquired the knowledge of the French language. He was afterwards employed as an usher and tutor in several different parts of England; during which time he became acquainted with heraldry and botany. He also ventured upon Chaldee and Arabic; the former of which he found easy from its near connexion with the Hebrew.

He then investigated the Celtic in all its dialects; and, having begun to form collections, and make comparisons between the Celtic, the English, the Latin, the Greek, and the Hebrew, and found a great affinity between them, he resolved to proceed through all these languages, and to form a comparative Lexicon. But, amid these learned labours and inquiries, it appears that Aram committed a crime which could not naturally have been expected from a man of so studious a turn, as the inducement that led him to it was merely the gain of wealth, of which the scholar is seldom covetous. On the 8th of February, 1745, he, in conjunction with a man named Richard Houseman, murdered one Daniel Clarke, a shoemaker at Knaresborough.

This unfortunate man, having lately married a woman of a good family, industriously circulated a report that his wife was entitled to a considerable fortune, which he should soon receive. In consequence of this, Aram, and Richard Houseman, conceiving hopes of making advantage of this circumstance, persuaded Clarke to make an ostentatious show of his own riches, to induce his wife's relations to give him that fortune of which he had boasted. There was sagacity, if not honesty, in this advice; for the world in general are more free to assist persons in affluence than those in distress.

Clarke was easily induced to comply with a hint so agreeable to his own desires; on which he borrowed, and bought on credit, a large quantity of silver plate, with jewels, watches, rings, &c. He told the persons of whom he purchased that a merchant in London had sent him an order to buy such plate for exportation; and no doubt was entertained of his credit till his sudden disappearance in February, 1745, when it was imagined that he had gone abroad, or at least to London, to dispose of his ill-acquired property.

When Clarke was possessed of these goods, Aram and Houseman determined to murder him, in order to share the booty; and, on the night of the 8th of February, 1745, they persuaded Clarke to take a walk with them, in order to consult upon the proper method to dispose of the effects.

On this plan they walked into a field, at a small distance from the town, well known by the name of St. Robert's Cave. When they came into this field Aram and Clarke went over a hedge towards the cave; and, when they had got within six or seven yards of it, Houseman (by the light of the moon) saw Aram strike Clarke several times, and at length beheld him fall, but never saw him afterwards. This was the state of the affair if Houseman's testimony on the trial might be credited.

The murderers, going home, shared Clarke's ill-gotten treasure, the half of which Houseman concealed in his garden for a twelvemonth, and then took it to Scotland, where he sold it. In the mean time Aram carried his share to London, where he sold it to a Jew, and then engaged himself as an usher, as already mentioned, at the Rev. Mr. Plainblanc's academy, in Piccadilly.

140

After this he was usher at other schools in different parts of the kingdom; but, as he did not correspond with his friends in Yorkshire, it was presumed that he was dead.

Fourteen years passed without the smallest clue being found to account for the sudden exit of Clarke, till in the year 1758 a labourer was employed to dig for stone to supply a lime-kiln at a place called Thistle Hill, near Knaresborough; and, having dug about two feet deep, he found the bones of a human body, still joined to each other by the ligatures of the joints, the body appearing to have been buried double. This incident immediately became the subject of general curiosity and inquiry. Some hints had been formerly thrown out by Aram's wife that Clarke was murdered; and it was well remembered that his disappearance was very sudden.

This occasioned Aram's wife to be sent for, as was also the coroner, and an inquisition was entered into, it being believed that the skeleton found was that of Daniel Clarke. Mrs. Aram declared that she believed Clarke had been murdered by her husband and Richard Houseman. The latter, when he was brought before the coroner, appeared to be in great confusion, trembling, changing colour, and faltering in his speech, during the examination. The coroner desired him to take up one of the bones, probably to observe what further effect that might produce; and Houseman, accordingly taking up one of the bones, said, ' This is no more Daniel Clarke's bone than it is mine.'*

* Murder may, for a while, be concealed; but the foul deed rarely remains long in darkness. About the time when this guilty wretch, taken by surprise, betrayed that which led to his accusation and punishment, the chambermaid of a lady of distinction at Valenciennes murdered her mistress. Her lady looking into the cellar, the maid pushed her down stairs, and, immediately following her, stopped her mouth, and beat her over the head with a brick till she killed her : the murderess then went up stairs,

141

These words were pronounced in such a manner as convinced those present that they proceeded not from Houseman's supposition that Clarke was alive, but from his certain knowledge where his bones really lay. Accordingly, after some evasions, he said that Clarke was murdered by Eugene Aram, and that the body was buried in St. Robert's Cave, near Knaresborough. He added, further, that Clarke's head lay to the right, in the turn, at the entrance of the cave; and a skeleton was accordingly found there exactly in the posture he described. In consequence of this confession search was made for Aram, and at length he was discovered in the situation of usher to an academy at Lynn, in Norfolk. He was taken from thence to York Castle, and on the 13th of August, 1759, was brought to trial at the county assizes. He was found guilty on the testimony of Richard Houseman, who, being arraigned, and acquitted, became an evidence against Aram; and whose testimony was corroborated by Mrs. Aram, and strong circumstantial evidence. The

dressed herself, attended vespers, and gave out that her mistress was gone alone to Annain, a village about a league off; that she was to go along the river Scheld, and that the next day she was to carry her watch and jewels. In the evening she returned home, cut the body to pieces, and next morning carried part of it in a bag, and threw it into the Scheld; and, towards the evening, she did the same with the remainder. The same day she carried the watch and jewels to the clergyman's at Annain, expressed much concern at her mistress's not being there, and, leaving the watch and jewels, went to look for her, as she pretended. On the 5th she returned, took away the watch and jewels, and carried them to her mistress's sister; and that day some pieces of the body being found in the Scheld, the unhappy wretch, in her guilty confusion, was the first who said that they must belong to her mistress, who, without doubt, had been murdered in going to Annain. However, she was taken up and examined, and people sent to the house, who discovered several traces of murder: upon which she was again examined, and, after much prevarication in her answers, she at last acknowledged the whole affair, and was executed.

plunder which Aram was supposed to have derived from the murder was not estimated at more than one hundred and sixty pounds.

His defence, for ingenuity and ability, would have done credit to the best lawyers at the bar. He thus addressed the Court and jury:

'My Lord,—I know not whether it is of right, or through some indulgence of your lordship, that I am allowed the liberty at this bar, and at this time, to attempt a defence, incapable and uninstructed as I am to speak; since, while I see so many eyes upon me, so numerous and awful a concourse, fixed with attention, and filled with I know not what expectancy, I labour not with guilt, my lord, but with perplexity; for, having never seen a Court but this, being wholly unacquainted with law, the customs of the bar, and all judiciary proceedings, I fear I shall be so little capable of speaking with propriety in this place, that it exceeds my hope if I shall be able to speak at all.

'I have heard, my lord, the indictment read, wherein I find myself charged with the highest crime, with an enormity I am altogether incapable of; a fact, to the commission of which there goes far more insensibility of heart, more profligacy of morals, than ever fell to my lot; and nothing possibly could have admitted a presumption of this nature but a depravity not inferior to that imputed to me. However, as I stand indicted at your lordship's bar, and have heard what is called evidence adduced in support of such a charge, I very humbly solicit your lordship's patience, and beg the hearing of this respectable audience, while I, single and unskilful, destitute of friends, and unassisted by counsel, say something, perhaps, like argument, in my defence. I shall consume but little of your lordship's time: what I have to say will be short; and this brevity, probably, will be the best part of it: however, it is offered with all possible regard and the greatest submission to your lordship's consideration, and that of this honourable Court.

' First, my lord, the whole tenour of my conduct in life contradicts every particular of the indictment : yet had I never said this, did not my present circumstances extort it from me, and seem to make it necessary. Permit me here, my lord, to call upon malignity itself, so long and cruelly busied in this prosecution, to charge upon me any immorality of which prejudice was not the author. No, my lord, I concerted no schemes of fraud, projected no violence, injured no man's person or property ; my days were honestly laborious, my nights intensely studious ; and I humbly conceive my notice of this, especially at this time, will not be thought impertinent or unseasonable, but, at least, deserving some attention ; because, my lord, that any person, after a temperate use of life, a series of thinking and acting regularly, and without one single deviation from sobriety, should plunge into the very depth of profligacy precipitately and at once, is altogether improbable and unprecedented, and absolutely inconsistent with the course of things. Mankind is never corrupted at once ; villainy is always progressive, and declines from right, step after step, till every regard of probity is lost, and every sense of all moral obligation totally perishes.

' Again, my lord, a suspicion of this kind, which nothing but malevolence could entertain and ignorance propagate, is violently opposed by my very situation at that time, with respect to health ; for, but a little space before, I had been confined to my bed, and suffered under a very long and severe disorder, and was not able, for half a year together, so much as to walk. The distemper left me, indeed—yet slowly, and in part ; but so macerated, so enfeebled, that I was reduced to crutches ; and, so far from being well about the time I am charged with this fact, that I never, to this day, perfectly recovered. Could, then, a person in this

144

condition take any thing into his head so unlikely, so extravagant? I, past the vigour of my age, feeble and valetudinary, with no inducement to engage, no ability to accomplish, no weapon wherewith to perpetrate such a fact; without interest, without power, without motive, without means.

'Besides, it must needs occur to every one that an action of this atrocious nature is never heard of but, when its springs are laid open, it appears that it was to support some indolence, or supply some luxury; to satisfy some avarice, or oblige some malice; to prevent some real or some imaginary want: yet I lay not under the influence of any one of these. Surely, my lord, I may, consistently with both truth and modesty, affirm thus much; and none who have any veracity, and knew me, will ever question this.

'In the second place, the disappearance of Clarke is suggested as an argument of his being dead; but the uncertainty of such an inference from that, and the fallibility of all conclusions of such a sort from such a circumstance, are too obvious, and too notorious, to require instances; yet, superseding many, permit me to produce a very recent one, and that afforded by this castle.

'In June, 1757, William Thompson, for all the vigilance of this place, in open daylight, and double-ironed, made his escape; and, notwithstanding an immediate inquiry set on foot, the strictest search, and all advertisement, was never seen or heard of since. If then Thompson got off unseen, through all these difficulties, how very easy was it for Clarke, when none of them opposed him? But what would be thought of a prosecution commenced against any one seen last with Thompson?

'Permit me next, my lord, to observe a little upon the bones which have been discovered. It is said (which, perhaps, is saying very far) that these are the skeleton of a man. It is possible, indeed, it may; but is there any certain known criterion which incontestably distinguishes the sex in human bones? Let it be considered, my lord, whether the ascertaining of this point ought not to precede any attempt to identify them.

'The place of their depositum, too, claims much more attention than is commonly bestowed upon it; for, of all places in the world, none could have mentioned any one wherein there was greater certainty of finding human bones than a hermitage, except he should point out a church-yard; hermitages, in time past, being not only places of religious retirement, but of burial too: and it has scarce, or never, been heard of, but that every cell now known contains, or contained, these relics of humanity; some mutilated, and some entire. I do not inform, but give me leave to remind your lordship, that here sat solitary Sanctity, and here the hermit or the anchoress hoped that repose for their bones, when dead, they here enjoyed when living.

'All the while, my lord, I am sensible this is known to your lordship, and many in this Court, better than to me; but it seems necessary to my case that others, who have not at all, perhaps, adverted to things of this nature, and may have concern in my trial, should be made acquainted with it. Suffer me then, my lord, to produce a few of many evidences that these cells were used as repositories of the dead, and to enumerate a few in which human bones have been found, as it happened in this question; lest, to some, that accident might seem extraordinary, and, consequently, occasion prejudice.

'1. The bones, as was supposed, of the Saxon Saint, Dubritius, were discovered buried in his cell at Guy's Cliff, near Warwick, as appears from the authority of Sir William Dugdale.

'2. The bones, thought to be those of the anchoress Rosia, were but lately discovered in a cell at Royston, entire, fair, and undecayed, though they must have lain interred for several centuries, as is proved by Dr. Stukely.

'3. But my own country, nay, almost this neighbourhood, supplies another instance; for in January, 1747, were found, by Mr. Stovin, accompanied by a reverend gentleman, the bones, in part, of some recluse, in the cell at Lindholm, near Hatfield. They were believed to be those of William of Lindholm, a hermit, who had long made this cave his habitation.

'4. In February, 1744, part of Woburn Abbey being pulled down, a large portion of a corpse appeared, even with the flesh on, and which bore cutting with a knife; though it is certain this had lain above two hundred years, and how much longer is doubtful; for this abbey was founded in 1145, and dissolved in 1538, or 1539.

'What would have been said, what believed, if this had been an accident to the bones in question?

'Farther, my lord:—it is not yet out of living memory that at a little distance from Knaresborough, in a field, part of the manor of the worthy and patriot baronet who does that borough the honour to represent it in parliament, were found, in digging for gravel, not one human skeleton only, but five or six, deposited side by side, with each an urn placed at its head, as your lordship knows was usual in ancient interments.

'About the same time, and in another field, almost close to this borough, was discovered also, in searching for gravel, another human skeleton; but the piety of the same worthy gentleman ordered both pits to be filled up again, commendably unwilling to disturb the dead.

'Is the invention of these bones forgotten, then, or industriously concealed, that the discovery of those in question may appear the more singular and extraordinary? whereas, in fact, there is nothing extraordinary in it. My lord, almost every place conceals such remains. In fields, in hills, in highway sides, in

147

commons, lie frequent and unsuspected bones; and our present allotments for rest for the departed are but of some centuries.

'Another particular seems not to claim a little of your lordship's notice, and that of the gentlemen of the jury; which is, that perhaps no example occurs of more than one skeleton being found in one cell: and in the cell in question was found but one; agreeable, in this, to the peculiarity of every other known cell in Britain. Not the invention of one skeleton, but of two, would have appeared suspicious and uncommon. But it seems another skeleton has been discovered by some labourer, which was full as confidently averred to be Clarke's as this. My lord, must some of the living, if it promotes some interest, be made answerable for all the bones that earth has concealed and chance exposed? and might not a place where bones lay be mentioned by a person by chance as well as found by a labourer by chance? or is it more criminal accidentally to name where bones lie than accidentally to find where they lie?

'Here too is a human skull produced, which is fractured; but was this the cause, or was it the consequence, of death? was it owing to violence, or was it the effect of natural decay? If it was violence, was that violence before or after death? My lord, in May, 1732, the remains of William, lord archbishop of this province, were taken up, by permission, in this cathedral, and the bones of the skull were found broken; yet certainly he died by no violence offered to him alive that could occasion that fracture there.

'Let it be considered, my lord, that, upon the dissolution of religious houses, and the commencement of the Reformation, the ravages of those times affected both the living and the dead. In search after imaginary treasures, coffins were broken up, graves and vaults dug open, monuments ransacked, and shrines demolished; and it ceased about the beginning of the

148

reign of Queen Elizabeth. I entreat your lordship, suffer not the violence, the depredations, and the iniquities of those times, to be imputed to this.

'Moreover, what gentleman here is ignorant that Knaresborough had a castle, which, though now a ruin, was once considerable both for its strength and garrison? All know it was vigorously besieged by the arms of the parliament; at which siege, in sallies, conflicts, flights, pursuits, many fell in all the places round it, and, where they fell, were buried; for every place, my lord, is burial earth in war; and many, questionless, of these rest yet unknown, whose bones futurity shall discover.

'I hope, with all imaginable submission, that what has been said will not be thought impertinent to this indictment; and that it will be far from the wisdom, the learning, and the integrity of this place, to impute to the living what zeal in its fury may have done—what nature may have taken off, and piety interred—or what war alone may have destroyed, alone deposited.

'As to the circumstances that have been raked together, I have nothing to observe but that all circumstances whatever are precarious, and have been but too frequently found lamentably fallible; even the strongest have failed. They may rise to the utmost degree of probability, yet they are but probability still. Why need I name to your lordship the two Harrisons recorded by Dr. Howel, who both suffered upon circumstances because of the sudden disappearance of their lodger, who was in credit, had contracted debts, borrowed money, and went off unseen, and returned a great many years after their execution? Why name the intricate affair of Jacques de Moulin, under King Charles II. related by a gentleman who was counsel for the crown? and why the unhappy Coleman, who suffered innocently, though convicted upon positive evidence; and whose children perished for want, because the world uncharitably believed the father

149

guilty? Why mention the perjury of Smith, incautiously admitted king's evidence; who, to screen himself, equally accused Faircloth and Loveday of the murder of Dun; the first of whom, in 1749, was executed at Winchester; and Loveday was about to suffer at Reading, had not Smith been proved perjured, to the satisfaction of the Court, by the surgeon of Gosport hospital?

'Now, my lord, having endeavoured to show that the whole of this process is altogether repugnant to every part of my life; that it is inconsistent with my condition of health about that time; that no rational inference can be drawn that a person is dead who suddenly disappears; that hermitages were the constant repositories of the bones of a recluse; that the proofs of this are well authenticated; that the revolutions in religion, or the fortune of war, have mangled or buried the dead; the conclusion remains, perhaps, no less reasonably than impatiently wished for. I, at last, after a year's confinement, equal to either fortune, put myself upon the candour, the justice, and the humanity of your lordship; and upon yours, my countrymen, gentlemen of the jury.'

Judge Noel, before whom he was tried, summed up the evidence with great perspicuity, and, in his comments on the prisoner's defence, declared it to be one of the most ingenious pieces of reasoning that had ever fallen under his notice. The jury, with little hesitation, found him guilty, and he received sentence of death.

After his conviction he confessed the justice of his sentence to two clergymen, who were directed to attend him in York Castle, to whom he acknowledged that he murdered Clarke. Being asked by one of them what was his motive for committing that action, he answered 'that he suspected Clarke of having an unlawful commerce with his wife; that he was persuaded, at the time when he committed the murder, he did right; but that since he thought it wrong.' In hopes of eluding the course of justice, he made an attempt upon his own life, by cutting his arm in two places with a razor, which he had concealed for that purpose. On a table, in his cell, was found the following paper, containing his reasons for the above attempt:—' What am I better than my fathers? To die is natural and necessary. Perfectly sensible of this, I fear no more to die than I did to be born. But the manner of it is something which should, in my opinion, be decent and manly. I think I have regarded both these points. Certainly nobody has a better right to dispose of a man's life than himself; and he, not others, should determine how. As for any indignities offered to my body, or silly reflections on my faith and morals, they are (as they always were) things indifferent to me. I think, though contrary to the common way of thinking, I wrong no man by this; and hope it is not offensive to that eternal Being that formed me and the world: and, as by this I injure no man, no man can be reasonably offended. I solicitously recommend myself to that eternal and almighty Being, the God of Nature, if I have done amiss. But perhaps I have not; and I hope this thing will never be imputed to me. Though I am now stained by malevolence, and suffer by prejudice, I hope to rise fair and unblemished. My life was not polluted, my morals irreproachable, and my opinions orthodox. I slept sound till three o'clock, awaked, and then writ these lines:—

' Come, pleasing rest! eternal slumbers, fall!
Seal mine, that once must seal the eyes of all.
Calm and composed my soul her journey takes;
No guilt that troubles, and no heart that aches.
Adieu, thou sun! all bright, like her, arise!
Adieu, fair friends, and all that's good and wise!'

These lines, found with the following letter, were supposed to have been written by Aram just before he attempted his own life.

'My dear friend,—Before this reaches you I shall be no more a living man in this world, though at present in perfect bodily health; but who can describe the horrors of mind which I suffer at this instant? Guilt—the guilt of blood shed without any provocation, without any cause but that of filthy lucre—pierces my conscience with wounds that give the most poignant pains! 'Tis true the consciousness of my horrid guilt has given me frequent interruptions in the midst of my business or pleasures; but yet I have found means to stifle its clamours, and contrived a momentary remedy for the disturbance it gave me by applying to the bottle or the bowl, or diversions, or company, or business; sometimes one, and sometimes the other, as opportunity offered: but now all these, and all other amusements, are at an end, and I am left forlorn, helpless, and destitute of every comfort; for I have nothing now in view but the certain destruction both of my soul and body. My conscience will now no longer suffer itself to be hoodwinked or browbeat; it has now got the mastery; it is my accuser, judge, and executioner; and the sentence it pronounceth against me is more dreadful than that I heard from the bench, which only condemned my body to the pains of death, which are soon over; but Conscience tells me plainly that she will summon me before another tribunal, where I shall have neither power nor means to stifle the evidence she will there bring against me; and that the sentence which will then be denounced will not only be irreversible, but will condemn my soul to torments that will know no end.

'Oh! had I but hearkened to the advice which dear-bought experience has enabled me to give, I should not now have been plunged into that dreadful gulf of despair which I find it impossible to extricate myself from; and therefore my soul is filled with horror inconceivable. I see both God and man my enemies, and in a few hours shall be exposed a public spectacle for the world to gaze at. Can you conceive any condition more horrible than mine? O, no! it cannot be! I am determined, therefore, to put a short end to trouble I am no longer able to bear, and prevent the executioner by doing his business with my own hand, and shall by this means at least prevent the shame and disgrace of a public exposure, and leave the care of my soul in the hands of eternal mercy. Wishing you all health, happiness, and prosperity, I am, to the last moment of my life, yours, with the sincerest regard,

'EUGENE ARAM.'

When the morning appointed for his execution arrived the keeper went to take him out of his cell, when he was surprised to find him almost expiring through loss of blood, having cut his left arm above the elbow, and near the wrist, with a razor; but he missed the artery. A surgeon, being sent for, soon stopped the bleeding; and when he was taken to the place of execution he was perfectly sensible, though so very weak as to be unable to join in devotion with the clergyman who attended him.

He was executed at York, August the 6th, 1759, and his body afterwards hung in chains in Knaresborough Forest.

More than thirty years had passed since the death of Eugene Aram, when his name was inserted, among the literary characters of our country, in the Biographia Britannica. There his high erudition is handed down to posterity. This tribute to departed genius, it however appears, raised the spleen of a meaner scholar, who arraigned the conduct of the editors in naming Aram, and omitting Bishop Atherton, who also met an ignominious death. The answer it produced, corroborating many of our observations on the life of the unfortunate Aram, and which we think will prove a highly acceptable conclusion to our narrative, we shall beg permission to quote.

153

'Objections are made to the admission of Eugene Aram into the Biographia Britannica, and the exclusion of Bishop Atherton; but it appears to me that the remarks on this subject are far from being just. The insertion of Aram is objected to because he was a man of bad principles, and ended his life at the gallows; but it should be remembered that it was never understood that in the Biographia Britannica the lives only of virtuous men were to be recorded.

'In the old edition are the lives of several persons who ended their days by the hands of the executioner. Bonner was not a virtuous character, and yet was very properly inserted, as well as Henry Cuff, who was executed at Tyburn in the reign of Queen Elizabeth.

'As to Eugene Aram, it is truly said of him in the Biographia, in the article objected to, that the progress he made in literature, allowing for the little instruction that he had received, may justly be considered as astonishing; and that his powers of mind were uncommonly great cannot reasonably be questioned.

'Eugene Aram possessed talents and acquisitions that might have classed him among the most respectable of human characters if his moral qualities had been equal to his intellectual.

'It was certainly the extraordinary talents and acquirements of Aram that occasioned his introduction into the Biographia; and I know that by persons of undoubted taste and judgment the account of him in that work has been thought a curious and interesting article. His singular defence alone was well worthy of being preserved in such a work.

'With respect to Bishop Atherton, he never had the least claim to insertion in such a work as the Biographia Britannica, and was therefore very properly omitted in the new edition. He was not in the least distinguished for genius or learning; his merely being a bishop could give him no just pretensions, and still less the unnatural crime for which he suffered.

'The friends of Bishop Atherton say that his reputation was suspected to have been destroyed, and his catastrophe effected, more by the contrivance of a party than by the aggravated guilt with which he was charged. If this were perfectly just, which, however, may be reasonably questioned, it would not give Atherton the least claim to insertion in the Biographia Britannica. Aram was inserted on account of his uncommon talents and learning; but Atherton, who was not distinguished for either, never had the least pretension to be recorded in such a work.'

JOHN PRICE, COMMONLY CALLED JACK KETCH,

EXECUTED FOR THE MURDER OF ELIZABETH WHITE.

WHEN we commenced our labours among the musty records of criminal convictions, little did we imagine that we should find the public executioner, vulgarly called Jack Ketch, to have been himself suspended on that fatal tree to which he had tied up such a number of sinners. Here have we the fullest proof of the hardness of heart created by repeatedly witnessing executions. The dreadful fate attending those who had died by his hands, their sufferings of mind, confessions and exhortations to the spectators to be warned by their example against the violation of the law, it seems, had no effect on Jack Ketch.

The callous wretch who, in the year 1718, filled this office, was named John Price. He was born in the parish of St. Martin's in the Fields, London, of reputable parents; his father having been in the service of his country, but unfortunately blown up at the demolishing of Tangier. From her loss, the widow was reduced to poverty, which rendered her unable of giving an education to her orphan children : but she succeeded in putting John apprentice to a dealer in rags; a business by which he might have earned an honest livelihood. When he had served two years of his apprenticeship his master died, and soon after he ran away from his mistress, and got employment in the loading of waggons with rags for other dealers. He then went to sea, and served with credit, on board different ships in the royal navy, for the space of eighteen years; but at length was paid off and discharged from further service.

The office of public executioner becoming vacant, it was given to Price, who, but for his extravagance, might have long continued in it, and subsisted on its dreadfully-earned wages. On returning from an execution, in the cart which had delivered some criminals into his hands, he was arrested in Holborn for debt, which he discharged, in part, with the wages he had that day earned, and the remainder from the produce of three suits of clothes, which he had taken from the bodies of the executed men. Not long afterwards he was lodged in the Marshalsea prison for other debts, and there remained for want of bail; in consequence whereof, being unable to attend his business at the next sessions of the Old Bailey, one William Marvel was appointed in his stead.

Having continued some time longer in the Marshalsea, he and a fellow-prisoner broke a hole in the wall, through which they made their escape; and soon after this Price committed the horrid murder for which his life paid the forfeit.

John Price was indicted at the Old Bailey on the 24th of April, 1718, for the murder of Elizabeth, the wife of William White, on the 13th of the preceding month.

In the course of the evidence it appeared that Price met the deceased near ten at night in Moorfields, and attempted to ravish her; but the poor woman (who was the wife of a watchman, and sold gingerbread in the streets) doing all in her power to resist his villainous attacks, he beat her so cruelly that streams of blood issued from her eyes and mouth, one of her arms was broken, some of her teeth knocked out, her head bruised in a most dreadful manner, one of her eyes forced from the socket; and he otherwise so ill treated her that the language of decency cannot describe it.

Some persons, hearing the cries of the unhappy creature, repaired to the spot, took Price into custody, and lodged him in the watch-house; then conveyed the woman to a house, where a surgeon and nurse were sent for to attend her. Being unable to speak, she answered the nurse's questions by signs, and in that manner described what had happened to her. She died, after having languished four days.

The prisoner, on his trial, denied being guilty of the fact; and said that, as he was crossing Moorfields, he found something lying in his way; that he kicked at it, but discovered that it was a woman: he lifted her up, but she could not stand on her legs; and he said that he was taken into custody while he was thus employed. This defence, however, could not be credited, from what some former evidences had sworn; and the jury did not hesitate to find him guilty.

After sentence of death was passed on him, he abandoned himself to the drinking of spirituous liquors to such a degree as rendered him totally incapable of all the exercises of devotion. He obstinately denied the fact till the day of his execution, when he confessed that he had been guilty of it; but said that the crime was perpetrated when he was in a state of intoxication. He was executed in Bunhill-fields, on the 31st of May, 1718, and, in his last moments, begged the prayers of the multitude, and hoped they would take warning by his untimely end. He was afterwards hung in chains near Holloway.

One would imagine that the dreadful scenes of calamity to which this man had been witness, if they had not taught him humanity, would at least have given him wisdom enough not to have perpetrated a crime that must necessarily bring him to a similarly fatal end to what he had so often seen of others : but perhaps his profession tended rather to harden his mind than otherwise.

The murder of which Price was guilty appears to have been one of the most barbarous and unprovoked we ever remember to have read of : and his pretence that he was drunk when he perpetrated it was no sort of excuse, since drunkenness itself is a crime, and one which frequently leads to the commission of others.

The lesson to be learnt from the fate of this man is to moderate our passions of every kind, and to live by the rules of temperance and sobriety. We are told, from the best authority, that ' hands that shed innocent blood are an abomination to the Lord.'

RICHARD TURPIN,

EXECUTED FOR HORSE-STEALING.

THIS man was the son of John Turpin, a farmer at Thackstead, in Essex ; and, having received a common school education, was apprenticed to a butcher in Whitechapel ; but was distinguished from his early youth for the impropriety of his behaviour, and the brutality of his manners.

On the expiration of his apprenticeship he married a young woman of East Ham, in Essex, named Palmer ; but he had not been long married before he took to the practice of stealing his neighbours' cattle, which he used to kill and cut up for sale.

Having stolen two oxen belonging to Mr. Giles, of Plaistow, he drove them to his own house ; but two of Giles's servants, suspecting who was the robber, went to Turpin's, where they saw the carcasses of two beasts of such size as had been lost; but, as the hides were stripped from them, it was impossible to say that they were the same: learning, however, that Turpin used to dispose of his hides at Waltham Abbey, they went thither, and saw the hides of the individual beasts that had been stolen.

No doubt now remaining who was the robber, a warrant was procured for the apprehension of Turpin;

Turpin placing an old Woman on the Fire, to compel the Discovery of her Treasure.

but, learning that the peace-officers were in search of him, he made his escape from the back window of his house at the very moment they were entering at the door.

Having retreated to a place of security, he found means to inform his wife where he was concealed: she accordingly furnished him with money, with which he travelled into the hundreds of Essex, where he joined a gang of smugglers, with whom he was for some time successful; till a set of the Custom-house officers, by one fortunate stroke, deprived him of all his ill-acquired gains.

Thrown out of this kind of business, he connected himself with a gang of deer-stealers, the principal part of whose depredations were committed on Epping Forest, and the parks in its neighbourhood: but, this business not succeeding to the expectation of the robbers, they determined to commence housebreakers.

Their plan was, to fix on houses that they presumed contained any valuable property; and, while one of them knocked at the door, the others were to rush in, and seize whatever they might deem worthy of their notice.

The first attack of this kind was at the house of Mr. Strype, an old man who kept a chandler's shop at Watford, whom they robbed of all the money in his possession, but did not offer him any personal violence.

Turpin now acquainted his associates that there was an old woman at Loughton who was in possession of seven or eight hundred pounds; whereupon they agreed to rob her; and when they came to the door one of them knocked, and the rest, forcing their way into the house, tied handkerchiefs over the eyes of the old woman and her maid.

This being done, Turpin demanded what money was in the house; and the owner hesitating to tell him, he threatened to set her on the fire if she did not make an immediate discovery. Still, however, she refused to give the desired information: on which the villains actually placed her on the fire, where she sat till the tormenting pains compelled her to discover her hidden treasure; so that the robbers possessed themselves of above four hundred pounds, and decamped with the booty.

Some little time after this they agreed to rob the house of a farmer near Barking; and, knocking at the door, the people declined to open it: on which they broke it open; and having bound the farmer, his wife, his son-in-law, and the servant-maid, they robbed the house of above seven hundred pounds; which delighted Turpin so much, that he exclaimed, ' Ay, this will do, if it would always be so ! ' and the robbers retired with their prize, which amounted to above eighty pounds for each of them.

This desperate gang, now flushed with success, determined to attack the house of Mr. Mason, the keeper of Epping Forest; and the time was fixed when the plan was to be carried into execution: but Turpin, having gone to London to spend his share of the former booty, intoxicated himself to such a degree that he totally forgot the appointment.

Nevertheless, the rest of the gang resolved that the absence of their companion should not frustrate the proposed design; and, having taken a solemn oath to break every article of furniture in Mason's house, they set out on their expedition.

Having gained admission, they beat and kicked the unhappy man with great severity. Finding an old man sitting by the fire-side, they permitted him to remain uninjured; and Mr. Mason's daughter escaped their fury by running out of the house, and taking shelter in a hog-sty.

After ransacking the lower part of the house, and doing much mischief, they went up stairs, where they broke every thing that fell in their way, and, among the rest, a china punch-bowl, from which dropped one hundred and twenty guineas, which they made prey of, and effected their escape. They now went to London in search of Turpin, with whom they shared the booty, though he had not taken part in the execution of the villainy.

On the 11th of January, 1735, Turpin and five of his companions went to the house of Mr. Saunders, a rich farmer at Charlton, in Kent, between seven and eight

161

in the evening, and, having knocked at the door, asked if Mr. Saunders was at home. Being answered in the affirmative, they rushed into the house, and found Mr. Saunders, with his wife and friends, playing at cards in the parlour. They told the company that they should remain uninjured if they made no disturbance. Having made prize of a silver snuff-box which lay on the table, part of the gang stood guard over the rest of the company, while the others attended Mr. Saunders through the house, and, breaking open his escrutoires and closets, stole above a hundred pounds, exclusive of plate.

During these transactions the servant-maid ran up stairs, barred the door of her room, and called out 'Thieves!' with a view of alarming the neighbourhood; but the robbers broke open the door, secured her, and then robbed the house of all the valuable property they had not before taken. Finding some mince-pies, and some bottles of wine, they sat down to regale themselves; and, meeting with a bottle of brandy, they compelled each of the company to drink a glass of it.

Mrs. Saunders fainting through terror, they administered some drops, in water, to her, and recovered her to the use of her senses. Having staid in the house a considerable time, they packed up their booty and departed, having first declared that if any of the family gave the least alarm within two hours, or advertised the marks of the stolen plate, they would return and murder them at a future time.

Retiring to a public house at Woolwich, where they had concerted the robbery, they crossed the Thames to an empty house in Ratcliffe Highway, where they deposited the stolen effects till they found a purchaser for them.

The division of the plunder having taken place, they, on the 18th of the same month, went to the house of Mr. Sheldon, near Croydon, in Surrey, where they arrived about seven in the evening. Having got into the yard, they perceived a light in the stable, and, going into it, found the coachman attending his horses. Having immediately bound him, they quitted the stable, and, meeting Mr. Sheldon in the yard, they seized him, and compelled him to conduct them into the house, whence they stole eleven guineas, with jewels, plate, and other things of value, to a large amount. Having committed this robbery, they returned Mr. Sheldon two guineas, and apologized for their conduct.

This being done, they hastened to the Black Horse, in the Broadway, Westminster, where they concerted the robbery of Mr. Lawrence, of Edgware, near Stanmore, in Middlesex, for which place they set out on the 4th of February, and arrived at a public house in that village about five o'clock in the evening. From this place they went to Mr. Lawrence's house, where they arrived about seven o'clock, just as he had discharged some people who had worked for him.

Having left their horses at the outer gate, one of the robbers, going forwards, found a boy who had just returned from folding his sheep: the rest of the gang following, a pistol was presented, and instant destruction threatened if he made any noise. They then took off his garters, tied his hands therewith, and told him to direct them to the door, and, when they knocked, to answer, and bid the servants open it, in which case they would not hurt him: but, when the boy came to the door, he was so terrified that he could not speak; on which one of the gang knocked, and a man-servant, imagining it was one of the neighbours, opened the door, whereupon they all rushed in, armed with pistols.

Having seized Mr. Lawrence and his servant, they threw a cloth over their faces, and, taking the boy into another room, demanded what fire-arms were in the house; to which he replied, only an old gun, which they broke in pieces. They then bound Mr. Lawrence and his man, and made them sit by the boy; and Turpin, searching the gentleman, took from him a

163

guinea, a Portugal piece, and some silver; but, not being satisfied with this booty, they forced him to conduct them up stairs, where they broke open a closet, and stole some money and plate : but, that not being sufficient, they threatened to murder Mr. Lawrence, each of them destining him to a different death, as the savageness of his own nature prompted. At length one of them took a kettle of water from the fire, and threw it over him; but it providentially happened not to be hot enough to scald him.

In the interim, the maid-servant, who was churning butter in the dairy, hearing a noise in the house, apprehended some mischief, on which she blew out her candle to screen herself; but, being found in the course of their search, one of the miscreants compelled her to go up stairs, where he gratified his brutal passion by force. They then robbed the house of all the valuable effects they could find, locked the family into the parlour, threw the key into the garden, and took their ill-gotten plunder to London.

The particulars of this atrocious robbery being represented to the king, a proclamation was issued for the apprehension of the offenders, promising a pardon to any one of them who would impeach his accomplices; and a reward of fifty pounds was offered, to be paid on conviction. This, however, had no effect; the robbers continued their depredations as before; and, flushed with the success they had met with, seemed to bid defiance to the laws.

On the 7th of February six of them assembled at the White Bear inn, in Drury Lane, where they agreed to rob the house of Mr. Francis, a farmer near Marylebone. Arriving at the place, they found a servant in the cow-house, whom, threatening to murder if he was not perfectly silent, they bound fast. This being done, they led him into the stable, where, finding another of the servants, they bound him in the same manner.

In the interim Mr. Francis happening to come home,

they presented their pistols to his breast, and threatened instant destruction to him if he made the least noise or opposition.

Having bound the master in the stable with his servants, they rushed into the house, tied Mrs. Francis, her daughter, and the maid-servant, and beat them in a most cruel manner. One of the thieves stood as a sentry while the rest rifled the house, in which they found a silver tankard, a medal of Charles I., a gold watch, several gold rings, a considerable sum of money, and a variety of valuable linen and other effects, which they conveyed to London.

Hereupon a reward of one hundred pounds was offered for the apprehension of the offenders; in consequence of which two of them were taken into custody, tried, convicted on the evidence of an accomplice, and hanged in chains: and the whole gang being dispersed, Turpin went into the country to renew his depredations on the public.

On a journey towards Cambridge, he met a man genteelly dressed, and well mounted; and, expecting a good booty, he presented a pistol to the supposed gentleman, and demanded his money. The party thus stopped happened to be one King, a famous highwayman, who knew Turpin; and, when the latter threatened instant destruction if he did not deliver his money, King burst into a fit of laughter, and said, 'What, dog eat dog?—Come, come, brother Turpin, if you don't know me I know you, and shall be glad of your company.'

These brethren in iniquity soon struck the bargain, and, immediately entering on business, committed a number of robberies; till at length they were so well known that no public house would receive them as guests. Thus situated, they fixed on a spot between the King's Oak and the Loughton road, on Epping Forest, where they made a cave which was large enough to receive them and their horses.

This cave was enclosed within a sort of thicket of bushes and brambles, through which they could look and see passengers on the road, while themselves remained unobserved.

From this station they used to issue, and robbed such a number of persons, that at length the very pedlars who travelled the road carried fire-arms for their defence : and, while they were in this retreat, Turpin's wife used to supply them with necessaries, and frequently remained in the cave during the night.

Having taken a ride as far as Bungay, in Suffolk, they observed two young countrywomen receive fourteen pounds for corn, on which Turpin resolved to rob them of the money. King objected, saying it was a pity to rob such pretty girls : but Turpin was obstinate, and obtained the booty.

Upon their return home, on the following day, they stopped a Mr. Bradle, of London, who was riding in his chariot with his children. The gentleman, seeing only one robber, was preparing to make resistance, when King called to Turpin to hold the horses. They took from the gentleman his watch, money, and an old mourning-ring; but returned the latter, as he declared that its intrinsic value was trifling; yet he was very unwilling to part with it.

Finding that they readily parted with the ring, he asked them what he must give for the watch : on which King said to Turpin, ' What say you, Jack? Here seems to be a good honest fellow; shall we let him have the watch ? ' Turpin replied, ' Do as you please ; ' on which King said to the gentleman, ' You must pay six guineas for it : we never sell for more, though the watch should be worth six-and-thirty.' The gentleman promised that the money should be left at the Dial, in Birchin Lane.

On the 4th of May, 1737, Turpin was guilty of murder, which arose from the following circumstance : —A reward of a hundred pounds having been offered for apprehending him, one Thomas Morris, a servant of Mr. Thompson, one of the keepers of Epping Forest, accompanied by a higgler, set off in order to apprehend him. Turpin seeing them approach near his dwelling, Mr. Thompson's man having a gun, he mistook them for poachers; on which he said there were no hares near that thicket. 'No,' said Morris; 'but I have found a Turpin;' and, presenting his gun, required him to surrender.

Hereupon Turpin spoke to him as in a friendly manner, and gradually retreated at the same time, till, having seized his own gun, he shot him dead on the spot, and the higgler ran off with the utmost precipitation.

This murder being represented to the secretary of state, the following proclamation was issued by government, which we give a place to, from its describing the person of this notorious depredator:

'It having been represented to the king that Richard Turpin did, on Wednesday, the 4th of May last, barbarously murder Thomas Morris, servant to Henry Thompson, one of the keepers of Epping Forest, and commit other notorious felonies and robberies near London, his majesty is pleased to promise his most gracious pardon to any of his accomplices, and a reward of two hundred pounds to any person or persons, that shall discover him, so that he may be apprehended and convicted. Turpin was born at Thackstead, in Essex, is about thirty, by trade a butcher, about five feet nine inches high, very much marked with the small-pox, his cheek-bones broad, his face thinner towards the bottom, his visage short, pretty upright, and broad about the shoulders.'

Turpin, to avoid the proclamation, went farther into the country in search of his old companion, King; and in the mean time sent a letter to his wife, to meet him at a public house at Hertford. The woman attended according to this direction; and her husband coming

167

into the house soon after she arrived, a butcher, to whom he owed five pounds, happened to see him; on which he said, ' Come, Dick, I know you have money now; and, if you will pay me, it will be of great service.'

Turpin told him that his wife was in the next room; that she had money, and that he should be paid immediately; but, while the butcher was hinting to some of his acquaintance that the person present was Turpin, and that they might take him into custody after he had received his debt, the highwayman made his escape through a window, and rode off with great expedition.

Turpin having found King, and a man named Potter, who had lately connected himself with them, they set off towards London in the dusk of the evening; but, when they came near the Green Man, on Epping Forest, they overtook a Mr. Major, who being mounted on a very fine horse, while Turpin's beast was jaded, the latter obliged him to dismount, and exchange.

The robbers now pursued their journey towards London; and Mr. Major, going to the Green Man, gave an account of the affair; on which it was conjectured that Turpin had been the robber, and that the horse which he exchanged must have been stolen.

It was on a Saturday evening that this robbery was committed; but, Mr. Major being advised to print hand-bills immediately, notice was given to the landlord of the Green Man that such a horse as Major had lost had been left at the Red Lion, in Whitechapel. The landlord, going thither, determined to wait till some person came for it; and, at about eleven at night, King's brother came to pay for the horse, and take him away; on which he was immediately seized, and conducted into the house.

Being asked what right he had to the horse, he said he had bought it; but the landlord, examining a whip which he had in his hand, found a button at the end of the handle half broken off, and the name of Major on the remaining half. Upon this he was given into the custody of a constable; but, as it was not supposed that he was the actual robber, he was told that he should have his liberty if he would discover his employer.

Hereupon he said that a stout man, in a white duffil coat, was waiting for the horse in Red Lion Street; on which the company, going thither, saw King, who drew a pistol, and attempted to fire it, but it flashed in the pan: he then endeavoured to pull out another pistol, but he could not, as it got entangled in his pocket.

At this time Turpin was watching at a small distance, and, riding towards the spot, King cried out, 'Shoot him, or we are taken;' on which Turpin fired, and shot his companion, who called out, 'Dick, you have killed me!' which the other hearing, rode off at full speed.

King lived a week after this affair, and gave information that Turpin might be found at a house near Hackney Marsh; and, on inquiry, it was discovered that Turpin had been there on the night that he rode off, lamenting that he had killed King, who was his most faithful associate.

For a considerable time did Turpin skulk about the forest, having been deprived of his retreat in the cave since he shot the servant of Mr. Thompson. On the examination of this cave there were found two shirts, two pair of stockings, a piece of ham, and part of a bottle of wine.

Some vain attempts were made to take this notorious offender into custody; and, among the rest, the hunts-man of a gentleman in the neighbourhood went in search of him with bloodhounds. Turpin perceiving them, and recollecting that King Charles II. evaded his pursuers under covert of the friendly branches of the oak, mounted one of those trees, under which the hounds passed, to his inexpressible terror, so that he determined to make a retreat into Yorkshire.

Going first to Long Sutton, in Lincolnshire, he stole

some horses, for which he was taken into custody, but escaped from the constable as he was conducting him before a magistrate, and hastened to Welton, in Yorkshire, where he went by the name of John Palmer, and assumed the character of a gentleman.

He now frequently went into Lincolnshire, where he stole horses, which he brought into Yorkshire, and either sold or exchanged them.

He often accompanied the neighbouring gentlemen on their parties of hunting and shooting; and one evening, on a return from an expedition of the latter kind, he wantonly shot a cock belonging to his landlord. On this Mr. Hall, a neighbour, said, ' You have done wrong in shooting your landlord's cock; ' to which Turpin replied, that, if he would stay while he loaded his gun, he would shoot him also.

Irritated by this insult, Mr. Hall informed the landlord of what had passed; and, application being made to some magistrates, a warrant was granted for the apprehension of the offender, who being taken into custody, and carried before a bench of justices, then assembled at the quarter-sessions, at Beverley, they demanded security for his good behaviour, which being unable or unwilling to give, he was committed to Bridewell.

On inquiry, it appeared that he made frequent journeys into Lincolnshire, on his return always abounding in money, and that he was likewise in possession of several horses, so that it was conjectured that he was a horse-stealer and a highwayman.

On this the magistrates went to him on the following day, and demanded who he was, where he had lived, and what was his employment? He replied, in substance, ' That about two years ago he had lived at Long Sutton, in Lincolnshire, and was by trade a butcher: but that, having contracted several debts for sheep that proved rotten, he was obliged to abscond, and come to live in Yorkshire.'

The magistrates, not being satisfied with this tale, commissioned the clerk of the peace to write into Lincolnshire, to make the necessary inquiries respecting the supposed John Palmer. The letter was carried by a special messenger, who brought an answer from a magistrate in the neighbourhood, importing that John Palmer was well known, though he had never carried on trade there: that he had been accused of sheep-stealing, for which he had been in custody, but had made his escape from the peace-officers: and that there were several informations lodged against him for horse-stealing.

Hereupon the magistrates thought it prudent to remove him to York Castle, where he had not been more than a month when two persons from Lincolnshire came and claimed a mare and foal, and likewise a horse, which he had stolen in that county.

After he had been about four months in prison, he wrote the following letter to his brother in Essex:

'York, Feb. 6, 1739.

'Dear Brother,

'I am sorry to acquaint you that I am now under confinement in York Castle for horse-stealing. If I could procure an evidence from London to give me a character, that would go a great way towards my being acquitted. I had not been long in this country before my being apprehended, so that it would pass off the readier. For Heaven's sake, dear brother, do not neglect me; you will know what I mean when I say,

'I am yours,
'JOHN PALMER.'

This letter, being returned, unopened, to the post-office in Essex, because the brother would not pay the postage of it, was accidentally seen by Mr. Smith, a schoolmaster, who, having taught Turpin to write, immediately knew his hand, on which he carried the letter to a magistrate, who broke it open, and it was thus discovered that the supposed John Palmer was the real Richard Turpin.

Hereupon the magistrates of Essex dispatched Mr. Smith to York, who immediately selected him from all the other prisoners in the Castle. This Mr. Smith, and another gentleman, afterwards proved his identity on his trial.

On the rumour that the noted Turpin was a prisoner in York Castle, persons flocked from all parts of the country to take a view of him, and debates ran high whether he was the real person or not. Among others who visited him was a young fellow who pretended to know the famous Turpin, and, having regarded him a considerable time with looks of great attention, he told the keeper he would bet him half a guinea that he was not Turpin; on which the prisoner, whispering the keeper, said ' Lay him the wager, and I'll go your halves.'

When this notorious malefactor was brought to trial, he was convicted on two indictments, and received sentence of death.

After conviction he wrote to his father, imploring him to intercede with a gentleman and lady of rank, to make interest that his sentence might be remitted, and that he might be transported. The father did what was in his power; but the notoriety of his character was such, that no persons would exert themselves in his favour.

This man lived in the most gay and thoughtless manner after conviction, regardless of all considerations of futurity, and effecting to make a jest of the dreadful fate that awaited him.

Not many days before his execution he purchased a new fustian frock and a pair of pumps, in order to wear them at the time of his death; and on the day before he hired five poor men, at ten shillings each, to follow the cart as mourners: he gave hatbands and gloves to several other persons; and also left a ring, and some other articles, to a married woman in Lincolnshire, with whom he had been acquainted.

On the morning of his death he was put into a cart, and being followed by his mourners, as above mentioned, he was drawn to the place of execution, in his way to which he bowed to the spectators with an air of the most astonishing indifference and intrepidity.

When he came to the fatal tree he ascended the ladder; and, on his right leg trembling, he stamped it down with an air of assumed courage, as if he was ashamed to be observed to discover any signs of fear. Having conversed with the executioner about half an hour, he threw himself off the ladder, and expired in a few minutes. Turpin suffered at York, April 10, 1739.

The spectators of the execution seemed to be much affected at the fate of this man, who was distinguished by the comeliness of his appearance. The corpse was brought to the Blue Boar, in Castle Gate, York, where it remained till the next morning, when it was interred in the churchyard of St. George's parish, with an inscription on the coffin, bearing the initials of his name, and his age. The grave was made remarkably deep, and the people who acted as mourners took such measures as they thought would secure the body: yet, about three o'clock on the following morning, some persons were observed in the churchyard, who carried it off; and the populace, having an intimation whither it was conveyed, found it in a garden belonging to one of the surgeons of the city.

Hereupon they took the body, laid it on a board, and having carried it through the streets in a kind of triumphal manner, and then filled the coffin with unslacked lime, buried it in the grave where it had been before deposited.—It is difficult to conceive the reason of all this concern and sympathy; for surely a more heartless and depraved villain than Turpin never existed. Independently of the brutal murders perpetrated by him, it is impossible to overlook the mean rascality of his robbing the two country girls (which even his fellow-thief objected to), or the barbarity of placing an old woman on the fire, because she refused directing his gang to the little hoard which had probably been laid by as the support of her declining years.

JOHN SMITH,

CONVICTED OF ROBBERY.

THOUGH the crimes committed by this man were not particularly atrocious, nor his life sufficiently remarkable for a place in this work, yet the circumstances attending his fate at the place of execution are perhaps more singular than any we may have to record. He was the son of a farmer at Malton, about fifteen miles from the city of York, who bound him apprentice to a packer in London, with whom he served out his time, and afterwards worked as a journeyman. He then went to sea in a merchant-man, after which he entered on board a man of war, and was at the famous expedition against Vigo; but on the return from that expedition he was discharged.

He had not been long disengaged from the naval service when he enlisted as a soldier in the regiment of guards commanded by Lord Cutts; but in this station he soon made bad connexions, and engaged with some of his dissolute companions as a housebreaker.

On the 5th of December, 1705, he was arraigned on four different indictments, on two of which he was convicted. While he lay under sentence of death, he seemed very little affected with his situation, absolutely depending on a reprieve, through the interest of his friends.

However, an order came for his execution on the 24th day of the same month, in consequence of which he was carried to Tyburn, where he performed his devotions, and was turned off in the usual manner; but when he had hung near fifteen minutes, the people present cried out, ' A reprieve ! ' Hereupon the malefactor was cut down, and, being conveyed to a house in the neighbourhood, he soon recovered, in consequence of bleeding and other proper applications.

When he perfectly recovered his senses, he was asked what were his feelings at the time of execution; to which he repeatedly replied, in substance, as follows: ' That when he was turned off, he, for some time, was sensible of very great pain, occasioned by the weight of his body, and felt his spirits in a strange commotion, violently pressing upwards; that having forced their way to his head, he, as it were, saw a great blaze, or glaring light, which seemed to go out at his eyes with a flash, and then he lost all sense of pain. That after he was cut down, and began to come to himself, the blood and spirits, forcing themselves into their former channels, put him, by a sort of pricking or shooting, to such intolerable pain that he could have wished those hanged who had cut him down.' From this circumstance he was called ' Half-hanged Smith.'

After this narrow escape from the grave, Smith pleaded to his pardon on the 20th of February; yet such was his propensity to evil deeds, that he returned to his former practices, and, being apprehended, was tried at the Old Bailey, for housebreaking; but some difficulties arising in the case, the jury brought in a special verdict, in consequence of which the affair was left to the opinion of the twelve judges, who determined in favour of the prisoner.

After this second extraordinary escape, he was a third time indicted; but the prosecutor happening to die before the day of trial, he once more obtained that liberty which his conduct showed he had not deserved.

We have no account what became of this man after this third remarkable incident in his favour; but Christian charity inclines us to hope that he made a proper use of the singular dispensation of Providence evidenced in his own person.

When once the mind has consented to the commission of sin, it is hard to be reclaimed. The memory of the pangs of an ignominious death could not deter this man from following the evil course he had begun. Thus, by giving way to small propensities, we imperceptibly go on to enormities which lead us to a shameful fate. Let us, therefore, at once resolve never to depart from the path of rectitude.

LAURENCE EARL FERRERS,

EXECUTED FOR MURDER.

From the royal blood of the Plantagenets was the house of Ferrers descended, and had been distinguished for ages. One of the family was slain, while fighting on behalf of the crown, at the memorable battle of Shrewsbury, in the beginning of the reign of Henry IV.—a circumstance that is mentioned by the immortal Shakspeare.

Laurence Earl Ferrers was a man of an unhappy

disposition. Though of clear intellects, and acknowledged abilities when sober, yet an early attachment to drinking greatly impaired his faculties; and, when drunk, his behaviour was that of a madman.

Lord Ferrers married the youngest daughter of Sir William Meridith, in the year 1752, but behaved to her with such unwarrantable cruelty that she was obliged to apply to Parliament for redress; the con-

Earl Ferrers shooting Mr. Johnson, his Steward.

sequence of which was that an act passed for allowing her a separate maintenance, to be raised out of his estates.

The following will afford a specimen of the brutality of Lord Ferrers' behaviour: Some oysters had been sent from London, which not proving good, his lordship directed one of the servants to swear that the carrier had changed them; but the servant declining to take such an oath, the earl flew on him in a rage, stabbed him in the breast with a knife, cut his head with a candlestick, and kicked him on the groin with such severity, that he was incapable of a retention of urine for several years afterwards.

Lord Ferrers' brother and his wife paying a visit to him and his countess at Stanton-Harold, some dispute arose between the parties; and Lady Ferrers being absent from the room, the earl ran up stairs with a large clasp-knife in his hand, and asked a servant whom he met where his lady was. The man said, ' In her own room! ' and, being directed to follow him thither, Lord Ferrers ordered him to load a brace of pistols with bullets. This order was complied with; but the servant, apprehensive of mischief, declined priming the pistols, which Lord Ferrers discovering, he swore at him, asked him for powder, and primed them himself. He then threatened that, if he did not immediately go and shoot his brother, the captain, he would blow his brains out. The servant hesitating, his lordship pulled the trigger of one of the pistols; but it missed fire. Hereupon the countess dropped on her knees, and begged him to appease his passions; but in return he swore at her, and threatened her destruction if she opposed him. The servant now escaped from the room, and reported what had passed to his lordship's brother, who immediately called his wife from her bed, and they left the house, though it was then two o'clock in the morning.

The unfortunate Mr. Johnson, who fell a sacrifice to the ungovernable passions of Lord Ferrers, had been bred up in the family from his youth, and was distinguished for the regular manner in which he kept his accounts, and his fidelity as a steward.

When the law had decreed a separate maintenance for the countess, Mr. Johnson was proposed as receiver of the rents for her use; but he declined this office till urged to take it on him by the earl himself. It appears that Johnson now stood high in his lordship's opinion: but a different scene soon ensued; for, the earl having conceived an opinion that Johnson had combined with the trustees to disappoint him of a contract for coal mines, he came to a resolution to destroy the honest steward.

From this time he spoke of him in opprobrious terms, said he had conspired with his enemies to injure him, and that he was a villain. With these sentiments he gave him warning to quit an advantageous farm which he held under his lordship; but, finding that the trustees under the act of separation had already granted him a lease of it, it having been promised to him by the earl or his relations, he was disappointed, and probably from that time he meditated a more cruel revenge.

He thought proper, however, to dissemble his malice to the man, as the most probable method to facilitate the gratification of it; so that poor Johnson was deceived into an opinion that he never was upon better terms with his lord in his life than at the very time he was contriving to destroy him.

His lordship at this time lived at Stanton, a seat about two miles from Ashby de la Zouch, in Leicestershire, and his family consisted of himself, Mrs. Clifford, a lady who lived with him, and her four natural daughters; and five servants—an old man and a boy, and three maids. Mr. Johnson lived at the house belonging to the farm, which he held under his lordship, called the Lount, about half a mile distant from Stanton.

On Sunday, the 13th of January, 1760, my lord went to the Lount, and, after some discourse with Mr. Johnson, ordered him to come to him at Stanton on the Friday following, the 18th, at three o'clock in the afternoon. My lord's hour of dinner was two; and soon after dinner, Mrs. Clifford being in the still-house, his lordship came to her, and told her that she and the children might fetch a walk. Mrs.

Clifford, who seems to have considered this an order to go out, prepared herself and the young ladies immediately, and asked whether they might go to her father's, which was not far off; to which he assented, and said they might stay till half an hour after five. The two men servants he also contrived to send out of the way, so that there was no one in the house but himself and the three maids.

In a very short time after the house was thus cleared Mr. Johnson came, and was let in by Elizabeth Burgeland, one of the maids. He asked if his lordship was within; and the girl replied Yes, he was in his room: Mr. Johnson immediately went, and knocked at the door; and my lord came to the door, and ordered him to wait in the still-house.

After he had been there about ten minutes his lordship came out again, and, calling him to his own room, went in with him, and immediately locked the door. When they were thus together, my lord first ordered him to settle an account, and, after a little time, produced a paper to him, purporting, as he said, to be a confession of his villainy, and required him to sign it. Johnson refused and expostulated, and his lordship then drawing a pistol, which he had charged and kept in his pocket for the purpose, presented it, and bid him kneel down. The poor man then knelt down upon one knee; but Lord Ferrers cried out, so loud as to be heard by one of the maids at the kitchen door, 'Down on your other knee; declare what you have acted against Lord Ferrers; your time is come —you must die;' and then immediately fired. The ball entered his body just below the last rib, yet he did not drop, but rose up, and expressed the sensations of a dying man both by his looks and by such broken sentences as are usually uttered in such situations. My lord, though he at first intended to shoot him again, upon finding he did not drop, was yet forced out of that resolution by involuntary remorse, upon the complaints of the poor man, and the dreadful change that he perceived in his countenance: he then came out of the room, having been shut up in it with the unhappy victim about half an hour; and the report of the pistol having alarmed the women in the wash-house, he called out, ' Who is there? ' One of them soon heard and answered him: he ordered her to see for one of the men, and another to assist in getting Mr. Johnson to bed.

At this time his lordship was perfectly sober; and, having dispatched a messenger for Mr. Kirkland, a surgeon, who lived at Ashby de la Zouch, he went back to the room where he had left Mr. Johnson with the maid, and asked him how he found himself. Johnson replied that he found himself like a dying man, and requested his lordship to send for his children: his lordship consented, and a messenger was dispatched to the Lount, to tell Miss Johnson that she must come to the hall directly, for that her father was taken very ill: upon coming to the hall she soon learned what had happened, and Lord Ferrers sent one of the maids with her up to the room into which her father had been removed, and immediately followed himself. Mr. Johnson was in bed, but did not speak to her: Lord Ferrers pulled down the clothes, and applied a pledget, dipped in arquebusade water, to the wound, and soon after left him. From the time the fact was committed Lord Ferrers continued to drink porter till he became drunk: in the mean time the messenger that had been sent for the surgeon, having at length found him at a neighbouring village about five o'clock, told him that his assistance was wanted for Mr. Johnson at Stanton: he came immediately with the messenger, but in his way to Stanton called at the Lount, where he first heard that Mr. Johnson had been shot, the rumour of the accident having by that time reached all the neighbouring parts.

When he came to the hall my lord told him that

he had shot Johnson, but believed that he was more frightened than hurt; that he had intended to shoot him dead, for that he was a villain, and deserved to die; ' but,' says he, ' now I have spared his life, I desire you would do what you can for him.' My lord at the same time desired that he would not suffer him to be seized, and declared, if any one should attempt it, he would shoot him.

Mr. Kirkland, who wisely determined to say whatever might keep Lord Ferrers, who was then in liquor, from any further outrages, told him that he should not be seized.

The patient complained of a violent pain in his bowels; and Mr. Kirkland preparing to search the wound, my lord informed him of the direction of it, by showing him how he held the pistol when he fired it. Mr. Kirkland found the ball had lodged in the body, at which his lordship expressed great surprise, declaring that he had tried that pistol a few days before, and that it then carried a ball through a deal board near an inch and a half thick.

Mr. Kirkland then went down stairs to prepare some dressings, and my lord soon after left the room. From this time, in proportion as the liquor, which he continued to drink, took effect, his passions became more tumultuous, and the transient fit of compassion, mixed with fear of himself, gave way to starts of rage, and the predominance of malice. He went up into the room where Johnson was dying, and pulled him by the wig, calling him villain, and threatening to shoot him through the head. The last time he went to him he was with great difficulty prevented from tearing the clothes off the bed, which he attempted with great fury, that he might strike him.

A proposal was made to my lord, by Mrs. Clifford, that Mr. Johnson should be removed to his own house; but he replied ' he shall not be removed; I will keep him here to plague the villain.' Many of these expressions were uttered in the hearing of Miss Johnson, whose sufferings in such a situation it is easier to conceive than express; yet, after his abuse of her father, he told her that if he died he would take care of her and of the family, provided they did not prosecute.

When his lordship went to bed, which was between eleven and twelve, he told Mr. Kirkland that he knew he could, if he would, set the affair in such a light as to prevent his being seized, desiring that he might see him before he went away in the morning, and declaring that he would rise at any hour.

Mr. Kirkland, for his own sake, was very solicitous to get Mr. Johnson removed, because, if he died where he was, contrary to the assurances he had given his lordship, he had reason to think his own life would be in danger. As soon as my lord was in bed, therefore, he went and told Mr. Johnson that he would take care he should be removed with all expedition.

He accordingly went to the Lount, and, having fitted up an easy chair, with two poles, by way of a sedan, and procured a guard, he returned about two o'clock, and carried Mr. Johnson to his house, without much fatigue, where he languished till about nine the next morning, and then expired.

As soon as he was dead the neighbours set about seizing the murderer: a few persons, armed, set out for Stanton, and, as they entered the hall-yard, they saw him going towards the stable, as they imagined, to take horse. He appeared to be just out of bed, his stockings being down, and his garters in his hand, having probably taken the alarm immediately on coming out of his room, and finding that Johnson had been removed.

One Springthorpe, advancing towards his lordship, presented a pistol, and required him to surrender; but my lord putting his hand to his pocket, Springthorpe imagined he was feeling for a pistol, and stopped short, being probably intimidated, and suffered his lordship to escape back into the house, where he fastened the doors, and stood upon his defence.

The concourse of people who had come to apprehend him beset the house, and their number increased very fast. In about two hours my lord appeared at the garret window, and called out 'How is Johnson?' Springthorpe answered 'He is dead;' upon which my lord insulted him, called him liar, and swore he would not believe any body but Kirkland. Upon being again assured he was dead, he desired the people might be dispersed, and said he would surrender; yet, almost in the same breath, he desired the people might be let in, and have some victuals and drink; but the issue was, he went away from the window, swearing he would not be taken.

The people, however, still continued near the house; and, about two hours after his lordship had appeared at the garret window, he was seen by one Curtis, a collier, upon the bowling-green: my lord was then armed with a blunderbuss, two or three pistols, and a dagger; but Curtis, so far from being intimidated, marched up boldly to him, in spite of his blunderbuss; and my lord was so struck with the determined resolution that appeared in this brave fellow, that he suffered him to seize him without making the least resistance; yet, the moment he was in custody, declared he had killed a villain, and that he gloried in the act.

He was carried from Stanton to a public house, kept by one Kinsey, at Ashby de la Zouch, where he was kept till the Monday following, during which time the coroner had sat upon the body, and the jury had brought in their verdict—'Wilful murder.'

From Ashby de la Zouch he was sent to Leicester gaol; from thence, about a fortnight afterwards, he was brought in his own landau and six, under a strong guard, to London, where he arrived on the 14th of

February, about noon, dressed like a jockey, in a close riding-frock, jockey boots and cap, and a plain shirt.

Being carried before the House of Lords, he was committed to the custody of the Black Rod, and ordered to the Tower, where he arrived about six o'clock in the evening, having behaved, during the whole journey, and at his commitment, with great calmness and propriety. He was confined in the Round Tower, near the drawbridge: two wardens were constantly in the room with him, and one at the door; two sentinels were posted at the bottom of the stairs, and one upon the drawbridge, with their bayonets fixed; and from this time the gates were ordered to be shut an hour sooner than usual.

Mrs. Clifford and the four young ladies, who had come up with him from Leicestershire, took a lodging in Tower Street, and for some time a servant was continually passing with letters between them; but afterwards this correspondence was permitted only once a day.

During his confinement he was moderate both in eating and drinking; his breakfast was a half-pint basin of tea, with a small spoonful of brandy in it, and a muffin; with his dinner he generally drank a pint of wine and a pint of water, and another pint of each with his supper. In general his behaviour was decent and quiet, except that he would sometimes suddenly start, tear open his waistcoat, and use other gestures, which showed that his mind was disturbed.

Mrs. Clifford came three times to the Tower to see him, but was not admitted; but his children were suffered to be with him some time.

On the 16th of April, having been a prisoner in the Tower two months and two days, he was brought to his trial, which continued till the 18th, before the House of Lords, assembled for that purpose; Lord Henley, Keeper of the Great Seal, having been created Lord High Steward upon the occasion.

The fact was easily proved, and his lordship, in his defence, examined several witnesses to prove his insanity; none of whom proved such an insanity as made him not accountable for his conduct. His lordship managed his defence himself, in such a manner as showed perfect recollection of mind, and an uncommon understanding; he mentioned the situation of being reduced to the necessity of attempting to prove himself a lunatic, that he might not be deemed a murderer, with the most delicate and affecting sensibility; and, when he found that his plea could not avail him, he confessed that he made it only to gratify his friends; that he was always averse to it himself; and that it had prevented what he had proposed, and what perhaps might have taken off the malignity, at least, of the accusation.

His lordship, immediately upon conviction, received sentence to be hanged on Monday, the 21st of April, and then to be anatomized; but, in consideration of his rank, the execution of this sentence was respited till Monday, the 5th of May.

During this interval he made a will, by which he left one thousand three hundred pounds to Mr. Johnson's children; one thousand pounds to each of his four natural daughters; and sixty pounds a year to Mrs. Clifford for her life. This will, however, being made after his conviction, was not valid; yet it was said that the same, or nearly the same, provision was made for the parties.

In the mean time a scaffold was erected under the gallows at Tyburn, and part of it, about a yard square, was raised about eighteen inches above the rest of the floor, with a contrivance to sink down upon a signal given; and the whole was covered with black baize.

In the morning of the 5th of May, about nine o'clock, his body was demanded of the keeper, at the gates of the Tower, by the sheriffs of London and

Middlesex. His lordship, being informed of it, sent a message to the sheriffs, requesting that he might go in his own landau, instead of the mourning coach which had been provided by his friends; and this request being granted, he entered his landau, drawn by six horses, with Mr. Humphries, Chaplain of the Tower, who had been admitted to his lordship that morning, for the first time : the landau was conducted to the outer gate of the Tower by the officers of that fortress, and was there delivered to the sheriffs.

Here Mr. Sheriff Vaillant entered the landau of his lordship, and, expressing his concern at having so melancholy a duty to perform, his lordship said ' He was much obliged to him, and took it kindly that he accompanied him.'

He was dressed in a suit of light-coloured clothes, embroidered with silver, said to be his wedding suit; and, soon after Mr. Vaillant came into the landau, he said ' You may, perhaps, Sir, think it strange to see me in this dress; but I have my particular reasons for it.'

The procession then began in the following order : —

A very large body of constables for the county of Middlesex, preceded by one of the high constables.

A party of horse-grenadiers, and a party of foot.

Mr. Sheriff Errington in his chariot, accompanied by his under-sheriff, Mr. Jackson.

The landau, escorted by two other parties of horse-grenadiers and foot.

Mr. Sheriff Vaillant's carriage, in which was his under-sheriff, Mr. Nichols.

A mourning-coach and six, with some of his lordship's friends.

A hearse and six, which was provided for the conveyance of his lordship's corpse from the place of execution to Surgeons' Hall.

The procession moved so slow, that my lord was two hours and three quarters in his landau; but during the whole time he appeared perfectly easy and composed, though he often expressed his desire to have it over, saying that ' the apparatus of death, and the passing through such crowds of people, were ten times worse than death itself.'

He told the sheriff that he had written to the king to beg ' that he might suffer where his ancestor, the Earl of Essex, had suffered; and was in greater hopes of obtaining that favour, as he had the honour of quartering part of the same arms, and of being allied to his majesty; and that he thought it was hard that he must die at the place appointed for the execution of common felons.'

Mr. Humphries took occasion to observe, that ' the world would naturally be very inquisitive concerning the religion his lordship professed, and asked him if he chose to say any thing upon that subject.' To which his lordship answered, ' That he did not think himself accountable to the world for his sentiments on religion; but that he had always believed in and adored one God, the Maker of all things;—that, whatever his notions were, he had never propagated them, or endeavoured to gain any persons over to his persuasion;—that all countries and nations had a form of religion by which the people were governed, and that he looked upon whoever disturbed them in it as an enemy to society.—That he very much blamed my Lord Bolingbroke for permitting his sentiments on religion to be published to the world.—That the many facts and disputes which happen about religion have almost turned morality out of doors.—That he never could believe what some sectaries teach, that faith alone will save mankind; so that if a man, just before he dies, should say only " I believe," that *that* alone will save him.'

As to the crime for which he suffered, he declared ' that he was under particular circumstances—that he had met with so many crosses and vexations, he

scarce knew what he did : ' and most solemnly pro-
tested ' that he had not the least malice against Mr.
Johnson.'

When his lordship had got to that part of Holborn
which is near Drury Lane, he said ' he was thirsty,
and should be glad of a glass of wine and water; '
upon which the sheriffs remonstrating to him, ' that
a stop for that purpose would necessarily draw a
greater crowd about him, which might possibly disturb and incommode him, yet, if his lordship still
desired it, it should be done,' he most readily
answered, ' that's true—I say no more—let us by no
means stop.'

When they approached near the place of execution,
his lordship told the sheriff ' that there was a person
waiting in a coach near there, for whom he had a
very sincere regard, and of whom he should be glad to
take his leave before he died; ' to which the sheriff
answered, that, ' if his lordship insisted upon it, it
should be so; but that he wished his lordship, for his
own sake, would decline it, lest the sight of a person,
for whom he had such a regard, should unman him,
and disarm him of the fortitude he possessed.'—
To which his lordship, without the least hesitation,
replied, ' Sir, if you think I am wrong, I submit : '
and upon the sheriff telling his lordship that if he
had any thing to deliver to that person, or any one
else, he would faithfully do it, his lordship delivered
to him a pocket-book, in which were a bank-note and
a ring, and a purse with some guineas, in order to
be delivered to that person, which were delivered
accordingly.

The landau being now advanced to the place of
execution, his lordship alighted from it, and ascended
upon the scaffold with the same composure and
fortitude of mind he had possessed from the time he
left the Tower. Soon after he had mounted the
scaffold, Mr. Humphries asked his lordship if he

chose to say prayers; which he declined; but, upon his asking him ' if he did not choose to join with him in the Lord's Prayer,' he readily answered ' he would, for he always thought it a very fine prayer; ' upon which they knelt down together upon two cushions, covered with black baize; and his lordship, with an audible voice, very devoutly repeated the Lord's Prayer, and afterwards, with great energy, the following ejaculation: ' O God, forgive me all my errors —pardon all my sins! '

His lordship, then rising, took his leave of the sheriff and the chaplain; and, after thanking them for their many civilities, he presented his watch to Mr. Sheriff Vaillant, which he desired his acceptance of; and requested that his body might be buried at Breden or Stanton, in Leicestershire.

His lordship then called for the executioner, who immediately came to him, and asked him forgiveness; upon which his lordship said ' I freely forgive you, as I do all mankind, and hope myself to be forgiven.' He then intended to give the executioner five guineas, but, by mistake, giving it into the hands of the executioner's assistant, an unseasonable dispute ensued between those unthinking and unfeeling wretches, which Mr. Sheriff Vaillant instantly silenced.

The executioner then proceeded to do his duty, to which his lordship, with great resignation, submitted. His neckcloth being taken off, a white cap, which he had brought in his pocket, being put upon his head, his arms secured by a black sash, and the cord put round his neck, he advanced by three steps to the elevated part of the scaffold, and, standing under the cross-beam which went over it, which was also covered with black baize, he asked the executioner ' Am I right? ' Then the cap was drawn over his face, and, upon a signal given by the sheriff, (for his lordship, upon being before asked, declined to give one himself,) that part upon which he stood instantly sunk down

191

from beneath his feet, and he was launched into eternity May the 5th, 1760.

From the time of his lordship's ascending upon the scaffold, until his execution, was about eight minutes; during which his countenance did not change, nor his tongue falter.

The accustomed time of one hour being past, the coffin was raised up, with the greatest decency, to receive the body; and, being deposited in the hearse, was conveyed by the sheriffs, with the same procession, to Surgeons' Hall, to undergo the remainder of the sentence.

A large incision was made from the neck to the bottom of the breast, and another across the throat; the lower part of the belly was laid open, and the bowels taken away. It was afterwards publicly exposed to view in a room up one pair of stairs at the Hall; and on the evening of Thursday, the 8th of May, it was delivered to his friends for interment.

The following verse is said to have been found in his apartment:

' In doubt I liv'd, in doubt I die,
  Yet stand prepared the vast abyss to try,
    And, undismayed, expect eternity.'

THOMAS ANDREWS,

CONVICTED OF AN UNNATURAL CRIME.

THIS miserable wretch, who had formerly lived in good credit, kept a public house at Pye Corner, near Smithfield, known by the sign of the Fortune of War, where he had as much business as enabled him to support his family in some degree of credit.

John Finnimore, a servant out of place, who had been acquainted with Andrews when he (Finnimore) lived with Mrs. Mead, in Red Lion Court, behind

Saint Sepulchre's church, called on Andrews, to inquire if he could help him to a service. Andrews's wife being now out of town, he told Finnimore that he was welcome to sleep at his house; but the other declined it for that night, as Mrs. Mead had given him permission to lodge at hers.

On the following day Finnimore went to Andrews's with an acquaintance; and, after they had drank together, Finnimore hinted that Mrs. Mead had not offered him a lodging for the second night; on which Andrews told him that, as his wife was still out of town, he was welcome to a share of his bed. Hereupon Finnimore went away with his acquaintance, and returned about nine o'clock in the evening.

There were at that time a considerable number of people in the house; and when they were gone, which was not till near one o'clock in the morning, Andrews locked the doors, and he and Finnimore went to bed together.

What passed, or was presumed to pass, till daylight, it is impossible to relate with any kind of regard to the laws of decency.

In the morning Andrews opened the door, and Finnimore, going out without exchanging a word with him, went to his acquaintance, whom he found at the George, in Leather Lane, looking after some horses, which he drove, being coachman to a gentleman who put up his cattle at that place.

The coachman asked Finnimore to carry a letter to Clapham; but he said he could not go, and assigned such reasons as accounted for his incapacity.

Hereupon the coachman advised Finnimore to have Andrews taken into custody; and on the following day a warrant was procured for this purpose; but, when the constable went to take Andrews into custody, he charged him likewise with Finnimore, on which the constable took charge of them both.

The constable conducted them to the Mansion-house;

but the lord mayor being absent, they were conveyed to the houses of two aldermen, neither of whom happening to be at home, Finnimore was lodged for that night in Bridewell, and Andrews in the Compter.

On the following day they were carried before Sir Robert Ladbroke, the sitting alderman at Guildhall, when Finnimore made such a charge against Andrews that he was committed to Newgate.

At the ensuing sessions Andrews was brought to his trial at the Old Bailey, when Finnimore gave such a clear account of the horrid transaction that the jury did not hesitate to find the prisoner guilty, and he received sentence of death.

Notwithstanding this conviction on evidence the most complete that the nature of such a case would allow, a conviction that left no doubt of Andrews's guilt in the mind of the public, yet such interest was made that he was indulged with a reprieve, and afterwards obtained a full **pardon.**

Andrews was discharged from Newgate in the month of July, 1761.

What sort of interest it was that procured a pardon for this man, it may be improper, because it could hardly be decent, to say. It is a subject that the delicate pen scarcely knows how to touch: but pardoned he was, to the astonishment of nine persons in ten who knew any thing of the case.

The writer of this narrative was well acquainted with two of the gentlemen that were of the jury that convicted Andrews; and he has been repeatedly assured by them that the strength of the evidence against him was such that no kind of doubt could remain of his guilt. Let the rest be buried, as it ought to be, in obscurity; and we believe our readers will thank us that this obnoxious story is one of the shortest in our collection.

MARY HAMILTON, *alias* CHARLES HAMILTON, *alias* GEORGE HAMILTON, *alias* WILLIAM HAMILTON,

WHIPPED FOR MARRYING WITH HER OWN SEX.

POLYGAMY, or a man marrying two or more wives, and, *vice versa*, a woman marrying two or more husbands, is a crime frequently committed; but a woman, according to the rites of the established Church, marrying a woman, is something strange and unnatural. Yet did this woman, under the outward garb of a man, marry fourteen of her own sex!

At the quarter-sessions held at Taunton, in Somersetshire, this woman was brought before the Court; but under what specific charge, or upon what penal statute she was indicted, we can neither trace by the mention of the circumstance, nor could we frame an indictment to meet the gross offence, because the law never contemplated a marriage among women. She was, however, tried, whether or not her case might have been cognizable, and Mary Price, the fourteenth wife, appeared in evidence (in such a case as this we must be pardoned for ambiguity) against her female husband. She swore that she was lawfully married to the prisoner, and that they bedded, and lived together as man and wife, for more than a quarter of a year; during all which time, so well did the impostor assume the character of man, that she still actually believed she had married a fellow-creature of the right and proper sex. At length, the prosecutrix added, she became mistrustful, and, comparing certain circumstances with the married Goodies, her neighbours, she was convinced that Mary had acted the part of Charles towards her by the vilest and most deceitful practices. The learned quorum of justices,

> ' In full-blown dignity of wigs,
> Mounted on blocks, thus cogitated '—

' That the he, she, prisoner at the bar, is an uncommon notorious cheat; and we, the Court, do sentence her or him, whichever he or she may be, to be imprisoned six months, and, during that time, to be whipped in the towns of Taunton, Glastonbury, Wells, and Shipton-Mallet, and to find security for good behaviour as long as they, the learned justices aforesaid, shall or may, in their wisdom and judgment, require;' and Mary, the monopolizer of her own sex, was imprisoned and whipped accordingly, in the severity of the winter of the year 1746.

THOMAS COLLEY

EXECUTED FOR MURDER.

THIS is not the only case which we shall be able to present arising out of the dregs of the superstition of witchcraft. In the days of the immortal Shakspeare this imbecility of the people was at its height. His writings, to suit the temper of the times, abound with ideal events. The scene in 'Macbeth,' of the Weird Sisters, is still represented in that inimitable tragedy.

The Ghost of Hamlet's father is made a principal speaking character in the magnificent play of 'Hamlet;' and, indeed, is absolutely necessary to the admirable plot which the work contains.

The 'Tempest' of the great bard has its spirits, and

Colley and the Mob ducking Osborne and his Wife for reputed Witchcraft.

the 'Comus' of Milton its enchantment. But it is hoped those times are past, and, Reason asserting her right in the mind of man, things supernatural have long been nearly disbelieved.

But not alone in Britain, and the then separate kingdom of Scotland, did this superstition prevail; all the civilized parts of Europe were tinctured with the same absurdity.

By the fanatics who first inhabited New England, in America, it was planted in all its terrors; and, before we proceed, we shall show that our brethren across the vast Atlantic put each other to death, under the forms of a court of law founded on the constitution of England, on charges of witchcraft.

The following copy of an indictment, furnished us by a friend who took it from the American Court record, must prove a matter of curiosity to the reader at the present enlightened era:—

'Essex, ss. (a town in the colony of Massachusets Bay, in New England.)

'The jurors of our sovereign lord and lady, the king and queen (King William and Queen Mary), present, that George Burroughs, late of Falmouth, in the province of Massachusets Bay, clerk (a Presbyterian minister of the Gospel), the ninth day of May, and divers other days and times, as well before as after, certain detestable arts, called witchcraft and sorceries, wickedly and feloniously hath used, practised, and exercised, at and in the town of Salem, in the county aforesaid, upon and against one Mary Walkot, single woman, by which said wicked arts the said Mary, on the day aforesaid, and divers other days and times, as well before as after, was, and is, tortured, afflicted, pined, consumed, wasted, and tormented, against the peace, &c.'

A witness, by name Ann Putnam, deposed as follows: 'On the 8th of May, 1692, I saw the apparition of George Burroughs, who grievously tormented me, and urged me to write in his book, which I refused. He then told me that his two first wives would appear to me presently, and tell me a great many lies, but I must not believe them. Then immediately appeared to me the forms of two women in winding-sheets, and napkins about their heads; at which I was greatly affrighted. They turned their faces towards Mr. Burroughs, and looked red and angry, and told him that he had been very cruel to them, and that their blood called for vengeance against him; and they also told him that they should be clothed with white robes in Heaven when he should be cast down into hell; and he immediately vanished away. And as soon as he was gone the women turned their faces towards me, and looked as pale as a white wall; and told me they were Mr. Burroughs's two wives, and that he had murdered them. And one told me she was his first wife, and he stabbed her under the left breast, and put a piece of sealing-wax in the wound; and she pulled aside the winding-sheet, and showed me the place: she also told me that she was in the house where Mr. Daris, the minister of Danvers, then lived, when it was done. And the other told me that Mr. Burroughs, and a wife that he hath now, killed her in the vessel as she was coming to see her friends from the eastward, because they would have one another. And they both charged me to tell these things to the magistrates before Mr. Burroughs's face; and, if he did not own them, they did not know but they should appear this morning. This morning, also, appeared to me another woman in a winding-sheet, and told me that she was Goodman Fuller's first wife, and Mr. Burroughs killed her, because there was a difference between her husband and him. Also, the ninth day of May, during his examination, he did most grievously torture Mary Walkot, Mercy Lewis, Elizabeth Hubbard, and Abigail Williams, by pinching, pricking, and choking them.'

Upon the above, and some other such evidence, was this unfortunate man condemned; and, horrible to relate, executed! Many other unhappy wretches suffered at the gallows on similar charges.

Having shown the mischief of this gross superstition in a world newly discovered, let us, before we proceed upon the trial of Colley, take a slight retrospect of the state of society in this respect, in the 16th century, on the more enlightened continent of Europe.

We find it asserted that, in the year 1562, a country-woman, named Michelle Chaudron, of the little territory of Geneva, met the devil in her way from the city! The devil gave her a kiss, received a homage, and imprinted on her upper lip and on her right breast the mark which he was wont to bestow upon his favourites. This seal of the devil was described to be a little sign upon the skin, which renders it insensible, as we are assured by all the demonographical civilians of those times.

The devil ordered Michelle Chaudron to bewitch two young girls. She obeyed her master punctually. The parents of the two girls accused her of dealing with the devil. The young women themselves, being confronted with the criminal, declared that they felt a continual prickling in some parts of their bodies, and that they were possessed. Physicians were called—at least men who passed for physicians in those days. They visited the girls. They sought for the seal of the devil on the body of Michelle, which seal is called, in the verbal process, the satanical mark. Into one of these marks they plunged a long needle, which was itself no small torture. Blood issued from the wound, and Michelle testified by her cries that the part was not insensible. The judges, not yet finding sufficient evidence that Michelle Chaudron was a witch, ordered her to be tortured, which infallibly produced the proof they wanted. The poor creature, overcome by pain, confessed at last every thing they desired.

The physicians sought again for the satanical mark, and found it in a little black spot on one of her thighs. Into this they plunged their needle. The poor creature, already exhausted, and almost expiring with the pain of the torture, was insensible to the needle, and did not cry out. She was instantly condemned to be burnt: but, the world beginning at this time to be a little more civilized, her murderers ordered her to be previously strangled.

In the year 1748, in the bishopric of Wurtsburg, an old woman was convicted of witchcraft, and burnt. This was an extraordinary phenomenon in the eighteenth century, particularly among a people who boasted of having trampled superstition under their feet, and flattered themselves that they had brought their reason to perfection.

On the 18th of April, 1751, a man named Nichols went to William Dell, the crier of Hemel-Hempstead, in Hertfordshire, and delivered to him a piece of paper, with four-pence to cry the words written thereon; a copy of which is as follows:—

'This is to give notice that on Monday next a man and a woman are to be publicly ducked at Tring, in this county, for their wicked crimes.'

This notice was given at Winslow and Leighton-Buzzard, as well as at Hemel-Hempstead, on the respective market-days, and was heard by Mr. Barton, overseer of the parish of Tring, who being informed that the persons intended to be ducked were John Osborne, and Ruth his wife, and having no doubt of the good character of both the parties, he sent them to the workhouse, as a protection from the rage of the mob.

On the day appointed for the practice of the infernal ceremony an immense number of people, supposed to be not fewer than five thousand, assembled near the workhouse at Tring, vowing revenge against Osborne and his wife, as a wizard and a witch, and demanding that they should be delivered up to their fury: they likewise pulled down a wall belonging to the workhouse, and broke the windows and window-frames.

On the preceding evening the master of the workhouse, suspecting some violence from what he heard of the disposition of the people, had sent Osborne and his wife to the vestry-room belonging to the church, as a place the most likely to secure them from insult.

The mob would not give credit to the master of the workhouse that the parties were removed, but, rushing into the house, searched it through, examining the closets, boxes, trunks, and even the salt-box, in search of them. There being a hole in the ceiling which appeared to have been left by the plasterers, Colley, who was one of the most active of the gang, cried out 'Let us search the ceiling!' This being done by Charles Young with similar want of success, they swore they would pull down the house, and set fire to the whole town of Tring, except Osborne and his wife were produced.

The master of the workhouse, apprehensive that they would carry their threats into execution, informed them at length where the poor people were concealed; on which the whole mob, with Colley at their head, went to the church, and brought them off in triumph.

This being done, the merciless brutes conducted them to a pond called Marlston-Mere, where the man and woman, having been stripped, were separately tied up in a cloth; a rope was then bound round the body of the woman, under her arm-pits, and two men dragged her into the pond, and through it several times; Colley going into the pond, and, with a stick, turning her from side to side.

Having ducked her repeatedly in this manner, they placed her by the side of the pond, and dragged the old man in, and ducked him: then he was put by, and the woman ducked again as before, Colley making the same use of his stick. With this cruelty the husband was treated twice over, and the wife three times; during the last of which the cloth in which she was wrapped came off, and she appeared quite naked.

Not satisfied with this barbarity, Colley pushed his stick against her breast. The poor woman attempted to lay hold of it; but, her strength being now exhausted, she expired on the spot. Then Colley went round the pond, collecting money of the populace for the *sport* he had shown them in ducking the old witch, as he called her.

The mob now departed to their several habitations; and the body, being taken out of the pond, was examined by Mr. Foster, a surgeon; and the coroner's inquest being summoned on the occasion, Mr. Foster deposed that, ' on examining the body of the deceased, he found no wound, either internal or external, except a little place that had the skin off on one of her breasts; and it was his opinion that she was suffocated with water and mud.'

Hereupon Colley was taken into custody, and, when his trial came on, Mr. Foster deposed to the same effect as above mentioned; and there being a variety of other strong proofs of the prisoner's guilt, he was convicted, and received sentence of death; previously to which, however, he made the following defence: ' I happened to be so unfortunate as to be at Marlston Green, among other people, out of curiosity to see what the mob would do with John Osborne and his wife; where, seeing that they used them very barbarously, I went into the pond as a friend, to save her if I could; for I knew both very well, and never had any occasion to fall out with them, but bore them good will. As for the money I collected by the pond-side, it was for the great pains I had taken in the pond to save both the man and the woman.'

This defence was artful enough; but, as he brought no witnesses to support any part of it, the jury paid no regard to it.

After conviction this man seemed to behold his guilt in its true light of enormity. He became, as far as could be judged, sincerely penitent for his sins, and made good use of the short time he had to live in a solemn preparation for eternity. On the day before his execution he received the sacrament, and then signed the following solemn declaration, which he requested might be dispersed through the several towns and villages in the county : —

'Good people,

' I beseech you all to take warning by an unhappy man's suffering, that you be not deluded into so absurd and wicked a conceit as to believe that there are any such beings upon earth as witches.

' It was that foolish and vain imagination, heightened and inflamed by the strength of liquor, which prompted me to be instrumental (with others as mad as myself) in the horrid and barbarous murder of Ruth Osborne, the supposed witch, for which I am now so deservedly to suffer death.

' I am fully convinced of my former error, and, with the sincerity of a dying man, declare that I do not believe there is such a thing in being as a witch; and pray God that none of you, through a contrary persuasion, may hereafter be induced to think that you have a right in any shape to persecute, much less endanger the life of, a fellow-creature. I beg of you all to pray to God to forgive me. and to wash clean my polluted soul in the blood of Jesus Christ, my Saviour and Redeemer.

' So exhorteth you all,
' The dying
' THOMAS COLLEY.'

The day before his execution he was removed from the gaol of Hertford, under the escort of one hundred men of the Oxford Blues, commanded by seven officers; and, being lodged in the gaol of St. Albans, was put into a chaise at five o'clock the next morning, with the hangman, and reached the place of execution about eleven, where his wife and daughter came to take leave of him; and the minister of Tring assisted him in his last moments, when he died exhibiting all the marks of unfeigned penitence.

204

He was executed the 24th of August, 1751, and his body afterwards hung in chains at a place called Gubblecut, near where the offence was committed.

It is astonishing that any persons could be so stupid as to believe in the ridiculous doctrine of witchcraft. How absurd to suppose that the power of Heaven is delegated to a weak and frail mortal; and, of all mortals, to a poor decrepid old woman! for we never hear of a young witch, but through the fascination of the eyes. Just when a woman has been poor and old enough to obtain the pity and compassion of every one; when nothing has remained to her but her innocence, her piety, and her tabby cat; then has she, by the voice of superstition, been dignified with the presumed possession of a power which the God of Heaven alone could exert!

It is remarkable, in the story before us, that the insurgents, in search of the presumed witch and wizard, had recourse to the salt-box. What a strange madness of credulity must have inflamed their minds! The reflection of a moment would have told them that, if the old folks had possessed power to have contracted themselves within the compass of a salt-box, they would have been able to have disappeared entirely; or even to have destroyed their persecutors by a mere effort of the will.

Pity is it, for the honour of common sense and true religion, and for the sake of example throughout the kingdom, that others, as well as Colley, had not been punished for this atrocious murder. As it is, however, his death has been of public service. We have heard of no ducking of witches presumptive since that time.

Those who are acquainted with history will observe, that what would have been deemed meritorious in the reign of James the First became criminal in that of George the Second; thanks to the increasing good sense, knowledge, and learning of the age!

The first-mentioned monarch wrote a book on the

subject of witchcraft, which he called 'Demonologia;' and the complaisant parliament of his days passed a bill to make it felony for any man or woman to be guilty of witchcraft! and in consequence thereof many innocent persons were murdered under the form of law: but this act has been repealed by the wisdom of later times.

Wheatley doing Penance in Church.

THE REVEREND MR. WHEATLEY,

SENTENCED TO DO PUBLIC PENANCE FOR ADULTERY.

WE consider it a part of our duty to give our readers occasionally an account of the various modes of punishment, for the commission of crimes, in distant nations.

No guilt is more frequent than adultery, and none, in its progress, more tending to fatal consequences, involving whole families in ruin, and driving others to seek revenge in the blood of the spoilers of their honour.

That adultery is a crime which has been detested by all wise and good people, as scandalous in its nature, pernicious to society, and destructive of religion, appears by the various severe laws and punishments by which legislators and magistrates have endeavoured to restrain it.

The histories of the ancient heathens tell us that they thought it a crime so very black and abominable, that they have compared it to sacrilege, or to robbing of temples; and their philosophers judged it to be worse than perjury. The old Ethiopians ranked it with treason, as a crime of the like nature and guilt; and the Egyptians had a law that the man guilty of it should have a thousand stripes, and that the woman should lose her nose, as a mark of perpetual infamy.

The ancient Athenians punished all adulterers with death, and even those who were only suspected with some less penalty. It was the custom of the Persians to throw the adulteress down headlong into a deep well; for, as adultery was, at one time, a common crime among the nobility and gentry in the court of ancient Persia, it became the frequent cause of rebellions, murders, and other dreadful calamities, in that empire.

The tragedy of Mejistes and his whole family, occasioned by the adultery of his wife with Xerxes the emperor, is most horrible to relate; and the punishment of Appodines the physician, for debauching Amytis, the widow of Megabyzus, is also most shocking and terrible.

The old lawgivers of Greece punished this crime with death.

Among the Lybians it was the custom to treat married women guilty of adultery in the most severe manner, without mercy and without pardon.

In a certain city of Crete, when an adulterer was caught in the fact, and judicially convicted, he was first adjudged to be covered with a crown of wool, in derision of his soft and effeminate nature, signified by that material and the animal whence it was taken, then publicly to pay a heavy fine, and to be rendered incapable of bearing any office in the government.

The King of the Tenideans made a law that the adulterer should be beheaded with an axe; and commanded his own son, found guilty of this fact, to be put to death in that manner.

The Lepreans made a law that the men should be led round the city for three days together, and then burnt in the face with a brand of indelible infamy; and that the women should stand in the market-place for eleven successive days, clothed only with a thin transparent garment, which should hang loose and untied, in order to expose them more to public shame, contempt, and laughter.

Hippomines, one of the kings of Athens, having caught an adulterer with his daughter Limona, ordered him to be tied to the wheel of a chariot, and her to one of the horses, and to be dragged about the streets till they died; a shameful and horrid spectacle to the whole city, but a public example of the most severe and impartial justice.

Dio the consul, the first King of the Romans, made a law that the faulty wife should be put to death after what manner her husband or relations thought fit; which law was afterwards confirmed, and continued in force many years. But the rigidly virtuous Cato allowed the husband to dispatch his wife immediately on finding her guilty, without staying for the forms of justice. Many also of the Roman emperors punished this crime with present death; though it must be confessed, indeed, that many others of them, with their empresses and daughters, and ladies of the highest quality, when Rome was declining, were notoriously guilty.

We read of many Julias and Messalinas in the reign of the twelve Cæsars, and so downwards, for a great length of time.

This vice soon after became very common among them in the days of their conquests, national influence, and prosperity; and yet, such diligence and labour had there been used to bring offenders to condign punishment, that Tacitus says, when he was a chief officer of Rome, he found in the public records the names of three thousand who had been put to death for committing adultery. Even the heathen Romans always punished malefactors convicted of this crime by banishment, and, in cases of the highest degree, with death.

The Hungarians, in those days when virtue was in more esteem than at present, made death the punishment, with dreadful infliction. The father was compelled to conduct and force his own daughter to the place of execution, the husband his wife, and the brother his sister.

In Old Saxony a woman convicted of this crime was punished precisely as the English law punished the murderer of her husband—strangled, and then burnt to ashes. The adulterer was then hung up over her grave; or else the chaste matrons of the town where the fact was committed had liberty to scourge him with whips and rods, from one village to another, until he died.

The Turks adopted the Levitical law, and stoned such offenders to death; though, before the law of Moses, the adulteress, when condemned, was burnt alive.

In holy writ, the prophet Jeremiah intimates that the King of Babylon was more cruel than any other monarch, for he roasted to death Zedekiah, the son of Maaseiah, and Ahad, the son of Kolaiah, because they had committed adultery with their neighbours' wives.

At this day, in Turkey, adulteries are often punished by drowning the guilty woman, and castrating the man.

The Spaniards and the Italians, by nature jealous and severe, wherever they suspect a man guilty with their wives, wait an opportunity of plunging a dagger secretly into his heart.

In France, five hundred years ago, two gentlemen of Normandy, who were brothers, were flayed alive, and hung upon gibbets, for adultery.

Modern writers have stigmatized this crime with the name it deserves—a most execrable villainy. Some of the old fathers of the Church have declared their minds with such sharpness and vehemence, as to pronounce it, in many cases, unpardonable.

If we look into the old books of the civil and canon laws we shall find that the several punishments made and ordained by them were either death by the sword or the loss of their noses, or some singular brand of infamy, or some large pecuniary mulct, or banishment; as we find by the old statutes of the Belgians and Hollanders. If a father caught his daughter in the fact, he might kill her and her gallant upon the spot; but a husband was empowered, in the like case, to put the latter only to death, but the wife was reserved to the judgment of the law.

Adultery, from being more immediately an offence against the Church, has been generally excepted out of the acts of pardon and indemnity, as an evil in itself, or of that nature which kings themselves cannot or will not pardon.

It would be endless to recount the many kingdoms and republics, with all their different laws and customs, where this abominable crime hath been, and still is, chastised and exposed with very signal, infamous, painful, and terrible punishments. In England, we are sorry to say, its commission now too often goes unpunished, whether in the prince or the pickpocket.

Let, however, this short extract from eminent authors, contrasted with its barefaced commission in our own country, give the immoral and incontinent a specimen of the opinion of the wise and sober part of mankind; and let them dread the examples of the downfall of mighty empires from profligacy, lest its general adoption hurl their country into the like fate.

Yet, in the present day, adultery, which we have shown to have been held in much abhorrence in ancient times, and punished with great severity, is degenerated into a kind of fashionable and expensive vice among the rich of all the polished nations of Europe; while the poor labourer, surrounded by children born in wedlock, and yet crying for bread, only heaves a sigh at such enormities.

A vice indulged in by the example of the great must spread like contagion, and every thoughtless young man become infected. When the great, though bound by the marriage vow, live in open and voluptuous adultery, lesser men will have their concubines too; and thus wives are deserted, and left either to pine under neglect, or, roused by their wrongs, desperately to seek retaliation.

The number of kept women in and about the metropolis have already been calculated. Most of them are maintained in affluence; and, having no kind of regard either for the person or the property of their dupe, they launch into every kind of extravagance and dissipation.

Corruption of morals in the people, though the progress be slow, will surely prove the downfall of their nation. When the hardy warriors of ancient

Rome quitted 'the trade of arms,' and, for the martial step, substituted

'Love's majesty to strut before a wanton ambling nymph,'

then commenced that degeneracy which in time overwhelmed their mighty empire, and left them an effeminate race, contemptible to those very nations they had formerly conquered.

About the year 1759 the crime of adultery was proved, with aggravated circumstances, against a profligate fellow, under the mask of Puritanism, of the name of Wheatley. This man was a Methodist preacher, who was styled Reverend, and a schoolmaster at Norwich.

He was brought to trial for adultery committed with several of his neighbours' wives, all professing Methodism, at the Ecclesiastical Court of the Bishop of Norwich.

Sufficient proof having been adduced, the judge declared the said Wheatley to be a lewd, debauched, incontinent, and adulterous man; and that he had committed the crimes of adultery, fornication, and incontinence, to the great scandal of good men, and pernicious to the example of others. He was then sentenced to do public penance in a linen cloth, in the parish church, with a paper pinned to his breast, denoting his crime; and condemned to pay the costs of the suit.

Formerly adulterers were exposed to public odium and derision, in white sheets, and in the parish church. The story in the 'Spectator,' of the adulteress riding on a black ram, is founded on fact:

'At East Bourne and West Bourne, in the county of Berks, if a customary tenant die, the widow shall have what the law calls her free bench in all his copyhold land, *dum sola et casta fuerit*; that is, *while she lives single and chaste*; but, if she commit incontinency, she forfeits her estate: yet, if she will come into court, riding backward upon a black ram, with his tail in her hand, and say the following words, the steward is bound by the custom to re-admit her to her free bench:

> ' Here I am,
> Riding upon a black ram,
> Like a whore as I am;
> And for my *crincum crancum*
> Have lost my *bincum bancum*,
> And for my tail's game
> Have done this worldly shame;
> Therefore I pray you, Mr. Steward,
> Let me have my land again.'

There is a like custom in the manor of Torre, in Devonshire, and other parts of the west.

—— M'CANNELLY AND —— MORGAN,

EXECUTED FOR BURGLARY.

As the time of harvest approaches numbers of the lowest order of Irish come over to the nearest counties in England, to offer themselves for hire, in getting in the hay and crops of corn, where they receive better wages, and live better, than in their own country. They would prove of infinite service, could they be kept to common honesty, but they are generally a wild, ferocious, and knavish set, and mix among the industrious and honest, for the purpose of plundering their employers.

The numerous depredations committed during the gathering of the harvest, more than at other seasons, leave little doubt of this fact; and farmers are therefore become extremely cautious whom they hire.

Mr. Porter, a wealthy farmer of Cheshire, had

engaged a number of these people, in the year 1751, in his harvest-fields. One evening his house was beset by the gang above mentioned, who forcibly broke open his doors, advanced to him while at his supper-table, seized, and bound him with cords, at the same time with horrid threats demanding his money.

They also seized his eldest daughter, pinioned her, and obliged her to show them where her father's money and plate were deposited. In the confusion, the youngest daughter, an heroic little girl of thirteen years of age, made her escape, ran into the stable, got astride the bare back of a horse, only haltered; but, not daring to ride past the house, beset by the rogues, she galloped over the fields, leaping hedges and ditches, to Pulford, to inform her eldest brother of the danger they were in at the village. He, and a friend named Craven, determined on attacking the villains, and for that purpose set off at full speed, the little girl accompanying them.

On entering his paternal roof, the son found one of the villains on guard, whom he killed so instantaneously that it caused no alarm. Proceeding to the parlour, they found the other four in the very act of setting his father on the fire, after robbing him of fourteen guineas, in order to extort more. They had stripped down his breeches to his feet, and his eldest daughter was on her knees, supplicating for his life.

What a sight was this for a son! Like an enraged lion, and backed by his brave friend, he flew upon the villains, who fired two pistols, and wounded both the father and the son, and a servant-boy whom they had also bound, but not so as to disable them, for the son wrested a hanger from one of them, cleft the villain to the ground, and cut the others.

The eldest daughter having unbound her father, the old man united his utmost efforts by the side of his son and friend; and so hard did they press, that the thieves jumped through a window, and ran off.

The young men pursued, and seized two more on Chester Bridge, who dropped a silver tankard. The fifth got on board a vessel at Liverpool, of which his brother was the cook, and bound for the West Indies; which sailed, but was driven back by adverse winds.

The account of the robbery, with the escape of the remaining villain, having reached Liverpool, a king's boat searched every vessel, and at length found the robber, by the wounds he had received, and sent him in fetters to Chester gaol.

Mr. Porter had a servant-man in the house at the time, a countryman of the robbers, who remained an unconcerned spectator, and, afterwards running away, was also sent to prison, charged with being an accomplice. They were brought to trial at Chester assizes, in March, 1752, and condemned.

Boyd, on account of his youth, and his having endeavoured to prevail upon the others not to murder Mr. Porter, had his sentence of death remitted for transportation.

The hired servant of Mr. Porter was not prosecuted.

Two or three days previous to that fixed for execution, Stanley slipped off his irons, and, changing his dress, escaped out of gaol, and got clear off.

On the 25th of May, 1752, M'Cannelly and Morgan were brought out of prison, in order to be hanged. Their behaviour was as decent as could be expected from such low-bred men. They both declared that Stanley, who escaped, was the sole contriver of the robbery.

They died in the Catholic faith, and were attended by a priest of that persuasion.

WILLIAM STROUD,

WHIPPED FOR SWINDLING.

HAD this man's offence been committed in Russia, his punishment would have been such as well might serve for the sake of example. It is there very severe, while (through the instrumentality of a guinea or so) it is often too leniently inflicted in England.

The *knout* of Russia would be well applied to the shoulders of an English swindler. The instrument with which whipping is inflicted in Russia is made of leather curiously twisted, and brought to a fine end like whipcord: with this whip the executioners dexterously carry off a slip of skin from the neck to the bottom of the back, laid bare to the waist; and, repeating their blows, in a little while rend away all the skin off the back in parallel stripes. In the common knout, the criminal receives the lashes suspended on the back of one of the executioners; but in the great knout, which is generally used on the same occasions as racking on the wheel in France, the criminal is hoisted into the air by means of a pulley fixed to the gallows, a cord fastened to the two wrists tied together, and another, of a crucial form, under his breast. Sometimes his hands are tied behind, over his back; and when he is pulled up in this position, his shoulders are dislocated. The executioners make this punishment more or less cruel; and it is said are so dexterous, that, when a criminal is condemned to die, they can make him expire at pleasure, either by one or several lashes.

As we shall have ample room left to comment on the all-accomplished swindlers of modern times, and as no mode of thieving has made so rapid a progress as this, we shall only here observe that Stroud displayed such dexterity in the infamous art as to keep his neck

PUNISHMENT OF WHIPPING
in the Press yard Old Bailey.

217

out of the halter, which, before swindling had arrived at its present degree of perfection, required considerable abilities.

This specious robber was well born and educated, but very early in life took to little tricks of cheating, which sufficiently marked his character. When but a schoolboy, he used to purloin blank leaves from the books of his companions, and was remarkable for robbing them of their marbles.

This disposition continued while he was an apprentice; and at length he embarked in business for himself: but he had not been long a master before he considered trade as a drudgery; on which he sold off his stock, took lodgings in Bond Street, and assumed the character of a fine gentleman.

He now lived in a most expensive manner, supplying the extravagances of women of ill fame; which soon reducing him to indigent circumstances, he fixed on a plan of defrauding individuals; for which purpose he got credit with a tailor for some elegant suits of apparel, took a genteel house, and hired some servants; thus imposing himself upon the public as a man of large estate.

An extensive credit, and splendid mode of living, were the consequences of his elegant appearance; but, some tradesmen bringing in bills which he was equally unable and unwilling to discharge, he sold off his household furniture, and privately decamped.

He now took handsome lodgings in Bloomsbury; and, dressing himself in velvet clothes, pretended to be the steward of a nobleman of high rank. He likewise took a house in Westminster, in which he placed an agent, who ordered in goods as for the nobleman; and the tradesmen who delivered these goods were directed to leave their bills for the examination of the steward; but the effects were no sooner in possession than they were sold to a broker, to the sheer loss of the respective tradesmen.

Stroud used to travel into the country in summer, and, having learned the names of London traders with whom people of fortune dealt, he used to write in their names for goods; but, constantly meeting the waggons that conveyed them, generally received the effects before they reached the places to which they were directed.

It would be endless to mention all the frauds of which he was guilty. London and the country were equally laid under contribution by him: and jewellers, watch-makers, lacemen, tailors, drapers, upholders, silversmiths, silk mercers, hatters, hosiers, &c. were by turns dupes to his artifices.

It was impossible for a man proceeding in this manner to evade justice. He was at length apprehended as a common cheat, and committed to the Gatehouse, Westminster. On his examination, a coachmaker charged him with defrauding him of a gilt chariot; a jeweller, of rings to the amount of a hundred pounds; a tailor, of a suit of velvet trimmed with gold; a cabinet-maker, of some valuable goods in his branch; and several other tradesmen of various articles.

The grand jury having found bills of indictment against him, he was tried at the Westminster sessions, when crowds of witnesses who had been duped and plundered by him appeared to give their evidence; and he was instantly found guilty.

The Court sentenced him to hard labour in Bridewell for six months, and in that time to be whipped through the streets six times, which was inflicted with the severity intended.

William York, aged Ten Years, murdering Susan Mahew, aged Five Years.

WILLIAM YORK,

CONVICTED OF MURDER.

THIS unhappy child was but just turned of ten years
of age when he committed the dreadful crime of which
he was convicted. He was a pauper in the poorhouse
belonging to the parish of Eye, in Suffolk, and was
committed, on the coroner's inquest, to Ipswich gaol,
for the murder of Susan Mahew, another child, of five
years of age, who had been his bedfellow. The following is his confession, taken and attested by a justice of
the peace, and which was, in part, proved on the trial,
with many corroborating circumstances of his guilt.

He said that a trifling quarrel happening between
them on the 13th of May, 1748, about ten in the
morning, he struck her with his open hand, and made
her cry: that she going out of the house to the dung-

hill, opposite to the door, he followed her, with a hook in his hand, with an intent to kill her; but before he came up to her he set down the hook, and went into the house for a knife: he then came out again, took hold of the girl's left hand, and cut her wrist all round to the bone, and then threw her down, and cut her to the bone just above the elbow of the same arm. That, after this, he set his foot upon her stomach, and cut her right arm round about, and to the bone, both on the wrist and above the elbow. That he still thought she would not die, and therefore took the hook, and cut her left thigh to the bone; and, observing she was not dead yet, his next care was to conceal the murder; for which purpose he filled a pail with water at a ditch, and, washing the blood off the child's body, buried it in the dunghill, together with the blood that was spilled upon the ground, and made the dunghill as smooth as he could; afterwards he washed the knife and hook, and carried them into the house, cleaned the blood off his own clothes, hid the child's clothes in an old chamber, and then came down and got his breakfast. When he was examined he showed very little concern, and appeared easy and cheerful. All he alleged was, that the child fouled the bed in which they lay together; that she was sulky, and that he did not like her. (Judge Hales ordered a boy of the same age to be hanged, who burnt a child in a cradle.*)

This 'boy murderer' was found guilty, and sentence of death pronounced against him; but he was respited from time to time, and, on account of his tender years, was at length pardoned.

If we were not well aware of the frequent negligence of keepers of poorhouses we should say that this

* Two boys, and small for their years, named John Bunn and Joseph Leech, the former fourteen, and the other fifteen years old, for a street robbery, were hanged at Tyburn. Let children beware of committing crimes, for their youth will not always save them.

premeditated and deliberate murder could not have been effected. Several hours must have elapsed during the shocking transaction; where, then, was the care over the infant paupers? The overseers of the poor, in many instances, are extremely attentive to their parish dinners; but, were they to employ the time lost in this sensuality in care and attendance to the morality of the individuals placed under their control, such crimes might be avoided, and the child of charity brought up in the paths of industry and virtue.

BENJAMIN TAPNER, JOHN COBBY, JOHN HAMMOND, WILLIAM JACKSON, WILLIAM CARTER, RICHARD MILLS THE ELDER, AND RICHARD MILLS THE YOUNGER (FATHER AND SON),

EXECUTED FOR MURDER.

> ——' Oh ! what are these ?
> Death's ministers, not men, who thus deal death
> Inhumanly to man, and multiply
> Ten thousand fold the sin of him who slew
> His brother ; for of whom such massacre
> Make they, but of their brethren—men of men ? '
> PARADISE LOST.

WHILE London and its environs were, about this time, beset with gangs of highwaymen, pickpockets, and swindlers, the country was infested with leagues of villains not less dangerous, and much more cruel. These were fellows who preyed upon the public by defrauding the revenue, in landing goods without a regular entry and payment of the duty. All mercantile nations have regulations of this nature; and indeed they are, in some measure, necessary for the regulation and protection of commerce, which in Britain is a main spring of the commonweal.

The smugglers on the sea-coast formerly went in

parties sufficiently strong to oppose the officers of the excise, and sometimes even to menace parties of the military sent to apprehend them. Whenever a custom-house officer unfortunately fell into their hands, he was barbarously tortured, and often murdered. A more cruel murder than this we are about to detail is not to be found in these volumes; and we much question

The Smugglers murdering Chater at Harris's Well.

whether the judicial annals of Europe can furnish any more diabolical.

The two unfortunate sufferers who were murdered by this desperate gang were William Galley the elder, a custom-house officer of Southampton, and Daniel Chater, a shoemaker of Fording-bridge. These men having been sent to give information respecting some circumstances attending the daring burglary at the custom-house at Poole, and not returning to their respective homes, a suspicion arose that they had been waylaid and murdered by the smugglers, and a search for them was therefore instituted.

Those employed for this purpose, after every inquiry, could hear no certain tidings of them, fear of the smugglers' resentment silencing such inhabitants on the road over which they had carried the unfortunate men as were not in connexion with them. At length a Mr. Stone, following his hounds, came to a spot which appeared to have been dug not long before, and, from the publicity of the circumstance of the men above mentioned being missed, he conjectured that there they might have been buried, and thereof gave immediate information. Upon digging there, nearly seven feet in the earth, the remains of Galley were found, but in so putrid a state as not to be known, except by the clothes. The search after Chater was now pursued with redoubled vigilance, and his body was found in a well (six miles distant from the burial-place of Galley) in Harris's Wood, near Lady Holt Park, with a quantity of stones, wooden rails, and earth, upon it.

At a special commission held at Chichester, on the 16th of January, 1749, Benjamin Tapner, John Cobby, John Hammond, William Carter, Richard Mills the elder, and Richard Mills the younger, were indicted for the murder of Daniel Chater; the three first as principals, and the others as accessories before the fact: and William Jackson and William Carter were indicted for the murder of William Galley.

Benjamin Tapner was a native of Adlington, in Sussex, and worked for some time as a bricklayer; but, being of an idle disposition, he soon quitted his business, and associated with a gang of smugglers, who had rendered themselves formidable to the neighbourhood by their lawless depredations.

John Cobby was an illiterate country fellow, the son of James Cobby, of the county of Sussex, labourer, and joined the smugglers a little time before he was thirty years of age.

224

John Hammond was a labouring man, born at Berstead, in Sussex, and had been a smuggler some time before he was apprehended for the above-mentioned murders, which was when he was almost forty years old.

William Jackson was a native of Hampshire, and had a wife and large family. He was brought up to the business of husbandry; but the hope of acquiring more money in an easier way induced him to engage with the smugglers, which at length ended in his ruin.

William Carter, of Rowland's Castle, in Hampshire, was the son of William Carter, of Eastmean, in the same county, thatcher. He was about the age of thirty-nine, and had practised smuggling a considerable time before the perpetration of the fact which led to his destruction.

Richard Mills, the elder, was a native of Trotton, in Sussex, and had been a horse-dealer by profession; but it is said that a failure in that business induced him to commence smuggler; and he had been long enough in that illicit practice to become one of the most hardened of the gang.

Richard Mills, the younger, lived at Stedham, in Sussex, and for some time followed his father's profession of horse-dealing; but unfortunately making a connexion with the smugglers, he came to the same ignominious end as his companions, in the thirty-seventh year of his age.

The two men, Galley and Chater, were proceeding on Sunday, February 14, 1748, to Major Battine, a justice of the peace, at Stanstead, in Sussex, with a letter written by Mr. Shearer, collector of the customs at Southampton, requesting him to take an examination of Chater concerning one Diamond, or Dymar, who was committed to Chichester gaol on suspicion of being one who broke the king's warehouse at Poole. Chater was engaged to give evidence, but with some reluctance, declaring that he saw Diamond, and shook

225

hands with him, who, with many others, was coming from Poole, loaded with tea, of which he threw him a bag. Having passed Havant, and come to the New Inn, at Leigh, they inquired their way, when George Austin, his brother, and brother-in-law, said that they were going the same road, and would accompany them to Rowland's Castle, where they might get better directions, it being just by the major's residence.

A little before noon they came to the White Hart, at Rowland's Castle, kept by Elizabeth Payne, widow, who had two sons, blacksmiths, in the same village. After some talk she told George Austin, privately, she was afraid that these two strangers were come to hurt the smugglers. He said, ' No, sure; they were only carrying a letter to Major Battine.' Upon this she sent one of her sons for William Jackson and William Carter, who lived near her house. Meanwhile Chater and Galley wanted to be going, and asked for their horses; but she told them that the major was not then at home, which, indeed, was true.

As soon as Jackson and Carter came, she told them her suspicions, with the circumstance of the letter. Soon after she advised George Austin to go away, lest he should come to some harm; he did so, leaving his brothers.

Payne's other son went and fetched in William Steele, Samuel Downer, otherwise Little Samuel, Edmund Richards, and Henry Sheerman, otherwise Little Harry, all smugglers, belonging to the same gang.

After they had drank a little while, Carter, who had some knowledge of Chater, called him into the yard, and asked him where Diamond was. Chater said he believed he was in custody, and that he was going to appear against him, which he was sorry for, but could not help it. Galley came into the yard to them, and, asking Chater why he would stay there, Jackson, who followed him, said, with a horrid imprecation, ' What is that to you?' and immediately struck him a blow in the face, which knocked him down, and set his nose and mouth bleeding. Soon after they all came into the house, when Jackson, reviling Galley, offered to strike him again, but one of the Paynes interposed.—Galley and Chater now began to be very uneasy, and wanted to be going; but Jackson, Carter, and the rest of them, persuading them to stay and drink more rum, and make it up, (for they were sorry for what had happened,) they sat down again; Austin and his brother-in-law being present. Jackson and Carter desired to see the letter, but they refused to show it. The smugglers then drank about plentifully, and made Galley and Chater fuddled; afterwards persuading them to lie down on a bed, which they did, and fell asleep: the letter was then taken away, read, and, the substance of it greatly exasperating them, it was destroyed.

One John Royce, a smuggler, now came in; and Jackson and Carter told him the contents of the letter, and that they had got the old rogue, the shoemaker of Fordingbridge, who was going to inform against John Diamond, the shepherd, then in custody at Chichester. Here William Steele proposed to take them both to a well, about two hundred yards from the house, and to murder and throw them in.

This proposal was not taken, as they had been seen in their company by the Austins, Mr. Garnet, and one Mr. Jenks, who was newly come into the house to drink. It was next proposed to send them to France; but that was objected against, as there was a possibility of their coming over again. Jackson's and Carter's wives, being present, cried out 'Hang the dogs, for they come here to hang you!' It was then proposed and agreed to keep them confined till they could know Diamond's fate, and, whatever it was, to treat these in the same manner; and each to allow threepence a week towards keeping them.

Galley and Chater continuing asleep, Jackson went in, and began the first scene of cruelty; for, having put on his spurs, he got upon the bed and spurred their foreheads, to wake them, and afterwards whipped them with a horse-whip, so that when they came out they were both bleeding. The abovesaid smugglers then took them out of the house; but Richards returned with a pistol, and swore he would shoot any person who should mention what had passed.

Meanwhile the rest put Galley and Chater on one horse, tied their legs under the horse's belly, and then tied the legs of both together. They now set forward, all but Royce, who had no horse. They had not gone above two hundred yards before Jackson called out 'Whip 'em, cut 'em, slash 'em, damn 'em!' upon which all began to whip except Steele, who led the horse, the roads being very bad. They whipped them for half a mile, till they came to Woodash, where they fell off, with their heads under the horse's belly; and their legs, which were tied, appeared over the horse's back. Their tormentors soon set them upright again, and continued whipping them over the head, face, shoulders, &c. till they came to Dean, upwards of half a mile farther: here they both fell again as before, with their heads under the horse's belly, which were struck at every step by the horse's hoofs.

Upon placing them again in the saddle, they found them so weak that they could not sit; upon which they separated them, and put Galley before Steele, and Chater before Little Sam; and then whipped Galley so severely, that, the lashes coming upon Steele, at his desire they desisted. They then went to Harris's well, near Lady Holt Park, where they took Galley off the horse, and threatened to throw him into the well: upon which he desired them to dispatch him at once, and put an end to his misery. 'No,' says Jackson, cursing, 'if that's the case, we have more to say to you;' then put him on a horse again, and whipped him over the Downs, till he was so weak that he fell off; when they laid him across the saddle, with his breast downwards, and Little Sam got up behind him; and as they went on he squeezed Galley's testicles so, that he groaned with the agony, and tumbled off. Being then put on astride, Richards got up behind him; but soon the poor man cried out 'I fall, I fall, I fall!' and Richards, pushing him, said, 'Fall and be damned!' Upon which he fell down and expired; and the villains, taking up the body, laid it again on the horse, and proposed to go to some proper place where Chater might be concealed till they heard the fate of Diamond.

Jackson and Carter called at one Pescod's house, desiring admittance for two sick men; but he absolutely refused it.

Being now one o'clock in the morning, they agreed to go to one Scardefield's, at the Red Lion, at Rake, which was not far. Here Carter and Jackson got admittance, after many refusals. While Scardefield went to draw liquor, he heard more company come in; but, though they refused to admit him into the room, he saw one man stand up very bloody, and another lie as dead. They said they had engaged some officers, lost their tea, and several of them were wounded, if not killed.

Jackson and Little Harry now carried Chater down to Old Mills's, which was not far off, and chained him in a turf-house; and Little Harry staying to watch him, Jackson returned again to the company. After they had drank gin and rum they all went out, taking the body of Galley with them. Carter compelled Scardefield to show them a place before used to bury smuggled tea, and to lend them spades, and a candle and lantern: there they began to dig, and, it being very cold, he helped to make a hole, where they buried 'something that lay across a horse like a dead man.'

They continued at Scardefield's, drinking, all that day, and in the night went to their own homes, in order to be seen on Tuesday, agreeing to meet again on Thursday at the same house, and bring more of their associates. They met accordingly, and brought old Richard Mills, and his sons Richard and John, Thomas Stringer, John Cobby, Benjamin Tapner, and John Hammond, who, with the former, made fourteen. They consulted now what was to be done with Chater; —it was unanimously agreed that he must be destroyed. Richard Mills, junior, proposed to load a gun, clap the muzzle to his head, tie a long string to the trigger, then all to pull it, that all might be equally guilty of his murder. This was rejected, because it would put him out of his pain too soon; and at length they came to a resolution to carry him up to Harris's well, which was not far off, and to throw him in.

All this while Chater was in the utmost horror and misery, being visited by one or other of them, who abused him both with words and blows. At last they all came, and, Tapner and Cobby going into the turf-house, the former pulled out a clasp-knife, and said, with a great oath, ' Down on your knees, and go to prayers, for with this knife I'll be your butcher! ' The poor man knelt down; and, as he was at prayers, Cobby kicked him, calling him ' informing villain.' Chater asking what they had done with Mr. Galley, Tapner, slashing the knife across his eyes, almost cut them out, and the gristle of his nose quite through : he bore it patiently, believing they were putting an end to his misery. Accordingly Tapner struck at him again, and made a deep cut in his forehead. Upon this old Mills said, ' Do not murder him here, but somewhere else.' Accordingly they placed him upon a horse, and all set out together for Harris's well, except Mills and his sons, they having no horses ready, and saying, in excuse, ' That there were enough without them to murder one man.' All the way Tapner whipped him till the blood came; and then swore that, if he blooded the saddle, he would torture him the more! which, as he could not stop his wounds from bleeding, was an incredible instance of barbarity.

When they were come within two hundred yards of the well, Jackson and Carter stopped, saying to Tapner, Cobby, Stringer, Steele, and Hammond, ' Go on and do your duty on Chater, as we have ours upon Galley.' In the dead of the night of the 18th they brought him to the well, which was nearly thirty feet deep, but dry, and paled close round. Tapner having fastened a noose round Chater's neck, they bade him get over the pales to the well. He was going through a broken place; but though he was covered with blood, and fainting with the anguish of his wounds, they forced him to climb up, having the rope about his neck, one end of which being tied to the pales, they pushed him into the well; but, the rope being short, he hung no farther within it than his thighs, and, leaning against the edge, he hung above a quarter of an hour, and was not strangled. They then untied him, and threw him head foremost into the well. They tarried some time, and, hearing him groan, they concluded to go to one William Comleah's, a gardener, to borrow a rope and ladder, saying they wanted to relieve one of their companions who had fallen into Harris's well. He said they might take them; but they could not manage the ladder, in their confusion, it being a long one.

They then returned to the well; and, still hearing him groan, and fearful that the sound thereof might lead to a discovery, the place being near the road, they threw upon him some of the rails and gate-posts fixed about the well; also great stones; when, finding him silent, they left him.

Their next consultation was how to dispose of their horses; when they killed Galley's, which was grey, and, taking his hide off, cut it into small pieces, and hid them so as to prevent any discovery; but a bay horse that Chater had rode on got from them.

On their return home these execrable murderers stopped at the house of one of their acquaintance to drink, where they were hardened enough to boast of the outrage they had committed, and even spoke of it as a circumstance that merited praise.

After a long and diligent search for the perpetrators of these crimes, some of the smugglers were taken up on suspicion, and, being examined in presence of the commissioners of the customs, were admitted evidences for the crown, on discovering all they knew of the horrid transaction.

In consequence hereof the prisoners were brought to trial at the time and place above mentioned; when Sir Michael Foster presided in Court.

The judge's charge to the grand jury was full of good sense, and highly reprobated the practice of smuggling, by which the fair trader is defrauded, and the revenue greatly injured.

When the trial came on, the evidence was very full and circumstantial against the prisoners; and the jury, after being out of Court about a quarter of an hour, brought in a verdict of guilty against all the prisoners: whereupon the judge pronounced sentence on the convicts in one of the most pathetic addresses that was ever heard; representing the enormity of their crime, and exhorting them to make immediate preparation for the awful fate that awaited them; adding, ' Christian charity obliges me to tell you that your time in this world will be very short.'

The heinousness of the crime of which these men had been convicted rendering it necessary that their punishment should be exemplary, the judge ordered that they should be executed on the following day; and the sentence was accordingly carried into execution against all but Jackson, who died in prison on the evening that he was condemned. They were attended by two ministers; and all, except Mills and his son, (who took no notice of each other, and thought themselves not guilty because they were not present at the finishing of the inhuman murder,) showed great marks of penitence. Tapner and Carter gave good advice to the spectators, and desired diligence might be used to apprehend Richards, whom they charged as the cause of their being brought to this wretched end. Young Mills smiled several times at the executioner, who was a discharged marine, and, having ropes too short for some of them, was puzzled to fit them. Old Mills, being forced to stand tip-toe to reach the halter, desired that he might not be hanged by inches. The Mills's were so rejoiced at being told that they were not to be hanged in chains after execution, that death seemed to excite in them no terror; while Jackson was so struck with horror at being measured for his irons, that he soon expired.

They were hanged at Chichester on the 18th of January, 1749, amidst such a concourse of spectators as is seldom seen on occasions of a public execution.

Carter was hung in chains near Rake, in Sussex; Tapner on Rook's Hill, near Chichester; and Cobby and Hammond at Cesley Isle, on the beach where they sometimes landed their smuggled goods, and where they could be seen at a great distance east and west.

Jackson had lived some years a Roman Catholic; and, from the following popish relic found in his pocket, there is little doubt but he died such, as far as such a scoundrel could be said to belong to any religion:

' Sancti tres reges,
Gaspar, Melchior, Belthazar,
Orate pro nobis, nunc et in hora
Mortis nostræ.
Ces billets ont touché aux trois
tetes de
S. S. Rois a Cologne.

Ils sont pour des voyageurs, contre
les malheurs de chemins, maux
de tete, mal caduque, fievres,
socellerie, toute sorte de
malefice, et mort
subite.'

The English of which is,

' Ye three holy kings,
Gaspar, Melchior, Belthazar,
Pray for us now, and in the hour of death.
These papers have touched the three heads of
The holy kings of Cologne.
They are to preserve travellers from
accidents on the road, head-aches,
falling sickness, fevers, witch-
craft, all kinds of mischief,
and sudden death.'

The body of the above-mentioned Jackson was
thrown into a hole near the place of execution; as
were those of Mills, the father and son, who had no
friends to take them away: and at a small distance
from this spot is erected a stone, on which is the
following inscription :

' Near this place was buried the body of William
Jackson, who, upon a special commission of Oyer and
Terminer, held at Chichester on the 16th day of
January, 1748-9, was, with William Carter, attainted
for the murder of William Galley, custom-house
officer; and who likewise was, together with Benjamin
Tapner, John Cobby, John Hammond, Richard Mills
the elder, Richard Mills the younger, his son, attainted
for the murder of Daniel Chater; but, dying in a few
hours after sentence of death was pronounced upon
him, he thereby escaped the punishment which the

234

heinousness of his complicated crimes deserved, and
which was, the next day, most justly inflicted upon his
accomplices.

' As a memorial to posterity, and a
warning to this and succeeding generations,
This stone is erected,
A. D. 1749.'

To comment upon these odious and loathsome
transactions is impossible; the imagination is glad to
escape from scenes of such unrivalled atrocity and
horror. We would rather contemplate the wretched
victims of undeserved ferocity at length relieved by the
friendly hand of Death; while the still more wretched
victims of their own evil passions are, by the memorial
stone above described, held up by name to the scorn
and detestation of posterity.

ANN WILLIAMS,

EXECUTED FOR THE MURDER OF HER HUSBAND.

THE behaviour of this fiend had long been a prelude to
the diabolical crime which she committed. She was
in her family turbulent and dictatorial; her husband
the very reverse. His mild and quiet disposition served
only to nurse her opposition and violence. He had

long given way to her in all things, and she, in return, ruled him with a rod of iron.

Before the commission of this horrid deed we have found women make use of man's unqualified indulgence. Hence arose the vulgar saying of 'the grey mare being the better horse,' of 'hen-pecked husbands,' and many other irritating observations on men troubled with shrews.

Ann Williams burnt at the Stake.

One of the wisest of the ancient philosophers had his Xantippe: and the poet sings,

> 'When man to woman gives the sway,
> To what is right they oft say Nay.'

The pliancy of the more unfortunate man in question could not shield him from the consequence of the ascendancy she had over him; it sunk into contempt, and she determined to rule alone. To effect

236

this, her wicked heart suggested the death of her husband. For this horrid purpose she prevailed on their servant-man to purchase some white mercury, which she mixed in some gruel, and caused him to eat it. This mode of administering the poison, it was conjectured, was adopted in contempt of him; for it appeared the poor man did not like gruel. She then directed him to draw her some ale, of which he also drank; and was immediately seized with violent purgings and vomiting. She told the man, whom it seems she meant afterwards to share her bed, that she 'had given her husband the stuff he brought, and that it was operating purely.'

The dying man, in his agonies, said his wife was a wicked woman; that he was well until she made him eat some pap, which had done his business, and that he should be a dead man on the morrow; and, in spite of medical aid, he died next day, his body being in a state of mortification.

The horrid crime being fully proved against her, she received sentence to be burnt at the stake, which sentence was accordingly carried into execution at Gloucester, April 13, 1753, among a number of spectators, who showed little pity for her fate, and which became still more shocking from denying the fact, so incontrovertibly proved, to the very last moment of her existence.

Brown holding his Wife to the Fire till he caused her Death.

NICHOL BROWN,

EXECUTED FOR THE MURDER OF HIS WIFE.

In the account given of this man there is a savage
ferocity which has not before come under our notice;
for, though we read in Captain Cook's, and other
accounts of circumnavigators, of their meeting with
cannibals; and, further, that even civilized men, by
the dire dint of the excruciating pains of hunger, have
slain, and, with horrible compunction, eaten one of
their companions, to support life in the rest; yet where
shall we find, except in this instance, a savage, in the
land of civilization and of plenty, eat human flesh?
After this it no longer remains astonishingly horrible
that such a brute could force his wife into the fire, and
burn her to death.

This atrocious monster was a native of Cramond, a small town near Edinburgh, where he received a school education. At a proper age he was placed with a butcher in that city, and, when his apprenticeship was expired, went to sea in a man of war, and continued in that station four years. The ship being paid off, Brown returned to Edinburgh, and married the widow of a butcher, who had left her a decent fortune.

Soon after this marriage Brown commenced dealer in cattle, in which he met with such success, that, in the course of a few years, he became possessed of a considerable sum. His success, however, did not inspire him with sentiments of humanity. His temper was so bad, that he was shunned by all serious people of his acquaintance; for he delighted in fomenting quarrels among his neighbours.

Taking to a habit of drinking, he seldom came home sober at night; and, his wife following his example, he used frequently to beat her for copying his own crime. This conduct rendered both parties obnoxious to their acquaintance; and the following story of Brown, which may be relied on as a fact, will incontestably prove the unfeeling brutality of his nature.

About a week after the execution of Norman Ross for murder, Brown had been drinking with some company at Leith, till, in the height of their jollity, they boasted what extravagant actions they could perform. Brown swore that he would cut off a piece of flesh from the leg of the dead man, and eat it. His companions, drunk as they were, appeared shocked at the very idea; while Brown, to prove that he was in earnest, procured a ladder, which he carried to the gibbet, and, cutting off a piece of flesh from the leg of the suspended body of Ross, brought it back, broiled, and ate it.

This circumstance was much talked of, but little credit was given to it by the inhabitants of Edinburgh till Brown's companions gave the fullest testimony of its truth. It will be now proper that we recite the particulars of the shocking crime for which this offender forfeited his life.

After having been drinking at an alehouse in the Cannongate, he went home about eleven at night, in a high degree of intoxication. His wife was also much in liquor; but, though equally criminal himself, he was so exasperated against her, that he struck her so violently that she fell from her chair. The noise of her fall alarmed the neighbours; but, as frequent quarrels had happened between them, no immediate notice was taken of the affair.

In about fifteen minutes the wife was heard to cry out 'Murder! help! fire! the rogue is murdering me! help, for Christ's sake!' The neighbours, now apprehending real danger, knocked at the door; but, no person being in the house but Brown and his wife, no admission was granted; and the woman was heard to groan most shockingly.

A person, looking through the key-hole, saw Brown holding his wife to the fire; on which he was called on to open the door, but refused to do so. The candle being extinguished, and the woman still continuing her cries, the door was at length forced open; and, when the neighbours went in, they beheld her a most shocking spectacle, lying half-naked before the fire, and her flesh in part broiled. In the interim Brown had got into bed, pretended to be asleep, and, when spoken to, appeared ignorant of the transaction. The woman, though so dreadfully burnt, retained her senses, accused her husband of the murder, and told in what manner it was perpetrated. She survived till the following morning, still continuing in the same tale, and then expired in the utmost agony.

The murderer was now seized, and, being lodged in the gaol of Edinburgh, was brought to trial, and capitally convicted.

After sentence he was allowed six weeks to prepare

himself for a future state, agreeably to the custom in Scotland.

He was visited by several divines of Edinburgh, but steadily persisted in the denial of his guilt, affirming that he was ignorant of his wife being burnt till the door was broke open by the neighbours.

Among others who visited the criminal was the Reverend Mr. Kinloch, an ancient minister, who, urging him to confess his crime, received no other reply than that, ' if he was to die to-morrow, he would have a new suit of clothes, to appear decently at the gallows.' Mr. Kinloch was so affected by his declaration, that he shed tears over the unhappy convict.

On the following day, August the 14th, 1754, he was attended to the place of execution at Edinburgh by the Reverend Dr. Brown; but to the last he denied having been guilty of the crime for which he suffered.

After execution he was hung in chains; but the body was stolen from the gibbet, and thrown into a pond, where, being found, it was exposed as before. In a few days, however, it was again stolen; and, though a reward was offered for its discovery, no such discovery was made.

It is impossible to express sufficient horror at the crime of which this man was guilty; and it is therefore the less necessary to make any remarks on his case, as no one can be tempted to think of committing a similar crime till he is totally divested of all the feelings of humanity. From a fate so wretched as this may the God of infinite mercy deliver us!

Price defrauding Mr. Spilsbury under the assumed Name of Wilmot.

CHARLES PRICE,

APPREHENDED ON A CHARGE OF FORGERY.

THE depredations of artful and designing men upon
the credulity of the honest and industrious have sometimes been carried to such a pitch as almost to exceed
the conceptions of the most acute and discerning; and
few have practised with more success, for a time, the
grossest impositions on society, than the subject of our
present notice. Varying and accommodating himself
to the circumstances in which he may be placed, man
is scarcely ever the same for any long period of
duration: characters, however, there are, who add to
these traits of variation by their dissimulation and
hypocrisy; and such an one was Charles Price, who, on

242

account of this circumstance, attained to a singular celebrity.

In the life of this extraordinary impostor we may learn the progress of iniquity, teach the rising generation to guard against its first approaches, and warn our readers against those depredations which are daily infesting society. Such examples of depravity are indeed humiliating to our natures, but at the same time hold forth instructive lessons, and consequently are well deserving of our serious contemplation.

Charles Price was born about the year 1730. His father lived in Monmouth Street, and carried on the business of a dealer in old clothes : here he died, in the year 1750, of a broken heart, occasioned, as it is said, by the bad conduct of his children.

Charles began early to manifest those traits of duplicity for which he afterwards became so greatly distinguished :—one remarkable instance deserves to be mentioned as an example of juvenile hypocrisy scarcely to be paralleled. He ripped off some gold lace from a suit of old clothes which his father had bought, and, putting on his elder brother's coat, went to sell it to a Jew. The Jew became a purchaser, and, in the way of trade, most unfortunately afterwards offered it to the father for sale. He instantly knew it, and insisted on the Jew's informing him from whom he received it. The boys coming in at the time, and the Jew recollecting the coat of the elder, immediately declared he was the person from whom he purchased it; in consequence of which he was directly seized and severely flogged, notwithstanding his protestations of innocence : the father was inflexible, while the conscious depredator, with an abominable relish for hypocrisy, witnessed the suffering of his brother, and inwardly rejoiced in the castigation.

By a continued series of tricks and knaveries, practised under the eye of the father, he at length grew tired of his son, and placed him with a hosier in St.

James's Street. Here he continued but for a short time, indulging in all the vagaries of his prolific imagination, and exercising himself in all the arts and deceptions of which he eventually made himself master. He robbed his father of an elegant suit of clothes, in which having dressed himself, he went in that disguise to the hosier, and bought about ten pounds' worth of the most fashionable and expensive silk stockings, desiring them to be sent home for him in an hour, and assuming the name of Henry Bolingbroke, Esq. The cheat was successful, for his master did not know him; but this was not enough, for in about half an hour after he appeared in the shop in his usual dress, and was desired to take the goods home, which he actually pretended to do : thus both his father and master were robbed. He was, however, soon discovered and dismissed. From this period we shall have to consider him at large in society, where he continued to practise the most outrageous acts of duplicity for many years.

Soon after this he set off for Holland, under the name of Johnson. Forging a recommendation to a Dutch merchant, he became his clerk, debauched his daughter, and was offered her hand in marriage;—robbed his master, and returned to England. Upon his arrival he contrived to get himself engaged in his majesty's small-beer brewery near Gosport. In this situation he conducted himself so well as to gain the confidence of his employer; and was upon the point of forming a matrimonial connexion with his daughter. This match, however, was prevented by an accidental discovery: the Jew, to whom he had formerly sold the gold lace, happened to reside at Portsmouth, and by his means the character of Price was soon disclosed, his schemes frustrated, and he was again thrown upon the world.

His wits, however, were not exhausted, nor did they ever slumber long, though always employed for some deceptive end. He determined upon a trial to establish a new brewery, by obtaining a partner with money; and as a first step towards it, in the year 1775, he issued the following curious advertisement:—

'Wanted,—A partner of character, probity, and extensive acquaintance, upon a plan permanent and productive. Fifty per cent. without risk, may be obtained. It is not necessary he should have any knowledge of the business, which the advertiser possesses to its fullest extent; but he must possess a capital of between five hundred and one thousand pounds to purchase materials, with which, to the knowledge of the advertiser, a large fortune must be made in a very short time. Address to P. C. Cardigan Head, Charing Cross.

'P. S. None but principals, and those of liberal ideas, will be treated with.'

By means of this advertisement, the famous comedian, Samuel Foote, was brought into the sphere of our hero's depredation. Eager to seize what he conceived to be a golden opportunity, he was induced to advance five hundred pounds for a brewery. This sum did not last long; and, instead of the rapid fortune which the advertiser appeared so certain of, Foote was glad to disengage himself from the concern with the loss of his capital, and retired, wrung with the anguish of disappointment. Notwithstanding which, Price had the impudence, not long afterwards, to apply to him again, under the idea of getting him to embark in the baking trade: the witty comedian, however, by this time knew his *Price*, and archly replied, 'As you have *brewed*, so you may bake; but I'll be cursed if ever you *bake* as you have *brewed*.'

Price, after this unfortunate business, assumed a new character, and appeared as a Methodist preacher, in which disguise he defrauded several persons of large sums of money. He issued advertisements, offering to procure gentlemen wives, and swindled a person of the name of Wigmore of fifty guineas: this turned out more serious than he expected, for Mr. Wigmore brought an indictment against him; but he found means to refund a part of the money, and effected his escape. These, and other fraudulent means, were long the objects of his ambition, though they were all the certain roads to infamy.

Still undismayed in his career, he had the astonishing impudence to set up again as a brewer, in Gray's Inn Lane : here, however, after committing a variety of frauds, he became a bankrupt in the year 1776. With ingenuity ever fruitful, he now set out for Germany, and engaged in a smuggling scheme, for which he was thrown into a prison in Holland, after realizing three hundred pounds. From this confinement he had address enough, by an artful defence, to extricate himself, and immediately returned to his native country. Here he again engaged himself in a sham brewery at Lambeth, where he was married; still continuing his depredations, till at length he found it necessary to decamp :—he actually went to Copenhagen. After some time he came back to England, where he was doomed to close his days.

His brewing attempts having all failed, he was obliged to study some new mode of plundering society; and, under the pretence of charity, he obtained money, for which he was imprisoned; and, having obtained liberation, he, in the character of a clergyman, succeeded in various depredations, which eventually brought him to the King's Bench, from the walls of which he had dexterity enough to extricate himself.

His next scheme was to try his success among the schemers in the lottery, and made his efforts answer his purpose for a time; but, absconding with a ticket of very considerable value, his attempts in this way were brought to a termination; indeed, his arts and his tricks were so various, that to recount them all would extend our memoir of him beyond the limits of a publication of this kind—Alas for human depravity!

We are now arrived at that period of our hero's life when, by connecting himself with the Bank of England, he immortalized himself, by recording his name on the lists of notoriety, as one of the most artful, and, for a time, the most successful of impostors; but the result was as might be expected—the loss of his life, after practising a series of the most iniquitous devices that were ever brought to play upon mankind.

In the year 1780, memorable for the riots in London, he assumed the name of Brant, and engaged a plain, simple, honest fellow, as a servant, whom he converted into the instrument of passing his forged notes, without detection. He advertised for this servant, and conducted himself in a manner truly curious towards him. The young man, having answered the advertisement, heard nothing relative to it for about a week. One evening, however, just about dusk, a coachman was heard inquiring for him, saying there was a gentleman over the way in a coach who wanted to speak to him. On this the young fellow was called, and went to the coach, where he was desired to step in: there he found an apparently old man, affecting the foreigner, seemingly very much afflicted with the gout, as he was completely wrapped up in flannel about the legs, and wore a camlet surtout, buttoned over his chin, close up to his mouth; a large black patch over his left eye; and almost every part of his face so hid, that the young fellow could scarcely discover a feature except his nose, his right eye, and a part of that cheek. The better to carry on this deception, Price took care to place the young man on his left side, on which the patch was; so that the old gentleman could take a look askance at the young fellow with his right eye, and by that means discover only a portion of his face. In this disguise he appeared to be between sixty and seventy years of age; and when this man whom he engaged saw him afterwards, not much under six feet high, his surprise and astonishment were so great, that he could scarcely believe his own senses; and, in addition to the deceptive dress in which he has been described, he sometimes wore boots or shoes with heels very little less than three inches high, and appeared so buttoned up and straitened as to look quite lank. While we are thus remarking upon the expedients to which he resorted, the better to effect his shameful purposes, it may not be ill-timed to give a true description of his person : he was in reality about five feet six inches high; a compact neat-made man, square shouldered, inclined to corpulency; his legs were firm and well set, but by nature his features gave him a look of more age than really belonged to him, which, at the time we are describing him, was near upon fifty, his nose was aquiline, and his eyes small and grey; his mouth stood very much inward, with very thin lips; his chin pointed and prominent, with a pale complexion; but what favoured in the greatest degree his disguise of speech was the loss of his teeth. His walk was exceedingly upright, and his manner active; in a word, he was something above what the world in general would term a *dapper made man.*

The honest simplicity of the young man whom he had thus duped into his service was such, that Price found no difficulty whatever in negotiating through his hands his forged bills, which were principally disposed of in the purchasing of lottery tickets and shares, at the same time taking care never fully to disclose to poor Samuel his real name, person, or history; and it must be confessed his plan was devised and executed with the utmost skill and ability. Samuel, who continued for some time the innocent and unsuspecting instrument of these nefarious practices, after passing bills to the amount of one thousand four hundred pounds, was detected, and taken into custody. Upon learning this, Price retired with his booty into the shades of the deepest obscurity, leaving poor Sam, who was terrified out of his wits at a contemplation of the consequences that might ensue from being an accomplice in such complicated villainy, to suffer near a twelvemonth's imprisonment.

Price, with a purse well lined, having sought refuge in some lone place of retirement, was heard nothing of till the year 1782, when, having, in all probability, exhausted his former acquisitions, he again sallied forth in search of new game with the most unparalleled audacity; and, as a first step to the accomplishment of his purpose, he engaged a smart active lad, of the name of Power, from a register-office. The father of this lad was a Scots Presbyterian, and, to ingratiate himself with the old man, Price professed high pretensions of religion, talked of virtue and morality, expressing a hope that the boy was well acquainted with the Lord's Prayer and the Ten Commandments. Having thus far succeeded, he now commenced his ravages on the well-known Mr. Spilsbury, of Soho Square, ordering large quantities of his drops in the name of Wilmot, and introduced himself to that gentleman as possessing all the symptoms of age and infirmity. He was wrapped up in a large camlet great coat, with a slouched hat on, the brim of which was large, and bent downward on each side of his head; a piece of red flannel covered his chin, and came up on each side of his face as high as his cheek-bones; he wore a large bush wig, and a pair of green spectacles on his nose; his legs and feet were completely enveloped in large wraps of flannel, and a green shade hung down from his hat; but upon this occasion he abandoned the black patch upon his eye, considering his features sufficiently disguised and obscured; and also that it would not be safe to resort to an old expedient. It is not a little remarkable that Mr. Spilsbury, who knew Price well, was not able to detect his villainy in the character of Wilmot; and it is a fact that, sitting together, side by side, in a coffee-house, Mr. Spilsbury was complaining to his coffee-house acquaintance of the notes which Wilmot had so artfully and successfully imposed upon him. Price actually favoured his own deceptions by pretending commiseration, frequently crying out ' Lack-a-day! good God!— is it possible?—who could conceive such knavery to exist?—But it is a wicked world, sir. What! and did the Bank refuse payment, sir?' staring through his spectacles with as much seeming surprise as an honest man would have done. ' Oh yes,' said Mr. Spilsbury, with some degree of acrimony; ' for you must know that it was upon the faith of the Bank of England that I and a great many others have been induced to take them; and they were so inimitably well done, that the nicest judges could not have distinguished them; but the old scoundrel will certainly be detected.' ' Good God!—lack-a-day! ' continued Price, ' he must have been an ingenious villain; what a complete old rascal!'

Price had frequently been at the shop of a Mr. Roberts, grocer, in Oxford Street, where he now and then bought a few articles, and took many opportunities of showing his importance. Upon one occasion he called in a hackney-coach, disguised as an old man, and bought some few articles: a day or two afterwards he repeated his visit; and, on a third day, when he knew Mr. Roberts was not in the way, went again, with his face so painted that he appeared to be diseased with the yellow jaundice. The shopman, to whom he enumerated his complaints, kindly informed him of a prescription for that disorder, by which his father had been cured of it. Price gladly accepted of the receipt, promising that, if it succeeded, he would call again, and handsomely reward him for his civility: in conformity with which he entered the shop a few days afterwards, apparently perfectly free from the complaint, and acknowledged his great obligations to the shopman; after which he expatiated freely on his affluent circumstances, the short time he had to live,

250

and the few relations he had to leave his property to; and made him a present of a ten pound bank-note. It will naturally be conceived this was a forgery, but it had the desired effect with Price; for at the same time he said he wanted cash for another, which was a fifty pound note. This the obliging and unsuspecting shopman got change for at an opposite neighbour's. The next day, during Mr. Roberts's absence, he called again, and entreated the lad to get small notes for five other notes of fifty pounds each: the lad, however, telling him his master was not at home, Price begged he would take them to his master's bankers, and there get them changed. This request was immediately complied with. The bankers, Messrs. Burchall and Co. complied with Mr. Roberts's supposed request, immediately changed them, and small notes were that day given to Price for them.

Having found out a fit object to practise his deceptions upon in the person of Mr. E——, who was an eminent merchant in the city, and having traced his connexions to Amsterdam, even to the obtaining a letter which was directed to him from a merchant there, he commenced his attack on that gentleman in the following manner:—He accosted him on 'Change in another disguised character, and told him that he had received a letter from a correspondent of theirs at Amsterdam, whose name he mentioned, informing him that a Mr. Trevors, who frequented the 'Change, had defrauded the Dutch merchant of one thousand pounds; that the latter requested Mr. E.'s assistance in the recovery of the whole, or any part of it he could obtain. With this prelude he opened the letter, and presented it to Mr. E. who, having read it, entertained no doubt of its being the handwriting of his Amsterdam correspondent; he therefore readily offered his assistance in any plan that might be pursued to favour his Dutch friend. After thus paving the way, he began to advise Mr. E. how to act. 'Trevors.' said he, ' will most likely be upon 'Change to-morrow; he always frequents the Dutch Walk, and is dressed in a red surtout, with a white wig; he has also square-toed shoes, and very small buckles. Your best way will be to accost him, draw him into a conversation upon the mercantile affairs of Amsterdam, and, by pretending he can be of service to you, invite him home to dinner with you. You will then have a good opportunity to mention the business, show him the letter, and inform him that, unless he refunds the whole or part of the money immediately, you will expose the affair to the merchants. By such a procedure you may probably procure the greater part of the property, as he is rich, and always has cash about him, and will rather comply with your demand than run the risk of exposure.' Mr. E. highly approved of this proposal, and was much pleased with the prospect he appeared to have of rendering such essential service to his Dutch friend. The next day our hero appeared on the Dutch Walk, in the dress he had so minutely described. Mr. E. followed the advice which had been given him, and, after a little conversation, invited the supposed Trevors to dine with him which was immediately accepted by Price.—After the cloth was removed, and the family had retired from table, Mr. E. began to open to Mr. Trevors, with as much delicacy as he could, the purpose of his invitation. Our hero affected surprise at this application, but acknowledged the charge in part; assured him of his intention to settle the whole account shortly, begged it might not be mentioned on 'Change, and, as a proof of his intention, he was willing to pay five hundred pounds down, if Mr. E. would bury the matter in oblivion. This being readily promised on Mr. E.'s part, Mr. Trevors produced a thousand pound bank-note from his pocket-book, which he said he would leave with Mr. E. if he would give him the difference. Not having sufficient cash and notes in the house, Mr. E. gave him a check on his banker for the remaining five hundred pounds, with which our hero very soon after took his leave. The next morning Mr. E. discovered that the thousand pound bank-note was a forgery, and ran to the bankers to stop the payment of his draft, but unfortunately too late; for a porter, who appeared to have been followed by a tall old woman into the banking-house, had obtained notes for the check four hours before Mr. E.'s application to stop payment.

Upon a variety of others in a similar way did Price exercise his deceptions; among the rest, Mr. Watt, hosier, and Mr. Reeves, a colourman, were sufferers; and such was his success, that in one day he negotiated sixty ten pound notes, changed fourteen fifty pound notes for seven one hundred pound notes; indeed, such were his tricks at this period, that it is scarcely possible to recount them.

The practices of evil-minded persons, who forget that useful and comprehensive commandment—' Do unto others as you would be done by '—seldom lead to happy or truly fortunate results, nor could it be expected to be the case with our present subject; he had assumed the character of an Irish linen-factor, under the name of Palton, and employed two young men to circulate his notes, whilst he still kept himself greatly disguised, and in obscurity. The notes were detected, and, by means of a pawnbroker, Price was with great difficulty at length discovered : when apprehended, however, he most solemnly declared he was innocent, and, when taken before the magistrate, conducted himself with great insolence. This took place on the 14th of January, 1786, and, notwithstanding his disguises, he was soon sworn to by more persons than one ; in consequence of which, and finding there was no means of escape from his present situation, he pretended to his wife, in particular, great and serious penitence; for which, however, there did not appear the least ground. The Bank were fully determined on prosecuting him, and there was little chance of his escaping an ignominious death by the hands of the public executioner; but even this he managed to avoid, for one evening he was found hanging against the post of his door, in the apartment allotted him in Tothillfields' Bridewell; thus ridding the world of as great a monster as ever disgraced civilized society.

In this situation he was discovered by the keeper of the prison, who cut him down quite dead, and found in his bosom three letters; in one of which, addressed to the directors of the Bank, he confessed every thing relative to the forgery, and the manner of circulating the notes; another, addressed to his wife, was written in a most affecting style; and in the third, directed to the keeper, he thanked him for the very humane treatment he had experienced during his confinement.

A coroner's jury was summoned, as usual in such cases, and returned a verdict of ' Self-Murder; ' in consequence of which his body was thrown into the ground in Tothillfields, and a stake driven through it.

In a box belonging to Price were found, after his death, two artificial noses, very curiously executed, in imitation of nature. These, it is obvious, he occasionally wore as a part of the various disguises by which he had been enabled so long to elude the hand of Justice. The counterfeit plates were found buried in a field near Tottenham Court Road, the turf being replaced on the spot. His wife, who had been confined with him as a supposed accomplice, was discharged, after making full confession of all she knew concerning his affairs; and the rolling-press, plates, and other materials, were destroyed by order of Sir Sampson Wright, the then presiding magistrate.

It has been calculated that the depredations of this artful villain on society amounted to upwards of one hundred thousand pounds! and yet, after his apprehension, he had the audacity to write a letter to a gentleman whom he had defrauded of more than two thousand pounds, recommending his wife and eight children to his protection.

Price's expenditure must have been great, or the imprudence of his female coadjutor excessive; for at her lodgings were fixed all the apparatus for manufacturing the paper and printing the bank-notes; the plates for which were also engraved by this ingenious culprit. Being thus paper-maker, engraver, printer, and circulator, it is not altogether surprising that he contrived to prolong his existence to the age of fifty-five; six years of which were passed in hostilities against the Bank directors, whose emoluments by fire, shipwreck, and other casualties, Price conceived were much too enormous.

It must appear extraordinary to the reader that this depraved impostor was so long able to escape discovery. But it should be added, such was the inventive ingenuity of his mind, that, in order to avoid detection, he took especial care, as well as by the multifarious disguises of his person and voice, to study the art of prevention, by combining the whole of the proceedings necessary for the accomplishment of his designs within his own power; seeing clearly that, if he had permitted a partner in his concerns, he could not have expected to remain so wholly unsuspected, at least, if not detected. He therefore became his own engraver, made his own paper, with the water-marks, and never suffered his negotiator to know him; nay, such was the secrecy with which he carried on his business, that Mrs. Price, his wife, had not the least knowledge or suspicion of his proceedings. Having by practice made himself master of engraving, he made his own ink to prove his own works; he then purchased implements, and manufactured the water-marks; he then set about to counterfeit handwritings, and in this he so far succeeded as to puzzle a part of the first body of men in the world; thus proving himself a most accomplished and wary adept in the art of deception. The abilities of the unhappy Ryland were exerted in his profession, and therefore the imposition was less to be wondered at; but in Price we find a novice in the art, capable of equal ingenuity in every department of the dangerous undertaking, from the engraving down to the publication.

An attentive perusal of this narrative must awaken in the breast of the reader a series of important and useful reflections, calculated to leave impressions that should excite a determination to resist every temptation that chance or opportunity may afford to indulge in a vice that eventually led to the destruction of this depraved man, who from his youth upwards appears to have had no object in view, but that of preying upon the credulity of his fellow-men.

That such talents should be appropriated to such an use must be deeply regretted; but that any individual should thus throughout life act the part of a wolf among his fellow-creatures deserves the utmost detestation. Society in general may also learn lessons of caution and vigilance from the contemplation of the extraordinary character here described. Vice appears in its most odious features—that of meditated imposition upon the honest and industrious part of the community: mark, however, its serpentine progress, and its wretched termination. Price has emphatically been termed the social monster; and it is sincerely hoped that a recital of his atrocities will have the effect of guarding the younger classes of our readers against the first inroads of deception. The Spartans used to teach young persons sobriety by placing before them a drunken man; and the contemplation of such a character as Price must tend to verify the assertion of a celebrated poet that

' An honest man's the noblest work of God.'

The fatal Encounter between Ward and Swain.

WILLIAM WARD,

CONVICTED OF MANSLAUGHTER.

' Boxing,' says a British writer, ' which is the setting
of the most worthless of the human species to batter
each other to mummy, to break jaws, to knock eye-
balls out of their sockets, to flatten the nose, beat out
teeth, or to dash each other on the ground, with such
dexterity as that they shall never rise again, if not a
royal sport, is, at least, a princely entertainment, and
manifests the *exalted* taste of its patrons.'

Of the subject of boxing, in his own country, the
American geographer, Dr. Morse, says, that, ' When
two boxers are wearied out with fighting and bruising
each other (in which encounters they kick and bite, as
well as strike,) they come, as it is called, to close

257

quarters, and each endeavours to twist his fore fingers into the earlocks of his antagonist. When these are fast clenched, the thumbs are extended each way to the nose, and the eyes gently turned out of their sockets. The victor, for his expertness, receives shouts of applause from the sporting throng, while his poor eyeless antagonist is laughed at for his misfortune.' This, in America, is called GOUGING.

The author of 'The Stranger in America,' in commenting upon the above passage, after adducing many instances of gouging, observes, ' But let us conclude this odious subject, which never should have stained these pages, had not the author alluded to (Morse) proclaimed to the world the cruel and unnatural facts, by observing that these barbarities appear not to have been the genuine growth of American soil. No such practice would be endured by an English mob; no such disgraceful revenge ever entered the breast of a Creek, a Cherokee, or a Kickapoo Indian.'

The sight is not the only sense endangered in these brutal contests in England; and life itself has oftener, than in the murder now in question, been lost in prize-fighting, as we shall show before we have done with the boxing of William Ward.

The barbarous and unlawful practice of fisticuffs, which the fools of fashion dignify by the name of pugilism, since the rude days of Broughton, had, until this period, happily become nearly out of use. Its renewal shows that there are periodical returns of fashion, even in amusements of cruelty.

The first public renewal of this species of cruelty was a battle between two low fellows, a Jew and a Christian, in outward form, but in heart, as Dr. Morse styles some of his countrymen, Nothingarians—that is, those who have not the fear of God before their eyes, through any medium of religion.

The fisticuffings between Humphries and Mendoza formed a treat for such fellows as may be daily seen lounging in Bond Street. Peers and pickpockets, *cheek by jowl*, scampered some score miles to witness the bloody spectacles which these two ruffians made of each other. As at a cock-fight, they made their bets, which, as between the ' grey and pile,' varied in proportion to the rounds, or knock-down blows, the failing eye, or the quantity of blood spilt.

The roads to this scene of inhumanity were thronged with all descriptions of idle fellows; some mounted upon the high-mettled racer, and others kicking and whipping miserable jack-asses, that they too might be in at the death, or giving in, as they term it, of the most exhausted of the two ruffian candidates for the gaining of public applause in prize-fighting.

Even royalty, which must ever be at the head of every fashion, was often in the motley mob collected to witness these disgraceful exhibitions; but, bad as are our youth, they will become still worse by following such pernicious examples.

His Majesty, when Prince of Wales, in one of these mortal conflicts, found one of the combatants made a corpse at his feet, upon the stage of pugilistic fight. The heir-apparent to the British crown turned pale away from the horrid sight, and made a vow never more to behold so savage and dangerous a contest, and to which he has conscientiously adhered.

Of the worst description of vagabonds, who run from one bloody stage to the other, was the fellow who now comes under our notice. His origin mean, his understanding totally uncultivated; arrogant of his savage prowess, vicious and cruel; he had often fought, and was the inglorious conqueror; but, in his turn, was shamefully vanquished, and, to the satisfaction of all who wished the downfall of such a desperado, by the fighting Jew, who had been considered his inferior in the despicable attainment.

William Ward, as we have already said, was once a pugilist, high in renown among the fashionable amateurs of that degrading pursuit. He, with several more of his infamous calling, had monopolized the outside of a stage-coach, journeying to Stilton, seventy-one miles from London, to attend another rencontre, between Jew Mendoza and Christian Humphries. They had not proceeded farther than Enfield, where, as the coach stopped to change horses, the bravado of Ward stimulated a drunken blacksmith, named Edwin Swain, to challenge him to combat.

Now, though there is no honour in the owner of a blood-horse, or a game cock, to match with a dung-hill, or an animal that had toiled in harness, yet Ward inhumanly accepted the foolish dolt's invitation; and, for a while, they did buffet each other with lusty sinews; but science soon overcame brute force, for, in fact, the blacksmith could not hit the trained bruiser. He therefore soon yielded the palm of victory, and retired into the public house, before which the coach and passengers waited the event of this shameful contest. This professed pugilist followed, and upon his unguarded antagonist dealt his fists, until the object of his cruelty was actually beaten to death!

Ward, conscious of the magnitude of his offence, hired a post-chaise, and, with his companions, set off to return to London, where they could best conceal themselves from offended justice; but they were pursued, and committed to prison.

The coroner's jury were divided in opinion, seven finding the crime 'wilful murder,' and nine 'man-slaughter;' and, from the circumstances attending the horrid deed, Ward was not admitted to bail; though he boasted that he could find security for his appearance to any amount. A poor mechanic, an useful member of society, might linger in gaol without a friend to bail him, while such ruffians have their aiders, abettors, and protectors, in men of property, rank, and title!

On the 5th of June, 1789, William Ward was

arraigned at the bar of the Old Bailey, for the murder of Edwin Swain, and, after a long trial, found guilty of manslaughter, fined one shilling, and sentenced to be imprisoned three months in Newgate.

The evidence did not amount to the proof of actual malice as the deceased first provoked the contest.

Mr. Justice Ashurst, who tried Ward, expressed his detestation of the inhuman and unlawful practice of boxing, and declared it to be a disgrace to a civilized nation.

At the expiration of his sentence, and when about to be liberated, Ward had the unparalleled effrontery to offer a public challenge to fight at the next Newmarket meeting. ' Is this,' says a monthly publication for September, 1789, commenting on this subject, ' the effect of the wholesome severity of the law? or are these gross violations of humanity to proceed till more homicides are committed? '

In the year 1809, John Jackson, late a prize-fighter, being apprehended on a warrant for assaulting Mr. James Savage, of Walsingham Place, St. George's Fields, stated, in his defence at the public office in Bow Street, that on the day on which he was charged with the assault, the 18th of September, at Covent Garden Theatre, he dined with General Gwynne, Colonel M'Donel, Captains Barclay and Hanbury, and others, at the Piazza Coffee-house; and *they went together* to the theatre!!!

THE REVEREND BENJAMIN RUSSEN,

EXECUTED FOR A RAPE.

THIS man was master of the subscription charity-school at Bethnal Green, in which had been bred up a poor girl named Anne Mayne.

At the sessions held at the Old Bailey in October, 1777, Benjamin Russen, clerk, was indicted for having committed a rape on the said Anne Mayne, on the 18th of June preceding. The girl deposed that, when Mrs. Russen lay in, the prisoner desired that she (Mayne) might stay below stairs with him, while he went to sleep after dinner, lest he should fall into the fire; and that he took this opportunity to perpetrate the fact with which he was charged; and, after it was committed, said that, if she told her mother, sister, or any body of it, he would flog her severely.

She proved a second commission of a similar fact, during which he looked out at the door, in apprehension that somebody was coming; but this did not happen to be the case. It appeared, likewise, that the crime was committed a third time; but it would be indelicate in the highest degree to recount the particulars of a fact of this nature.

A surgeon, who was present when Mr. Russen was carried before Justice Wilmot, deposed that, on examination of the girl, he did not discover that any absolute violence had been committed.

There were three other indictments against Russen of a similar nature, but he was acquitted of them all. He now proceeded to call several persons to his character, who spoke well of him as far as they knew.

In his defence he denied the fact, and pleaded the malice of his enemies, who, he said, had charged him with those offences to deprive him of his place. He urged the favourable representation of the surgeon, who had sworn that the child had not been materially injured; and insisted that, at the time the fact was charged to have been committed, he was so ill as to keep his chamber.

By endeavouring to prove this he proved too much; for the witness swore that he kept his chamber two months successively, contrary to the tenor of all the other witnesses; so that the jury were induced to think that he had not kept his chamber even one month.

The counsel for the prisoner laboured hard to adduce some proofs of his innocence; but the jury brought in a verdict that the prisoner was guilty; in consequence of which he received sentence of death.

After conviction the behaviour of Mr. Russen was exceedingly proper for a man in his unhappy situation. No very extraordinary exertions were made to obtain a pardon for him, because it was presumed it would not have been granted.

On the morning of execution Mr. Russen was taken from Newgate to Tyburn in a mourning-coach. Just before he left the prison, seeing a number of people about him, he made use of this emphatical expression, ' Stand clear! look to yourselves! I am the first hypocrite in Sion!' The parting scene between himself and his son was extremely affecting.

He was attended in the coach by the Ordinary of Newgate (the Reverend Mr. Hughes), a sheriff's officer, and an undertaker, who had engaged to conduct the funeral.

At the place of execution Russen seemed to have a proper sense of his past wicked life; but, in regard to the crime for which he suffered, he thought himself ill treated, as he always asserted that he had never been guilty of a rape, though he acknowledged, a day or two before his death, that he had taken liberties with the child which were highly unbecoming. Previous to the prayers commonly used at the place of execution he made a long extempore prayer, and earnestly exhorted the surrounding multitude to take warning by his fate. He likewise censured the indecency of the people, who stood near the gallows with their hats on, and with apparent unconcern, during the time of prayer; and observed that the place where unhappy victims are to suffer the sentence of the law should be held as sacred as a church. He therefore requested the spectators to be uncovered, and to join in their supplications for him to Almighty God, which accordingly several of them complied with; and, after having prayed for his wife and helpless children, he once more recommended his soul to the mercy of God, and was then launched into eternity.

On the way to execution the mob insulted Russen: but the propriety of his behaviour at the fatal tree had an evident effect on the spectators; and, when his body was cut down, it was put into a hearse, and delivered to his friends for interment.

Benjamin Russen was executed at Tyburn on the 12th of December, 1777.

It is with pain that the pen of delicacy touches a

subject of this nature; and this pain is increased when we consider that the object of our remarks was in a line of life that ought to have induced him to set the best example to others. A clergyman who is a schoolmaster is bound by a double tie to exhibit every mark of his attention to the duties of religion and morality; and, when he fails of this duty, his example is presumed to have a worse influence than that of a man differently situated.

Mr. Russen had a wife and six children, which was no slight aggravation of his crime.

JOHN HOLMES AND PETER WILLIAMS,

WHIPPED FOR STEALING DEAD BODIES.

THESE impious robbers are vulgarly termed, in London, resurrection men, but should rather be called sacrilegious robbers of our holy Church, not even confining the unnatural crime to men alone, for the gentler sex are connected in this horrid traffic, whose business it is to strip off the shroud, or whatever garments in which the body may have been wrapped, and to sell them, while the men, through the darkness of night, drag the naked bodies to be anatomized.

Though it matters little where we return to our original dust, yet there is something offensive to the living to hear of graves being violated for this base purpose; and to know that the remains of a parent, a wife, or a child, have been thus removed, is shocking to our nature.

When Hunter, the famous anatomist, was in full practice, he had a surgical theatre behind his house in Windmill Street, where he gave lectures to a very numerous class of pupils. To this place such numbers of dead bodies were brought, during the winter season, that the mob rose several times, and were upon the point of pulling down his house. He had a well dug in the back part of his premises, in which was thrown the putrid flesh, and with it alkalis, in order to hasten its consumption.

Numberless are the instances of dead bodies being seized on their way to the surgeons. Hackney coachmen, for an extra fare, and porters with hampers, are often employed by these resurrection men for this purpose.

A monthly publication, in March, 1776, says, ' The remains of more than twenty dead bodies were discovered in a shed in Tottenham Court Road, supposed to have been deposited there by traders to the surgeons; of whom there is one, it is said, in the Borough, who makes an open profession of dealing in dead bodies, and is well known by the name of the ' Resurrectionist.'

Still more shocking is it to be told that men who are paid for protecting the sacred deposit of the mortal remains of their fellow-parishioners are often confederates, as the present case will demonstrate.

Holmes, the principal villain in this case, was gravedigger of St. George's, Bloomsbury. Williams was his assistant; and a woman, named Esther Donaldson, an accomplice. They were all indicted for stealing the body of Mrs. Jane Sainsbury, who departed this life on the 9th of October then last past, and the corpse was interred in the burying-ground of St. George's, above mentioned, on the Monday following. They were detected before they could secure their booty; and the widower, however unpleasant, determined to prosecute them. In order to their conviction, he had to undergo the mental pain of viewing and identifying the remains of his wife!

The grave-digger and his deputy were convicted at the Middlesex court of quarter-sessions for December, 1777, on the fullest evidence; and the acquittal of the woman was much regretted, as no doubt remained of her equal guilt. She therefore was released, but Holmes and Williams were sentenced to six months' imprisonment, and to be whipped twice, on their bare backs, from the end of Kingsgate Street, Holborn, to Dyot Street, St. Giles's, being half a mile, and which was inflicted, with the severity due to so detestable an offence, through crowds of approving spectators.

JOHN RANN, COMMONLY CALLED SIXTEEN-STRING JACK,

EXECUTED FOR HIGHWAY ROBBERY.

THIS fellow was entitled to be classed among the impudent and arrogant self-created gentlemen who levied arbitrary contributions on the highway: he was also of considerable notoriety in acts of such species of depredations, having been regularly initiated, from the humble pickpocket.

John Rann was born at a village a few miles from Bath, of honest parents, who were in low circumstances, and incapable of giving him any kind of education. For some time he obtained a livelihood by vending goods, which he drove round the city and adjacent country on an ass.

A lady of distinction, who happened to be at Bath, took Rann into her service when he was about twelve years of age; and his behaviour was such, that he became the favourite of his mistress and fellow-servants.

At length he came to London, and got employment as a helper in the stables at Brooke's Mews, in which station he bore a good character. He then became the driver of a postchaise, after which he was servant to an officer, and in both these stations he was well spoken of.

About four years before his execution he was coachman to a gentleman of fortune near Portman Square, and it was at this period that he dressed in the manner which gave rise to the appellation of Sixteen-string Jack, by wearing breeches with eight strings at each knee.

After living in the service of several noblemen he lost his character, and turned pickpocket, in company

Rann on his Trial at the Old Bailey

with three fellows, named Jones, Clayton, and Colledge, the latter of whom, a mere boy, obtained the name of *Eight-stringed Jack*.

At the sessions held at the Old Bailey in April, 1774, Rann, Clayton, and one Shepherd, were tried for robbing Mr. William Somers on the highway, and acquitted for want of evidence. They were again tried for robbing Mr. Langford, but acquitted for the same reason.

For some time past Rann had kept company with a young woman named Roche, who, having been apprenticed to a milliner, and being seduced by an officer of the guards, was reduced to obtain bread by the casual wages of prostitution; and, at length associating with highwaymen, received such valuable effects as they took on the road.

> ' A woman's honour is a woman's all,
> You're lost for ever if perchance you fall;
> In this, wit, beauty, fortune, form, and mind,
> You give like atoms to the whistling wind;
> All worth, all pleasure, is with honour lost,
> A truth which thousands witness to their cost
> The fate of woman deeply we deplore,
> They fall like stars that set to rise no more.'

On the 30th of May Rann was taken into custody, and, being brought to Bow Street on the following Wednesday, was charged with robbing John Devall, Esq. near the nine-mile stone on the Hounslow road, of his watch and money. This watch he had given to Miss Roche, who had delivered it to Catharine Smith, by whom it was offered in pledge to Mr. Hallam, a pawnbroker, who, suspecting that it was not honestly obtained, caused all the parties to be taken into custody.

Miss Roche was now charged with receiving the watch, knowing it to have been stolen; and Miss Smith, being sworn, deposed that, on the day Mr. Devall was robbed, Roche told her that ' she expected Rann to bring her some money in the evening;' that he accordingly came about ten at night, and, having retired some time with Miss Roche, she, on her return, owned that she had received a watch and five guineas from him, which he said he had taken from a gentleman on the highway; and that she, Miss Smith, carried the watch to pawn to Mr. Hallam, at the request of Miss Roche.

Sir John Fielding asked Rann if he would offer any thing in his defence; on which the latter said, ' I know no more of the matter than you do, nor half so much neither.' On this occasion Rann was dressed in a manner above his style of life and his circumstances. He had a bundle of flowers in the breast of his coat almost as large as a broom; and his irons were tied up with a number of blue ribands.

For this offence Rann was tried at the sessions held at the Old Bailey, in July, 1774, and acquitted.

Two or three days after this acquittal Rann engaged to sup with a girl at her lodgings in Bow Street; but, not being punctual to his appointment, the girl went to bed, and Rann, not being able to obtain admittance at the door, attempted to get in at the window on the first floor, and had nearly accomplished his purpose, when he was taken into custody by the watchman.

For this burglarious attempt he was examined at Bow Street on the 27th of July, when the girl, whose apartments he had attempted to break open, declared that he could not have had any felonious intention, as he knew that he would have been a welcome guest, and have been readily admitted, if she had not fallen asleep. On this he was dismissed, after Sir John Fielding had cautioned him to leave his dangerous profession, and seek for some more honest means of support.

On the Sunday following Rann appeared at Bagnigge Wells, dressed in a scarlet coat, tambour waistcoat, white silk stockings, laced hat, &c. and publicly declared himself to be a highwayman. Having indulged pretty freely, he became extremely quarrelsome, and several scuffles ensued, in one of which he lost a ring from his finger, and, when he discovered his loss, he said it was but a hundred guineas gone, which one evening's *work* would replace. He became at length so troublesome that part of the company agreed to turn him out of the house: but they met with so obstinate a resistance that they were obliged to give up their design; when a number of young fellows, possessed of more spirit than discretion, attacked this magnanimous hero, and actually forced him through the window into the road. Rann was not much injured by this severe treatment; but he complained bitterly against those who could so affront a *gentleman* of his character.

Rann, being arrested for a debt of fifty pounds, which he was unable to pay, was confined in the Marshalsea prison, where he was visited by a number of men and women of bad character, some of whom paid his debt, and procured his discharge.

At another time, Rann being with two companions at an alehouse in Tottenham Court Road, two sheriff's officers arrested Rann, who, not having money to pay the debt, deposited his watch in the hands of the bailiffs, and his associates advanced three guineas, which together made more than the amount of the debt; and, as a balance was to be returned to Rann when the watch should be redeemed, he told the bailiffs that, if they would lend him five shillings, he would treat them with a crown bowl of punch. This they readily did; and, while they were drinking, Rann said to the officers, 'You have not treated me like a gentleman. When Sir John Fielding's people come after me they use me genteelly; they only hold up a finger, beckon me, and I follow them as quietly as a lamb.'

When the bailiffs were gone, Rann and his companions rode off; but our hero, soon returning, stopped at the turnpike, and asked if he had been wanted. 'No,' said the tollman. 'Why,' replied the other, 'I am Sixteen-string Jack, the famous highwayman—have any of Sir John Fielding's people been this way?' 'Yes,' said the man, 'some of them are but just gone through.' Rann replied, 'If you see them again, tell them I am gone towards London;' and then rode off with the utmost unconcern.

Soon afterwards Rann appeared at Barnet races,

dressed in a most elegant sporting style, his waistcoat being blue satin, trimmed with silver, and he was followed by hundreds of people, who were eager to gratify their curiosity by the sight of a man who had been so much the subject of public conversation.

A very short time before Rann was capitally convicted he attended a public execution at Tyburn, and, getting within the ring formed by the constables round the gallows, desired that he might be permitted to stand there, 'for,' said he, 'perhaps it is very proper that I should be a spectator on this occasion.'

On the 26th of September, 1774, Rann and William Collier went on the Uxbridge road, with a view to commit robberies on the highway; and on the Wednesday following they were examined at the public office in Bow Street, when Dr. William Bell, chaplain to the Princess Amelia, deposed that, between three and four o'clock in the afternoon of Monday, the 26th of September, as he was riding near Ealing, he observed two men of rather mean appearance, who rode past him; and that he remarked they had suspicious looks; yet neither at that time, nor for some little time afterwards, had he any idea of being robbed: that soon afterwards one of them, which he believed was Rann, crossed the head of his horse, and, demanding his money, said 'Give it to me, and take no notice, or I'll blow your brains out.' On this the doctor gave him one shilling and sixpence, which was all the silver he had, and likewise a common watch in a tortoise-shell case.

On the evening of the day on which the robbery was committed Eleanor Roche, who was kept by Rann, and her maid-servant, carried a watch to pledge with Mr. Cordy, pawnbroker, in Oxford Road, who, suspecting that it had not been honestly acquired, stopped it, and applied to Mr. Grignion, watchmaker, in Russell Street, Covent Garden, who had made the watch for Dr. Bell.

Mr. Clarke swore that, on going to Miss Roche's lodgings on the Monday night, he found two pair of boots wet and dirty, which had evidently been worn that day; and Mr. Haliburton swore that he waited at Miss Roche's lodgings till Rann and Collier came thither; in consequence of which they were taken into custody.

On the 5th of October, John Rann, William Collier, Eleanor Roche, and Christian Stewart (servant to Roche), were brought to Bow Street; when Dr. Bell deposed in substance as he had done the preceding week: and William Hills, servant to the Princess Amelia, swore that he saw Rann, whom he well knew, ascend the hill at Acton about twenty minutes before the robbery was committed—a circumstance which perfectly agreed with Dr. Bell's account of the time that he was robbed.

John Rann and William Collier were therefore committed to Newgate, to take their trials for the highway robbery; Miss Roche was sent to Clerkenwell Bridewell, and Christian Stewart, her servant, to Tothill Fields' Bridewell, to be tried as accessories after the fact.

The evidence given on this trial was, in substance, the same as that which had been given at Bow Street; but, some favourable circumstances appearing in behalf of Collier, he was recommended to mercy, and afterwards respited during the king's pleasure. Miss Roche was sentenced to be transported for fourteen years; her servant was acquitted; and Rann was left for execution.

When Rann was brought down to take his trial he was dressed in a new suit of pea-green clothes; his hat was bound round with silver strings; he wore a ruffled shirt; and his behaviour evinced the utmost unconcern.

Rann was so confident of being acquitted that he had ordered a genteel supper to be provided for the entertainment of his particular friends and associates on the joyful occasion; but their intended mirth was turned into mourning, and the madness of guilty joy gave way to the sullen melancholy of equally guilty grief.

When Rann received his sentence he attempted to force a smile, but it was evident that his mind was racked with pains that no language can express.

After conviction the behaviour of this malefactor was, for some time, very improper for one in his unhappy circumstances. On Sunday, the 23rd of October, he had seven girls to dine with him. The company were remarkably cheerful; nor was Rann less joyous than his companions.

His conduct was expressive of great unconcern till the time that the warrant for his execution arrived; after which he began to be somewhat serious in his preparation for a future state.

On the morning of execution he received the sacrament in the chapel of the prison, and at the fatal tree behaved with great decency, but did not appear so much affected by his approaching fate as some printed accounts have represented him. When he came near the gallows he turned round, and looked at it as an object which he had long expected to see, but not as one that he dreaded, as might reasonably have been expected.

He was turned off November the 30th, 1774, and, having hung the usual time, his body was delivered to his friends for interment.

The Duchess of Kingston's Interview with Foote, the Comedian.

THE DUCHESS OF KINGSTON,

CONVICTED OF BIGAMY.

FEW females have, in their time, attracted so large a portion of public notice as this celebrated lady, who was the daughter of Colonel Chudleigh, the descendant of an ancient family in the county of Devon. Her father dying while she was very young, the care of this, his only daughter, devolved on her mother, who had little more than the usual pension allotted to the widow of an officer for their mutual subsistence. Under these circumstances, Mrs. Chudleigh prudently availed herself of the best substitute for money—good connexions. These, the rank, situation, and habits of her husband had placed within

275

her power. She hired a house, fit, at that less refined period, for a fashionable town residence; and accommodated an inmate, for the purpose of adding to the scantiness of her income.

Her daughter Elizabeth was soon distinguished for a brilliancy of repartee, and for other qualities highly recommendatory, because extremely pleasing. An opportunity offered for the display of them to every advantage. The father of King George III. had his court at Leicester House. Mr. Pulteney, who then blazed as a meteor in the opposition, was honoured with the particular regard of the Prince of Wales. Miss Chudleigh was introduced to Mr. Pulteney, and he obtained for her, at the age of about eighteen, the appointment of maid of honour to the Princess of Wales; but he did more than thus place her in an elevated station; he endeavoured to cultivate her understanding : to him Miss Chudleigh read; and with him, when separated by distance, actually corresponded.

The station to which Miss Chudleigh was advanced, combined with many personal attractions, produced her a number of admirers; some with titles, and others in the expectation of them. Among the former was the Duke of Hamilton, whom Miss Gunning had afterwards the good fortune to obtain for a consort. The duke was passionately fond of Miss Chudleigh, and pressed his suit with such ardour as to obtain a solemn engagement, on her part, that on his return from a tour, for which he was preparing, she would become his wife. There was reasons why this event should not immediately take place; that the engagement would be fulfilled at the specified time both parties considered as a moral certainty. A mutual pledge was given and accepted; the duke commenced his proposed tour; and the parting condition was, that he should write by every opportunity, and Miss Chudleigh, of course, to answer his epistles. Thus the arrangement of Fortune seemed to have united a pair, who possibly might have experienced much happiness; for between the duke and Miss Chudleigh there was a similarity of disposition. Fate, however, had not destined them for each other.

Miss Chudleigh had an aunt, whose name was Hanmer: at her house the Hon. Mr. Hervey, son of the Earl of Bristol, and a captain in the royal navy, was a visitor. To this gentleman Mrs. Hanmer became so exceedingly partial; that she favoured his views on her niece, and engaged her efforts to effect, if possible, matrimonial connexion. There were two difficulties which would have been insurmountable, had they not been opposed by the fertile genius of a female—Miss Chudleigh disliked Captain Hervey, and she was betrothed to the Duke of Hamilton. To render this alliance nugatory, the letters of his grace were intercepted by Mrs. Hanmer; and, his supposed silence giving offence to her niece, she worked so successfully on her pride as to induce her to abandon all thoughts of her lover, whose passion she had cherished with delight. A conduct the reverse of that imputed to the duke was observed by Captain Hervey: he was all that assiduity could dictate, or attention perform. He had daily access to Miss Chudleigh, and each interview was artfully improved by the aunt to the promotion of her own views. The letters of his Grace of Hamilton, which regularly arrived, were as regularly suppressed; until piqued beyond endurance, Miss Chudleigh was prevailed on to accept the hand of Captain Hervey, and, by a private marriage, to ensure the participation of his future honours and fortune. The ceremony was performed in a private chapel adjoining the country mansion of Mr. Merrill, at Lainston, near Winchester, in Hampshire

On a review of life, the predominant evil experienced may be easily traced, by every reflecting mind, to some wilful error, or injudicious mistake, operating as a determinate cause, and giving the colour to our fate. This was the case with Miss Chudleigh; for the hour she became united with Captain Hervey proved to her the origin of every subsequent unhappiness. The connubial rites were attended with unhappy consequences, and, from the night following the day on which the marriage was solemnized, Miss Chudleigh resolved never to have further connexion with her husband. To prevail on him not to claim her as his wife required all the art of which she was mistress; and the best dissuasive was the loss of her situation as maid of honour, should the marriage be publicly known. The finances of Captain Hervey not enabling him, at the time, to compensate such a loss, this, most probably, operated as a prudential motive for his yielding to the entreaties of his wife, which he did in a manner that at times indicated a strong desire to play the tyrant. In fact, as she frequently expressed herself, ' Her misery commenced with the arrival of Captain Hervey in England, and the greatest joy she experienced was the intelligence of his departure.'

Miss Chudleigh, now Mrs. Hervey, a maid in appearance, a wife in disguise, seemed, to those who judge from external appearance only, to be in a most enviable situation. Of the higher circles she was the attractive centre; of gayer life the invigorating spirit. Her royal mistress smiled on her; a few friendships she cemented; and conquests she made in such abundance, that, like Cæsar in triumph, she had a train of captives at her heels: yet, with all this appearance of happiness, she wanted that, without which there is no happiness on earth—peace of mind. Her husband, quieted for a time, grew obstreperous as she became more the object of admiration; and, feeling his right, was determined to assert it. She endeavoured, by letters, to sooth him into peace; but her efforts were not successful; and he demanded an interview, enforcing his demand by threats of exposure in case of refusal: she was therefore obliged to comply. The meeting was at the apartment of Captain Hervey; a black servant only was in the house. On entering the room where he was, his first care was to prevent her retreat by locking the door. This interview ended, like every other which she had with Captain Hervey, unhappily for her—the fruit of it being the addition of a boy to the human race. Miss Chudleigh removed to Chelsea for a change of air, and returned to Leicester House, perfectly recovered from her indisposition. The infant, soon sinking into the arms of death, left only the tale of its existence to be related.

While these and a variety of other circumstances were passing between Miss Chudleigh and her husband, the Duke of Hamilton arrived from his travels. He lost not a moment in paying his homage to the idol of his affections, and obtaining an explanation of the reason why his letters were unanswered. Flighty as he was in other respects, to Miss Chudleigh his constancy remained unshaken. The interview placed Mrs. Hanmer in her true light, and the duke made a tender of his hand where his heart was already centred. The rejection of this offer, which it was impossible to accept, and almost as impossible to explain why it was rejected, occasioned emotions in the duke which the imagination may conceive better than the pen explain. Miss Chudleigh was even compelled to prohibit his visits. Several other nobles experienced a similar fate, which astonished the fashionable world: and the mother of Miss Chudleigh, who was a total stranger to the private marriage of her daughter, reprehended her folly in proper terms.

In order to relieve herself, at least for a time, from the embarrassments which environed her, Miss Chudleigh determined to travel, and embarked for the Continent, choosing Germany for the theatre of her peregrinations. She resided some time at Berlin; then went to Dresden; and, as she aspired to the acquaintance of crowned heads, she was gratified by that of the great Frederic of Prussia, who not only conversed, but corresponded, with her. In the Electress of Saxony she found a friend, whose affection for her continued to the latest period of life. The electress was a woman of sense, honour, virtue, and religion. Her letters were replete with kindness: while her hand distributed presents to Miss Chudleigh out of the treasury of abundance, her heart was interested for her happiness. This she afterwards evinced during her prosecution; for, at that time, a letter from the electress contained the following passage: ' You have long experienced my love; my revenue, my protection, my everything, you may command. Come then, my dear life, to an asylum of peace. Quit a country where, if you are bequeathed a cloak, some pretender may start up, and ruin you by law to prove it not your property. Let me have you at Dresden.'

On her return from the Continent Miss Chudleigh ran over the career of pleasure, enlivened the court circles, and each year became more ingratiated with the mistress whom she served. She was the leader of fashion, played whist with Lord Chesterfield, and revelled with Lady Harrington and Miss Ashe. She was a constant visitant at all public places, and, in 1742, appeared at a masked ball in the character of Iphigenia.

Reflection, however, put off for the day, too frequently intruded an unwelcome visit at night. Captain Hervey, like a perturbed spirit, was eternally crossing the path trodden by his wife. If in the rooms at Bath, he was sure to be there. At a rout, ridotto, or ball, this destroyer of her peace imbittered every pleasure, and even menaced her with an intimation that he would disclose the marriage to the princess. In this Miss Chudleigh anticipated him, by being the first relater of the circumstance. Her royal mistress pitied her, and continued her patronage to the hour of her death.

At length a stratagem was either suggested, or it occurred to Miss Chudleigh, at once to deprive Captain Hervey of the power to claim her as his wife. The clergyman who had married them was dead. The register-book was in careless hands. A handsome compliment was paid for the inspection, and, while the person in whose custody it was listened to an amusing story, Miss Chudleigh tore out the register. Thus imagining the business accomplished, she for a time bade defiance to her husband, whose taste for the softer sex subsiding, from some unaccountable cause, occasioned Miss Chudleigh a cessation of inquietude. Her better fate influenced in her favour the heart of a man who was the exemplar of amiability: this was the Duke of Kingston. Meanwhile Captain Hervey had succeeded to the earldom of Bristol. With rank he obtained fortune; and both were inviting objects to the mind of our heroine. When a succession to the family honours and revenue became highly probable, a short period before it took place Miss Chudleigh went to the house of Mr. Merrill, in whose chapel she was married. Her ostensible reason was a jaunt out of town; her real design was to procure, if possible, the insertion of her marriage with Captain Hervey in the book which, in order to destroy the written evidence of that marriage, she had formerly mutilated. With this view she dealt out promises with a liberal hand. The officiating clerk, who was a person of various avocations, was to be promoted to the extent of his wishes. The book was managed by the lady to her content, and she returned to London, secretly exulting in the excellence and success of her machination. She did, it is true, succeed, but it was laying the groundwork of that very evidence which operated afterwards to her conviction.

Such was the situation of Miss Chudleigh when the

Duke of Kingston became her admirer. Remarried, as it were, by her own stratagem, the participation of ducal honours became legally impossible. The chains of wedlock, which the lady had been so industrious in shaking off or putting on, as seemed most suitable to her views, were now galling to an excess. Every advice was taken, but the means of liberation were beyond the power of human device. To acquiesce in that which could not be remedied seemed the only alternative. The Duke of Kingston's attachment was ardent, and truly sincere. He mingled the friend with the lover; nor was there an endearing title under heaven he would not have assumed, could but the assumption have really advanced the happiness of Miss Chudleigh. For a series of years they cohabited; yet with such observance of external decorum, that their intimacy was not an evidenced certainty.

The Earl of Bristol, by time and attachments, had grown so weary of the connubial state, as to be cordially desirous of a change. At first, when sounded on the subject of a divorce, he said her vanity should not be gratified by being a duchess. Afterwards, however, there being a lady to whom he wished to offer his hand, he so altered his tone, as to express a readiness to consent to any possible means of annihilating the union subsisting between him and Miss Chudleigh. The civilians were consulted, a jactitation suit was instituted, but the evidence that could prove the marriage was kept back. Lord Bristol failing, as it was designed he should fail, in substantiating the marriage, a sentence of the Court, pronouncing the nullity of the claim, concluded the business. The object now to be obtained was, a legal opinion as to the operative power of such a sentence; and the civilians, highly tenacious of the rights of their own courts, adjudged the decree not liable to be disturbed by the interference of any extrinsic court of judicature. Under conviction of perfect safety, therefore, the marriage between his Grace of Kingston and Miss Chudleigh was publicly solemnized. The favours were worn by the highest personages in the kingdom; and, during the life of the duke, not any attempt was made to dispute the legality of the procedure. The fortune was not entailed; his grace had, therefore, the option to bequeath it as seemed best to his own inclination. The heirs since, were then expectants; the claims rested on hope, not certainty. The duchess figured without apprehension or control. She was raised to the pinnacle of her fortune, and for a very few years did she enjoy that which the chicanery of her life had been directed to accomplish, the parade of title, without that honour which integrity of character alone can ennoble.

At length she was checked in the career of enjoyment by the death of the Duke of Kingston. His will, excluding from every benefit an elder, and preferring a younger nephew as his heir in tail, gave rise to a prosecution of the duchess, which ended in the beggary of her prosecutor, and the exile of herself. The demise of the Duke of Kingston was not sudden or unexpected; being attacked with a paralytic affection, he lingered but a short time, and that time was employed by his consort in journeying his grace about, under the futile idea of prolonging his life by change of air and situation. At last, when real danger seemed to threaten, even in the opinion of the duchess, she dispatched one of her swiftest-footed messengers to her solicitor, Mr. Field, of the Temple, requiring his immediate attendance: he obeyed the summons, and, arriving at the house, the duchess privately imparted her wishes, which were, that he would procure the duke to execute, and be himself a subscribing witness to, a will made without his knowledge, and more to the taste of the duchess than that which he had executed. The difference between these two wills was this: the duke had bequeathed the income of his estates to his relict during her life, and expressly under condition of her continuing in a state of widowhood. Perfectly satisfied, however, as the duchess appeared with whatever was the inclination of her dearest lord, she could not resist the seeming opportunity of carrying her secret wishes into effect. She did not relish the temple of Hymen being shut against her. Earnestly, therefore, did she press Mr. Field to have her own will immediately executed, which left her at liberty to give her hand to the conqueror of her heart. The duchess, in her anxiety to have the restraint shaken off, had nearly deprived herself of every benefit derivable from the demise of the duke. When Mr. Field was introduced to his grace, his intellects were perceptibly affected: he knew the friends who approached him, and a transient knowledge of their persons was the only indication of mental exertion which seemed to be left him. Mr. Field very properly remonstrated on the impropriety of introducing a will for execution to a man in such a state. This occasioned a severe reprehension from the duchess, who reminded him that his business was only to obey the instructions of his employer: feeling, however, for his professional character, he positively refused either to tender the will, or be in any manner concerned in endeavouring to procure the execution. With this refusal he quitted the house, the duchess beholding him with an indignant eye as the annoyer of her scheme, when, in fact, by not complying with it, he was rendering her an essential service; for, had the will she proposed been executed, it would most indubitably have been set aside. The heirs would consequently have excluded the relict from everything, except that to which the right of dower entitled her; and, the marriage being invalidated, the lady in this, as in other respects, would have been ruined by her own stratagem. Soon after the frustration of this attempt the Duke of Kingston expired. No sooner were the funeral rites performed than the duchess adjusted her affairs, and embarked for the Continent, proposing Rome for her temporary residence. Ganganelli at that time filled the papal see. From the moderation of his principles, the tolerant spirit which he on every occasion displayed, and the marked attention he bestowed on the English, he acquired the title of the Protestant Pope : to such a character the duchess was a welcome visitor. Ganganelli treated her with the utmost civility—gave her, as a sovereign prince, many privileges—and she was lodged in the palace of one of the cardinals. Her vanity being thus gratified, her grace, in return, treated the Romans with a public spectacle. She had built an elegant pleasure-yacht; a gentleman who had served in the navy was the commander. Under her orders he sailed for Italy; and the vessel, at considerable trouble and some expense, was conveyed up the Tiber. The sight of an English yacht there was uncommon; it drew the people in crowds to the shore, and the applause was general through the city. This seemed to be the era of festivity and happiness; but, while the bark floated triumphantly on the undulation of the Tiber, a business was transacting in England which put an end to all momentary bliss.

Mrs. Cradock, who, in the capacity of a domestic, had been present during the ceremony of marriage between Miss Chudleigh and Lord Bristol, found herself so reduced in circumstances that she applied to Mr. Field for pecuniary relief. He saw her, and most injudiciously refused her every succour : in vain she urged her distress, and the absence of the duchess, who was the only person on whose munificence she had the justest claim. Field was deaf to her entreaties; she then told him what was in her power to discover. To many circumstances which she related he was an entire stranger, and he affected to discredit the rest. Mrs. Cradock ended the interview with a menace that she would make the relations of the Duke of Kingston acquainted with every important particular. Field set her at defiance : and, thus exposed to penury, she was exasperated to vengeance, and instantly set about the work of ruin.

His Grace of Kingston had borne a marked dislike to one of his nephews, Mr. Evelyn Meadows, one of the sons of his sister, Lady Frances Pierpoint. This gentleman, being excluded from the presumptive heirship, joyfully received the information that a method of doing himself substantial justice yet remained. He saw Mrs. Cradock; heard the detail of evidence which she offered; and, perfectly satisfied as to its accuracy, he had a bill of indictment, for bigamy, preferred against the reputed widow of the Duke of Kingston, and the bill was found. Mr. Field had notice of the procedure, and the duchess was properly advised to return instantly to England and appear to the indictment, to prevent an outlawry.

An immediate return to England was the only measure that could now be adopted by her grace, who, on recovering the little of her judgment which was left, drove to the house of Mr. Jenkins, at that time banker to all the British travellers who visited the Roman capital. The opponents of the duchess endeavoured to prevent her return to England by a species of artful policy exactly suited to the lady with whom they had to deal. The duchess had placed securities in the hands of Mr. Jenkins for the sums she might occasionally require, and he was perfectly safe in regard to any advance he might make. Yet, apprized that the duchess would call on him for money to defray the expense of her journey to England, he avoided seeing her. Aware of this, the duchess was incessant in her applications; and, finding all her efforts to see Mr. Jenkins fail, she pocketed a brace of pistols, returned to his house, and receiving the usual answer that he was not at home, she seated herself on the steps of the door, and declared her determination there to remain until he returned, were it for a week, a month, or a year. She knew that business would compel his return, and, finding it impracticable any longer to elude an interview, Mr. Jenkins appeared. As the duchess possessed that gift of utterance for which ladies of spirit are sometimes so eminent, it may be supposed that the conversation with the banker was not of the mildest kind. Money was demanded, not asked. A little prevarication ensued; but the production of a pistol served as the most powerful mode of reasoning; the necessary sum was instantly obtained, and the duchess quitted Rome. Her journey was retarded before she reached the Alps; a violent fever seemed to seize on her vitals: but she recovered, to the astonishment of her attendants. An abscess then formed in her side, which rendering it impossible for her to endure the motion of the carriage, a kind of litter was provided, in which she slowly travelled. In this situation nature was relieved by the breaking of the abscess; and, after a tediously painful journey, the duchess reached Calais. At that place she made a pause, and there it was that her apprehension got the better of her reason. In idea she was fettered and incarcerated in the worst cell of the worst prison in London. She was totally ignorant of the bailable nature of her offence, and by consequence expected the utmost that can be imagined. Colonel West, a brother of the late Lord Delaware, whom the duchess had known in England, became her principal associate; but he was not lawyer enough to satisfy her doubts. By the means of former connexions, and through a benevolence in his own nature, the Earl of Mansfield had a private meeting with the duchess. The venerable peer conducted himself in a manner which did honour to his heart and character.

Her spirits being soothed by the interview, the duchess embarked for Dover, landed, drove post to Kingston House, and found friends displaying both zeal and alacrity in her cause. The first measure taken was to have the duchess bailed: this was done before Lord Mansfield; the Duke of Newcastle, Lord Mountstuart, Mr. Glover, and other characters of rank, attended. The manner of adjusting this disagreeable matter was such as to solace the mind, and prepare it for a greater encounter. The prosecution and consequent trial of the duchess becoming objects of magnitude, the public curiosity and expectation were proportionably excited. The duchess had through life distinguished herself as a most eccentric character. Her turn of mind was original, and many of her actions were without a parallel, even when she moved in the sphere of amusement, it was in a style peculiarly her own. If others invited admiration by a partial display of their charms at a masquerade, she at once threw off the veil, and set censure at defiance. Thus, at midnight assemblies, where Bacchus revelled, and the altars of Venus were encircled by the votaries of Love, the duchess, then Miss Chudleigh, appeared almost in the unadorned simplicity of primitive nature.

The dilemma, therefore, into which she was thrown by the pending prosecution, was, to such a character, of the most perplexing kind. She had in a manner invited the disgrace, by neglecting the means of preventing it. Mrs. Cradock, the only existing evidence, against her, had personally solicited a maintenance for the remaining years of her life; and had voluntarily offered, in case a stipend should be settled on her, to retire to her native village, and never more intrude.—The offer was rejected by the duchess, who would only consent to allow her twenty pounds a year, on condition of her sequestering herself in some place near the Peak of Derbyshire. This the duchess considered as a most liberal offer; and she expressed her astonishment that she should have the assurance to reject it. It was, however, rejected with the utmost scorn; and she who was refused a paltry pittance, except on condition of banishing herself for life, might afterwards have received thousands to abscond.

Under the assurances of her lawyers, the duchess was as quiet as the troublesome monitor in her bosom would permit her to be. Reconciled, therefore, in some measure, to the encounter, her repose was on a sudden interrupted by an adversary from a different quarter. This was the celebrated Foote, who, mixing in the first circles of fashion, was perfectly acquainted with the leading transactions of the duchess's life. Besides this he had received much private information from some person who had been intimate with her, and resolved to turn it to his advantage. As, in the opinion of Mandeville, private vices are public benefits, so Foote deemed the crimes and vices of individuals lawful game for his wit. On this principle he proceeded with the Duchess of Kingston. He wrote a piece entitled ' A Trip to Calais.' The scenes were humorous, the character of the duchess admirably drawn, and the object was accomplished, namely, to make her ashamed of herself. The real design, however, of Foote, was to obtain money for suppressing the piece, and with this view he contrived to have it communicated to the duchess that the Haymarket theatre would open with an entertainment in which she was taken off to the life. Alarmed at this, she sent for Foote, who attended with the piece in his pocket; and, being desired to read part of it, he proceeded in the character of Lady Kitty Crocodile, until, no longer able to forbear, she rose in a violent passion, and exclaimed ' This is scandalous, Mr. Foote! Why, what a wretch you have made me.'—' You! ' replied the humorist : ' this is not designed for your grace; it is not you! ' After a few turns about the room the duchess became more composed, and, assuming a smile, entreated as a favour that Mr. Foote would leave the piece for her perusal, engaging at the same time to return it on the ensuing morning. He readily complied, and took his leave. Being thus left to consider her own picture, so much did her grace dislike it, that she determined, if possible, to prevent its exposure to public view. As the artist had no objection to sell it, she was inclined to be the purchaser. This was the next morning made known to Foote, who was questioned as to the sum which would satisfy him for suppressing the piece. Proportioning his expectations to her power of gratifying them, he demanded two thousand pounds, and a certain sum in compensation for a loss which he pretended would be sustained by the scenes, designed for the ' Trip to Calais,' being appropriated to other uses.—The magnitude of this demand staggered the duchess. She intimated her extreme surprise, and a wish that the request was moderated within the boundary of reason. Concluding that she must at last comply, Foote would not abate one guinea. She offered fourteen, then sixteen hundred pounds, and had actually signed a draft on Messrs. Drummond and Co. for that sum, for his acceptance. This compliance induced Foote to think he should finally succeed, till, by grasping at too much, he overstood his market, and lost every thing.

The demand of Foote might, at any other time, have passed among the indifferent events of the hour, as wholly undeserving of the public notice. Those long connected with the duchess, and in habits of intimacy, felt the attack made on her as directed by a ruffian hand at a moment when she was least able to make resistance. His grace the Duke of Newcastle was consulted. The chamberlain of the household was apprized of the circumstance; and his prohibitory interference was earnestly solicited. He sent for the manuscript copy of ' The Trip to Calais,' perused and censured it. This occasioned a remonstrating letter from Foote to the Earl of Hertford, at that time in office.

Besides these, and other powerful aids, the duchess

called in professional advice. The sages of the robe were consulted, and their opinions were that the piece was a malicious libel; and that, should it be represented, a short-hand writer ought to be employed to attend on the night of representation, to minute each offensive passage, as the groundwork of a prosecution. This advice was followed, and Foote was intimidated: he denied having made a demand of two thousand pounds; but the Rev. Mr. Foster contradicted him in an affidavit.

Thus defeated in point of fact, Foote found himself baffled also in point of design. The chamberlain would not permit the piece to be represented. Foote now had recourse to another expedient. He caused it to be intimated to her ' That it was in his power to publish, if not to perform; but, were his expenses reimbursed (and the sum which her grace had formerly offered would do the business), he would desist.' The being communicated to the duchess, she in this, as in too many cases, asked the opinion of her friends, with a secret determination to follow her own. Foote, finding that she began to yield, pressed his desire incessantly; and she had actually provided bills to the amount of one thousand six hundred pounds, which she would have given Foote but for the Rev. Mr. Jackson, who, being asked his opinion of the demand of Foote, returned this answer: ' Instead of complying with it, your grace should obtain complete evidence of the menace and demand, and then consult your counsel whether a prosecution will not lie for endeavouring to extort money by threats. Your grace must remember the attack on the first Duke of Marlborough, whom a stranger, who had formed a design either on his purse or his interest, endeavoured to menace into a compliance.'

This answer struck the Earl of Peterborough and Mr. Foster very forcibly, as in perfect coincidence with their own opinions. Mr. Jackson was then solicited to wait on Mr. Foote; Mr. Foster, the chaplain of the duchess, professing himself to be too far advanced in years to enter into the field of literary combat. Mr. Jackson consented to be the champion on the following condition, that the duchess would give her honour never to retract her determination, nor to let Foote extort from her a single guinea. Her grace subscribing to this condition, Mr. Jackson waited on Mr. Foote at his house in Suffolk Street, to whom he intimated the resolution of the duchess.

Foote, however, still wished to have matters compromised. To this end he addressed a letter to the duchess, which began with stating ' that a member of the privy council and a friend of her grace (by whom he meant the Duke of Newcastle) had conversed with him on the subject of the dispute between them; and that, for himself, he was ready to have every thing adjusted.' This letter afforded the duchess a triumph. There was a concession in every line. She sent for Mr. Jackson; thanked him ten thousand times for his interference; and declared that he had saved her one thousand six hundred pounds. She showed him the letter which she had received from Foote, and desired him, in her name, to answer it, and publish both. This he declined, alleging that a newspaper controversy would degrade her. She, however, thought otherwise. Foote's letter, her grace's answer, and the rejoinder of the wit, appeared. In the latter Foote compared the duchess to the weeping widow renowned in ancient story, converting her weeds into canonicals for Mr. Jackson, and applied the following line, as applicable to her supposed amorous condition :—

' So mourned the dame of Ephesus her love.'

This farce served to turn, for a time, the current of attention into a different channel: but it becoming necessary, in the progress of events, to adopt some serious measures, either to evade or meet the pending prosecution, the duchess openly affected an earnest desire to have the trial, if possible, accelerated. Secretly, however, she was employed in trying every stratagem which art could devise to elude the measures taken against her. A very favourable opportunity offered, which, had she embraced it, her purpose would have been accomplished. It became a matter of debate in the House of Peers whether the trial of her grace should or should not be carried on in Westminster Hall. The expense to be incurred by the nation was, by several peers, considered as introducing a burden wholly unnecessary. Lord Mansfield endeavoured to avail himself of this objection in favour of the duchess, whom it was his private wish to have saved from the exposure of a trial, and the ignominy of what he well knew must follow, a conviction. Here then was the critical instant in which the duchess might have extricated herself. A hint was privately conveyed to her that the sum of ten thousand pounds would satisfy every expectation, and put an end to the prosecution. This hint was improved into an authoritative proposal. The duchess was entreated by her friends to embrace the measure; but through a fatal confidence, either in her legal advisers, her own machinations, or in both, she refused the proposal with an air of insult. This was folly in the extreme; and yet it was deserving pity, because it was folly misguided. Under every assurance of safety, the duchess assumed an air of indifference about the business, which but ill accorded with her situation. She talked of the absolute necessity of setting out for Rome; affected to have some material business to transact with the Pope; and took, in consequence, every measure in her power to accelerate the trial, as if the regular pace of justice were not swift enough to overtake her. She did not, however, abandon her manœuvring. On the contrary, at the moment in which she had claimed her privilege as a peeress, and petitioned for a speedy trial, she was busied in a scheme to get rid of the principal evidence, Mrs. Cradock, and prevail on her to quit the kingdom. A near relation of this woman was a deliverer of penny-post letters. He was spoken to, and he engaged to let the duchess have an interview with Mrs. Cradock; but her grace was to be disguised, and to reveal herself only after some conversation. The stratagem was adopted: the duchess changed her sex in appearance, and waited at the appointed hour and place without seeing either Mrs. Cradock or the person who had promised to effect the meeting. The fact was, that every particular of this business had been communicated to the prosecutors, who instructed the letter-carrier to pretend an acquiescence in the scheme.

Thus baffled in a project which had a plausible appearance of success, the only method left was the best possible arrangement of matters preparatory to the trial. On the 15th day of April, 1776, the business came on in Westminster-hall, when the queen was present, accompanied by the Prince of Wales, princess-royal, and others of the royal family. Many foreign ambassadors were also present, as well as several of the nobility. These having taken their seats, the duchess came forward, attended by Mrs. Egerton, Mrs. Barrington, and Miss Chudleigh, three of the ladies of her bedchamber, and her chaplain, physician, and apothecary; and as she approached the bar she made three reverences, and then dropped on her knees, when the lord high steward said, ' Madam, you may rise.' Having risen, she courtesied to the lord high steward and the house of peers, and her compliments were returned.

Proclamation being made for silence, the lord high steward mentioned to the prisoner the fatal consequences attending the crime of which she stood indicted, signifying that, however alarming and awful her present circumstances, she might derive great consolation from considering that she was to be tried by the most liberal, candid, and august assembly in the universe.

The duchess then read a paper, setting forth that she was guiltless of the offence alleged against her, and that the agitation of her mind arose, not from the consciousness of guilt, but from the painful circumstance of being called before so awful a tribunal on a criminal accusation; begging, therefore, that, if she was deficient in the observance of any ceremonial points, her failure might not be understood as proceeding from wilful disrespect, but be attributed to the unfortunate peculiarity of her situation. It was added, in the paper, that she had travelled from Rome in so dangerous a state of health, that it was necessary for her to be conveyed in a litter; and that she was perfectly satisfied that she should have a fair trial, since the determination respecting her cause, on which materially depended her honour and fortune, would proceed from the most unprejudiced and august assembly in the world.

The lord high steward desired the lady to give attention while she was arraigned on an indictment for bigamy. Proclamation for silence being made, the duchess (who had been permitted to sit) arose, and read a paper, representing to the Court that she was advised by her counsel to plead the sentence of the ecclesiastical court in the year 1769 as a bar to her being tried on the present indictment. The lord high steward informed her that she must plead to the indictment; in consequence of which she was arraigned; and, being asked by the clerk of the crown whether she was guilty of the felony with which she stood charged, she answered, with great firmness, 'Not guilty, my lords.' The clerk of the crown then asking her how she would be tried, she said, 'By God and her peers;' on which the clerk said, 'God send your ladyship a good deliverance.'

Four days were occupied in arguments of counsel respecting the admission or rejection of a sentence of the spiritual court, which being decided in the negative, the trial proceeded. The first witness was Anne Cradock, who deposed as follows:—

'I have known her grace the Duchess of Kingston ever since the year 1742, at which time she came on a visit to Mr. Merrill's, at Lainston, in Hampshire, during the Winchester races. At that time I lived in the family of Mrs. Hanmer, Miss Chudleigh's aunt, who was then on a visit at Mr. Merrill's, where Mr. Hervey and Miss Chudleigh first met, and soon conceived a mutual attachment towards each other. They were privately married one evening, about eleven o'clock, in Launceston church, in the presence of Mr. Mountney, Mrs. Hanmer, the Reverend Mr. Ames, the rector, who performed the ceremony, and myself. I was ordered out of the church to entice Mr. Merrill's servants out of the way. I saw the bride and bridegroom put to bed together, and Mrs. Hanmer obliged them to rise again: they went to bed together the night following. In a few days Mr. Hervey was under the necessity of going to Portsmouth, in order to embark on board Sir John Danvers's fleet, in which he was a lieutenant; and, being ordered to call him at five o'clock in the morning, I went into the bedchamber at the appointed hour, and found him and his lady sleeping in bed together, and was unwilling to disturb them, thinking the delay of an hour or two would not be of any consequence. My husband, to whom I was not married till after the time I have mentioned, accompanied Mr. Hervey in the capacity of his servant. When Mr. Hervey returned from the Mediterranean, his lady and he lived together. I then thought her in a state of pregnancy. Some months after Mr. Hervey went again to sea; and, during his absence, I was informed that the lady was brought to bed. She herself told me she had a little boy at nurse, and that his features greatly resembled those of Mr. Hervey.'

The Duke of Grafton asked the witness whether she had seen the child; and she answered in the negative. His grace also asked, whether, as the ceremony was performed at night, there were any lights in the church? In answer to which she said Mr. Mountney had a wax light fixed to the crown of his hat. In reply to questions proposed by Lord Hillsborough, the witness acknowledged that she had received a letter from Mr. Fossard, of Piccadilly, containing a promise of a sinecure place on condition of her appearing to give evidence against the lady at the bar; and expressing that, if she thought proper, she might show the letter to Mr. Hervey.

On Saturday, the 20th of April, Anne Cradock was further examined. The Lords Derby, Hillsborough, Buckingamshire, and others, questioning her whether she had not been promised a reward by the prosecutor on condition of her giving evidence to convict the prisoner, her answers were evasive; but she was at length brought to acknowledge that pecuniary offers had been made to induce her to give evidence in support of the prosecution.

Mrs. Sophia Pettiplace, sister to Lord Howe, was next examined; but her evidence was of no consequence. She lived with her grace at the time when her supposed marriage took place with Mr. Hervey, but was not present at the ceremony; and she only believed that the duchess had mentioned the circumstance to her.

Cæsar Hawkins, Esq. deposed that he had been acquainted with the duchess several years, he believed not less than thirty. He had heard of a marriage between Mr. Hervey and the lady at the bar, which circumstance was afterwards mentioned to him by both parties, previous to Mr. Hervey's last going to sea. By the desire of her grace he was in the room when the issue of the marriage was born, and once saw the child. He was sent for by Mr. Hervey soon after his return from sea, and desired by him to wait upon the lady, with proposals for procuring a divorce, which he accordingly did; when her grace declared herself absolutely determined against listening to such terms; and he knew that many messages passed on the subject. Her grace some time after informed him, at his own house, that she had instituted a jactitation suit against Mr. Hervey in Doctors' Commons. On another visit she appeared very grave, and, desiring him to retire into another apartment, said she was exceedingly unhappy in consequence of an oath, which she had long dreaded, having been tendered to her at Doctors' Commons, to disavow her marriage, which she would not do for ten thousand worlds. Upon another visit, a short time after, she informed him that a sentence had passed in her favour at Doctors' Commons, which would be irrevocable, unless Mr. Hervey pursued certain measures within a limited time, which she did not apprehend he would do. Hereupon he inquired how she got over the oath; and her reply was, that the circumstance of her marriage was so blended with falsities, that she could easily reconcile the matter to her conscience; since the ceremony was a business of so scrambling and shabby a nature, that she could as safely swear she was *not* as that she *was* married.

Judith Philips, being called, swore that she was the widow of the Reverend Mr. Ames; that she remembered when her late husband performed the marriage ceremony between Mr. Hervey and the prisoner; that she was not present, but derived her information from her husband; that, some time after the marriage, the lady desired her to prevail upon her husband to grant a certificate, which she said she believed her husband would not refuse; that Mr. Merrill, who accompanied the lady, advised her to consult his attorney from Worcester; that, in compliance with the attorney's advice, a register-book was purchased, and the marriage inserted therein, with some late burials in the parish. The book was here produced, and the witness swore to the writing of her late husband.

The writing of the Reverend Mr. Ames was proved by the Reverend Mr. Inchin and the Reverend Mr. Dennis; and the entry of a caveat to the duke's will was proved by a clerk from Doctors' Commons. The book, in which the marriage of the Duke of Kingston with the lady at the bar was registered on the 8th of March, 1769, was produced by the Reverend Mr. Trebeck, of St. Margaret's, Westminster; and the Reverend Mr. Samuel Harpur, of the Museum, swore that he performed the marriage ceremony between the parties on the day mentioned in the book produced by Mr. Trebeck.

Monday, the 22d of April, after the attorney-general had declared the evidence on behalf of the prosecution to be concluded, the lord high steward called upon the prisoner for her defence, which she read; and the following are the most material arguments it contained to invalidate the evidence adduced by the prosecutor:—She appealed to the Searcher of all hearts, that she never considered herself as legally married to Mr. Hervey; she said that she considered herself as a single woman, and as such was addressed by the late Duke of Kingston; that, influenced by a legitimate attachment to his grace, she instituted a suit in the ecclesiastical court, where her supposed marriage with Mr. Hervey was declared null and void; but, anxious for every conscientious as well as legal sanction, she submitted an authentic state of her case to the Archbishop of Canterbury, who, in the most decisive and unreserved manner, declared that she was at liberty to marry, and afterwards granted, and delivered to Dr. Collier, a special license for her marriage with the late Duke of Kingston. She said that, on her marriage, she experienced every mark of gracious esteem from their majesties, and her late royal mistress, the Princess Dowager of Wales, and was publicly recognised as Duchess of Kingston. Under such respectable sanctions, and virtuous motives for the conduct she pursued, strengthened by a decision that had been esteemed conclusive and irrevocable for the space of seven centuries, if their lordships should deem her guilty, on any rigid principle of law, she hoped, nay, she was conscious, they would attribute her failure as proceeding from a mistaken judgment and erroneous advice, and not censure her for intentional guilt.

She bestowed the highest encomiums on the deceased duke, and solemnly assured the Court that she had in no one instance abused her ascendency over him; and that, so far from endeavouring to engross his possessions, she had declared herself amply provided for by that fortune for life which he was extremely anxious to bequeath in perpetuity. As to the neglect of the duke's eldest nephew, she said it was entirely the consequence of his disrespectful behaviour to her; and she was not dissatisfied at a preference to another nephew, whose respect and attention to her had been such as the duke judged to be her due on her advancement to the honour of being the wife of his grace.

The lord high steward desired Mr. Wallace to proceed with the evidence. The advocate stated the nature of the evidence he meant to produce to prove that Anne Cradock had asserted to different people that she had no recollection of the marriage between Mr. Hervey and the lady at the bar; and that she placed a reliance on a promise of having a provision made for her in consequence of the evidence she was to give on the present trial: and, to invalidate the depositions of Judith Philips, he ordered the clerk to read a letter, wherein she supplicated her grace to exert her influence to prevent her husband's discharge from the duke's service; and observed, that Mrs. Philips had, on the preceding day, swore that her husband was not dismissed, but voluntarily quitted his station in the household of his grace.

Mr. Wallace called Mr. Berkley, Lord Bristol's attorney, who said his lordship told him he was desirous of obtaining a divorce, and directed him to Anne Cradock, saying she was the only person then living who was present at his marriage; and that, a short time previous to the commencement of the jactitation suit, he waited upon Anne Cradock, who informed him that her memory was bad, and that she could remember nothing perfectly in relation to the marriage, which must have been a long time before.

Anne Pritchard deposed that about three months had elapsed since being informed by Mrs. Cradock that she expected to be provided for soon after the trial, and of being enabled to procure a place in the custom-house for one of her relations.

The lord high steward addressed himself to the Court; saying, that their lordships had heard the evidence on both sides, and that the importance and solemnity of the occasion required that they should severally pronounce their opinions in the absence of the prisoner, observing that the junior baron was to speak first.—Their lordships declared the prisoner to be guilty.

Proclamation being made for the usher of the black rod to bring the prisoner to the bar, she no sooner appeared than the lord high steward informed her that the lords had maturely considered the evidence adduced against her, and likewise all that had been advanced in her favour, and had pronounced her guilty of the felony for which she was indicted. He then requested whether she had any thing to urge against judgment being pronounced. Hereupon the lady delivered a paper, containing the following words, to be read by the clerk:—

'I plead the privilege of the peerage.'

After this the lord high steward informed her grace

that the lords had considered the plea, and agreed to allow it; adding words to this effect: 'Madam, you will be discharged on paying the usual fees.'

The lady appeared to be perfectly composed and collected during the greatest part of her long and important trial; but when sentence was pronounced she fainted, and was carried out of court.

Sentence was pronounced upon Elizabeth, Duchess of Kingston, on Monday, the 22d of April, 1776.

The solemn business being concluded, the prosecutors had a plan in embryo to confine the Countess of Bristol (for so, after conviction, she in reality was) to this country, and to have her deprived of her personal property. A writ of ' *Ne exeat regno* ' was preparing, of which the lady received private notice; and, being advised instantaneously to leave the kingdom, she caused her carriage to be driven about the most public streets of the metropolis, and invited a select party to dine at Kingston House, the better to cover her design, while in a hired post-chaise she travelled to Dover. Mr. Harding, the captain of her yacht, was there, and he conveyed her, in the first open boat that could be obtained, to Calais.

During her absence some incidents had happened at Rome, of which she received advice, and which rendered it necessary for her once more to visit that renowned city. In the public bank she had deposited her plate for safety when she set out for England; and in her palace she had left a Spanish friar, and an English girl, whom she had carried with her to Italy. The friar found means to seduce the girl, and to convert great part of the moveables to his own advantage, after which he absconded.

Of these transactions the duchess was informed by letter, on the receipt of which she set out for Rome, and, having withdrawn her plate out of the public bank, she returned to Calais.

The expeditious communication between that place

and England afforded the earliest intelligence relative to the proceedings of her opponents. Their business was now to set aside, if possible, the will of the Duke of Kingston. There was not a probability of their succeeding in the attempt; but still the attempt was to be made. This kept alive the apprehension of danger in the mind of the duchess: and, so long as that apprehension subsisted, it was necessary, in policy, to affect a particular regard for certain persons in England, who had the power of rendering her a service. Among these was Dr. Schomberg, who, in return for the zeal he manifested in her cause, was presented in her name with a ring, brilliantly encircled, the stone a deep blue, and upon it the words *'Pour l'Amitié.'* The intrinsic value was never once considered by Schomberg; it was the presumable tribute of gratitude which affected the mind. He wore the ring, and almost in every company he proclaimed the donor. But a short portion of time elapsed before one of the encircling brilliants fell out, and then he discovered it to be a mere bauble, which did not originally cost more than six-and-thirty shillings. The indignant Doctor threw it out of the window.

The will of his grace of Kingston receiving every confirmation which the courts of justice could give, to dissipate, rather than expend, the income of his estates, appeared to be the leading rule of her life. A house which she had purchased at Calais was not sufficient for the purpose of perplexities; a mansion at Mont Martre, near Paris, was fixed on, and the purchase of it negotiated in as short a time as the duchess could desire. There were only a few obstacles to enjoyment, which were not considered until the purchase was completed. The house was in so ruinous a condition as to be in momentary danger of falling. The land was more like the field of the slothful than the vineyard of the industrious. These evils were not perceived by the duchess till she was in possession of her wishes. A lawsuit with the owner of the estate was the consequence of the agreement. The duchess went to Petersburgh, and returned to France before it was finished. The manner in which this suit was decided proved the ultimate cause of her death.

Besides this trivial purchase, another was made by the duchess, the scale of which was truly grand. The brother of the then French monarch was the owner of a domain, according in every respect with his dignity. This was the territory of St. Assize, at a pleasant distance from Paris, abounding in game of different species, and rich in all the luxuriant embellishments of nature. The mansion was fit for the brother of a king; it contained three hundred beds. The value of such an estate was too considerable to be expected in one payment: she therefore agreed to discharge the whole of the sum demanded, which was fifty-five thousand pounds, by instalments. The purchase on the part of the duchess was a good one. It afforded not only game, but rabbits in plenty; and, finding them to be of superior quality and flavour, the duchess, during the first week of her possession, had as many killed and sold as brought her three hundred guineas. At Petersburgh she had been a distiller of brandy; and now at Paris she turned rabbit-merchant.

Such was her situation, when one day, while she was at dinner, her servants received the intelligence that judgment respecting the house near Paris had been awarded against her. The sudden communication of the news produced an agitation of her whole frame. She flew into a violent passion, and burst an internal blood-vessel : even this, however, she appeared to have surmounted, until a few days afterwards, when preparing to rise from her bed, a servant, who had long been with her, endeavoured to dissuade her from it. The duchess addressed her thus : 'I am not very well, but I will rise.' On a remonstrance being attempted, she said, 'At your peril disobey me : I will get up and walk about the room; ring for the secretary to assist me.' She was obeyed, dressed, and the secretary entered the chamber.—The duchess then walked about, complained of thirst, and said, ' I could drink a glass of my fine Madeira, and eat a slice of toasted bread. I shall be quite well afterwards; but let it be a large glass of wine.' The attendant reluctantly brought, and the duchess drank, the wine. She then said, ' I am perfectly recovered; I knew the Madeira would do me good. My heart feels oddly. I will have another glass.' The servant here observed that such a quantity of wine in the morning might intoxicate rather than benefit. The duchess persisted in her orders, and, the second glass of Madeira being produced, she drank that also, and pronounced herself to be charmingly indeed. She then walked a little about the room, and afterwards said, ' I will lie down on the couch; I can sleep, and after that I shall be entirely recovered.' She seated herself in the couch, a female having hold of each hand. In this situation she soon appeared to have fallen into a sound sleep, until the women felt her hands colder than ordinary, and the duchess was found to have expired, as the wearied labourer sinks into the arms of rest. She died August 26, 1796.

THE REVEREND JAMES HACKMAN,

EXECUTED FOR MURDER.

THIS shocking and truly lamentable case interested all ranks of people, who pitied the murderer's fate, conceiving him stimulated to commit the horrid crime through love and madness. Pamphlets and poems were written on the occasion, and the crime was long the common topic of conversation.

The object of Mr. Hackman's love renders his case still more singular.

Miss Reay had been the mistress of Lord Sandwich

near twenty years, was the mother of nine children, and nearly double the age of Mr. Hackman.

This murder affords a melancholy proof that there is no act so contrary to reason that men will not commit when under the dominion of their passions. In short, it is impossible to convey an idea of the impression it made; and the manner in which it was done created horror and pity in every feeling mind.

Mr. Hackman shooting Miss Reay and attempting Suicide.

The Rev. James Hackman was born at Gosport, in Hampshire, and originally designed for trade; but he was too volatile in disposition to submit to the drudgery of the shop or counting-house. His parents, willing to promote his interest as far as lay in their power, purchased him an ensign's commission in the 68th regiment of foot. He had not been long in the army when he was sent to command a recruiting party; and, being at Huntingdon, he was frequently invited to dine with Lord Sandwich, who had a seat in that neighbourhood. Here it was that he first became acquainted with Miss Reay, who lived under the protection of that nobleman.

This lady was the daughter of a staymaker in Covent Garden, and served her apprenticeship to a mantua-maker in George's Court, St. John's Lane, Clerkenwell. She was bound when only thirteen; and, during her apprenticeship, was taken notice of by the nobleman above mentioned, who took her under his protection, and treated her with every mark of tenderness. No sooner had Mr. Hackman seen her than he became enamoured of her, though she had then lived nineteen years with his lordship. Finding he could not obtain preferment in the army, he turned his thoughts to the church, and entered into orders. Soon after he obtained the living of Wiverton, in Norfolk, which was only about Christmas preceding the shocking deed which cost him his life; so that it may be said he never enjoyed it.

It is probable that Mr. Hackman imagined that there was a mutual passion—that Miss Reay had the same regard for him as he had for her. Love and madness are often little better than synonymous terms; for, had Mr. Hackman not been blinded by a bewitching passion, he could never have imagined that Miss Reay would have left the family of a noble lord at the head of one of the highest departments of the state, in order to live in an humble station. Those who have been long accustomed to affluence, and even profusion, seldom choose to lower their flags. However, he was still tormented by this unhappy, irregular, and ungovernable passion, which, in an unhappy moment, led him to commit the crime for which he suffered.

Miss Reay was extremely fond of music, and, as her noble protector was in a high rank, we need not be surprised to find that frequent concerts were performed both in London and at Hinchinbrook: at the latter place Mr. Hackman was generally of the party, and his attention to her at those times was very great. How long he had been in London previous to this affair is not certainly known, but at that time he lodged in Duke's Court, St. Martin's Lane. On the morning of the 7th of April, 1779, he sat some time in his closet, reading ' Blair's Sermons; ' but in the evening he took a walk to the Admiralty, where he saw Miss Reay go into the coach along with Signora Galli, who attended her. The coach drove to Covent Garden Theatre, where she staid to see the performance of ' Love in a Village.' Mr. Hackman went into the theatre at the same time; but, not being able to contain the violence of his passion, returned, and again went to his lodgings, and, having loaded two pistols, went to the playhouse, where he waited till the play was over. Seeing Miss Reay ready to step into the coach, he took a pistol in each hand, one of which he discharged against her, which killed her on the spot, and the other at himself, which, however, did not take effect.

He then beat himself with the butt end on his head, in order to destroy himself, so fully bent was he on the destruction of both. After some struggle he was secured, his wounds dressed, and then he was carried before Sir John Fielding, who committed him to Tothillfields' Bridewell, and next to Newgate, where a person was appointed to attend him, lest he should lay violent hands on himself. In Newgate, as he knew he had no favour to expect, he prepared himself for the awful change he was about to make. He had dined with his sister on the day the murder was committed; and, in the afternoon, wrote a letter to her husband, Mr. Booth, an eminent attorney, acquainting him of his resolution of destroying himself, desiring him to sell what effects he should leave behind him, to pay a small debt; but this letter was not sent, for it was found in his pocket.

On the trial Mr. Macnamara deposed that, on

Wednesday, the 7th day of April, on seeing Miss Reay, with whom he had some little acquaintance, in some difficulties in getting from the playhouse, he offered his assistance to hand her to her coach; and just as they were in the Piazzas, very near the carriage, he heard the report of a pistol, and felt an impression on his right arm, which arm she held with her left, and instantly dropped. He thought at first that the pistol had been fired through wantonness, and that she had fallen from the fright, and therefore fell upon his knees to help her up; but, finding his hands bloody, he then conceived an idea of what had happened, and, by the assistance of a link-boy, got the deceased into the Shakspeare Tavern, where he first saw the prisoner, after he was secured. He asked him some questions relative to the fact and the cause; and his answer was, that neither the time nor place were proper to resolve him. He asked his name, and was told Hackman: he knew a Mr. Booth, in Craven Street, and desired he might be sent for.

He asked to see the lady; to which he (the witness) objected, and had her removed to a private room. From the impression he felt, and the great quantity of blood about him, he grew sick, and went home; and knew nothing more about it.

Mary Anderson, a fruit-woman, deposed that, just as the play was over, she saw two ladies and a gentleman coming out of the playhouse, and a gentleman in black following them. Lord Sandwich's coach was called. When the carriage came up the gentleman handed the other lady into it. The lady that was shot stood behind, when the gentleman in black came up, laid hold of her gown, and pulled two pistols out of his pocket: the one in his right hand he discharged at the lady, and the other, in his left, he discharged at himself. They fell feet to feet. He beat himself violently over the head with his pistol, and desired somebody would kill him.

Richard Blandy, the constable, swore to the finding two letters in the prisoner's pocket, which he delivered to Mr. Campbell, the master of the Shakspeare Tavern, in Covent Garden.

Mr. Mahon, an apothecary, corroborated the evidence of the fruit-woman: he wrenched the pistol out of his hand, with which he was beating himself, as he lay on the ground—took him to his house, dressed his wounds, and accompanied him to the Shakspeare.

Denis O'Brian, a surgeon, examined the wound of the deceased, and found it mortal.

Being called upon for his defence, he addressed the Court in the following words:—

'I should not have troubled the Court with the examination of witnesses to support the charge against me, had I not thought that the pleading guilty to the indictment gave an indication of contemning death, not suitable to my present condition, and was, in some measure, being accessory to a second peril of my life; and I likewise thought that the justice of my country ought to be satisfied by suffering my offence to be proved, and the fact established by evidence.

'I stand here this day the most wretched of human beings, and confess myself criminal in a high degree; yet while I acknowledge, with shame and repentance, that my determination against my own life was formal and complete, I protest, with that regard to truth which becomes my situation, that the will to destroy her, who was ever dearer to me than life, was never mine till a momentary frenzy overcame me, and induced me to commit the deed I now deplore. The letter, which I meant for my brother-in-law after my decease, will have its due weight, as to this point, with good men.

'Before this dreadful act, I trust nothing will be found in the tenor of my life which the common charity of mankind will not excuse. I have no wish to avoid the punishment which the laws of my country

310

appoint for my crime; but, being already too unhappy to feel a punishment in death or a satisfaction in life, I submit myself with penitence and patience to the disposal and judgment of Almighty God, and to the consequences of this inquiry into my conduct and intention.'

Then was read the following letter:—

'My dear Frederic,—When this reaches you I shall be no more; but do not let my unhappy fate distress you too much: I have strove against it as long as possible, but it now overpowers me. You well know where my affections were placed: my having by some means or other lost hers (an idea which I could not support) has driven me to madness. The world will condemn me, but your good heart will pity me. God bless you, my dear Frederic! Would I had a sum to leave you, to convince you of my great regard! You was my only friend. I have hid one circumstance from you, which gives me great pain. I owe Mr. Knight, of Gosport, one hundred pounds, for which he has the writings of my houses; but I hope in God, when they are sold, and all other matters collected, there will be nearly enough to settle our account. May Almighty God bless you and yours with comfort and happiness; and may you ever be a stranger to the pangs I now feel! May Heaven protect my beloved woman, and forgive this act, which alone could relieve me from a world of misery I have long endured! Oh! if it should ever be in your power to do her an act of friendship, remember your faithful friend,

'J. HACKMAN.'

The jury immediately returned their fatal verdict. The unhappy man heard the sentence pronounced against him with calm resignation to his fate, and employed the very short time allowed murderers after conviction in repentance and prayer.

During the procession to the fatal tree at Tyburn he seemed much affected, and said but little; and when he arrived at Tyburn, and got out of the coach and mounted the cart, he took leave of Dr. Porter and the Ordinary.

After some time spent in prayer, he was turned off, on April the 19th, 1779; and, having hung the usual time, his body was carried to Surgeons' Hall for dissection.

Such was the end of a young gentleman who might have been an ornament to his country, the delight of his friends, and a comfort to his relations, had he not been led way by the influence of an unhappy passion.

RENWICK WILLIAMS, COMMONLY CALLED 'THE MONSTER,'

CONVICTED OF A BRUTAL AND WANTON ASSAULT ON MISS ANNE PORTER.

SEVERAL months previous to the apprehension of this man, a report ran through all ranks of society that young females had been secretly wounded in different parts of their bodies, in the public streets, and often in the day-time, by a monster, who, upon committing the brutal crime, effected his escape.

Sometimes, as reported, the villain presented a nosegay to a young female, wherein was concealed a sharp instrument; and, as he offered them the flowers to smell, stabbed them in the face. Other tales were told, of some being stabbed in the thigh, and behind; in fine, there was universal terror in the female world in London.

At length a man named Renwick Williams was apprehended on the charge of one of the young ladies thus brutally wounded, and his trial came on at the Old Bailey, on the 18th of July, 1790.

The indictment charged, that with force and arms, in the parish of St. James, on the king's highway,

Renwick Williams did, unlawfully, wilfully, and maliciously, make an assault upon, maim, and wound, Anne Porter, against the peace, &c. A second count charged the said Renwick Williams, that, on the same day and year, he did unlawfully, wilfully, and maliciously, tear, spoil, cut, and deface, the garments and clothes—to wit, the cloak, gown, petticoat, and shift,

Renwick Williams stabbing Miss Porter.

of the said Anne Porter, contrary to the statute, and against the peace, &c.

Miss Anne Porter deposed that she had been at St. James's, to see the ball, on the night of the 18th of January, 1790, accompanied by her sister, Miss Sarah Porter, and another lady; that her father had appointed to meet them at twelve o'clock, the hour the ball generally breaks up; but that it ended at eleven, and she was therefore under the necessity either of staying where she was, until her father came, or to return home at that time. Her father, she said, lived in St. James's Street, and that he kept a tavern and a cold bath. She agreed to go home with her party.

As they proceeded up St. James's Street her sister appeared much agitated, and called to her to hasten home, which she and her company accordingly did. Her sister was the first to reach the hall door. As the witness turned the corner of the rails, she received a blow on the right hip; she turned round, and saw the prisoner stoop down: she had seen him before several times, on each of which he had followed close behind her, and used language so gross, that the Court did not press on her to relate the particulars.

He did not immediately run away when he struck her, but looked on her face, and she thus had a perfect opportunity of observing him. She had no doubt, she said, of the prisoner being the man that wounded her. She supposed that the wound was inflicted with a sharp instrument, because her clothes were cut, and she was wounded through them.

Miss Porter farther deposed that on the 13th of June last she was walking in St. James's Park, with her mother and her two sisters, and a gentleman of the name of Coleman. The prisoner at the bar met and passed her; she was struck with his person, and knew him; she found he had turned to look after her. Upon appearing agitated, she was questioned, and pointed him out to Mr. Coleman. She said she knew him when he was brought up to the public office at Bow Street.

Her gown, of pink silk, and her shift, which she wore the night she was wounded, were produced in court, and were cut on the right side, a considerable length.

Miss Sarah Porter was next called. She swore that she had seen the prisoner at the bar prior to the 18th of June last, but had no acquaintance with him. He had followed her, and talked to her in language the most shocking and obscene. She had seen him four

314

or five different times. On that night, when her sister was cut, she saw him standing near the bottom of St. James's Street, and, spying her, he exclaimed, ' O ho! are you there?' and immediately struck her a violent blow on the side of the head. She then, as well as she was able, being almost stunned, called to her sister to make haste, adding, ' Don't you see the wretch behind us?' Upon coming to their own door, the prisoner rushed between them, and about the time he struck her sister he also rent the witness's gown. There were lights in the street, and she knew him.

Two more sisters, Miss Rebecca Porter and Miss Martha Porter, also bore unequivocal testimony as to the identity of the prisoner, with respect to his having accosted them, in company with their sisters, with the most obscene and indecent language.*

Mr. John Coleman was the next witness called. He swore that he was walking with Miss Anne Porter, and the rest of her family, in St. James's Park, on the evening of Sunday, the 13th of June, 1790. That, upon observing Miss Porter much agitated, and inquiring the cause, she pointed out the prisoner at the bar, and said ' the wretch had just passed her.' Having pointed him out, the witness followed him to the house of Mr. Smith, in South Moulton Street, and, upon going into the parlour where he was, expressed his surprise on the prisoner's not resenting the insults he (the witness) had offered him; and demanded his address. Mr. Smith and the prisoner both expressed their surprise at such a demand, without a reason given; he therefore said, that he, the prisoner, had insulted some ladies, who had pointed him out, and

* This is a practice among a set of scoundrels of the present day, in the public streets, wherever they find a modest, well-dressed, unprotected female. They not only whisper the most abominable bawdry in her chaste ear, but often pinch her on the side or behind, so as to put her in both bodily and mental pain. Such rascals ought to be whipped at the cart's tail through every street in London.

that he must have satisfaction. The prisoner denied having offered any insult; but, upon his persisting, they exchanged addresses.

The prisoner's address was produced by the witness, No. 52, Jermyn Street. The witness and the prisoner then mutually recognised each other, as having been in company with each other before, and the witness then departed. On his departure he repented having quitted him, and, turning back, he met with him at the top of St. James's Street: he then accosted him again, saying ' I don't think you are the person I took you for; you had better come with me now, and let the ladies see you.' The prisoner objected, as it was late at night; but, upon his saying it was close by, he went with him.

On his being introduced into the parlour, where the Miss Porters were sitting, two of them, Anne and Sarah, fainted away, exclaiming, ' Oh! my God! that's the wretch!' The prisoner then said, ' The ladies' behaviour is odd; they don't take me for the monster that is advertised?' The witness said they did.

The prisoner was there an hour before he was taken away, and in that time said nothing particular.

Mr. Tomkins, surgeon, was next called. By his description the wound must have been made by a very sharp instrument. He had also examined the clothes, and they must have been cut at the same time. The wound itself was, at the beginning, for two or three inches, but skin-deep; about the middle of it, three or four inches deep, and gradually decreasing in depth towards the end. The length of the wound, from the hip downwards, was nine or ten inches.

The prisoner, being called upon for his defence, begged the indulgence of the Court, in supplying the deficiency of his memory, upon what he wished to state, from a written paper. He accordingly read as follows :—

' He stood,' he said, ' an object equally demanding

the attention and compassion of the Court. That, conscious of his innocence, he was ready to admit the justice of whatever sufferings he had hitherto undergone, arising from suspicion. He had the greatest confidence in the justice and liberality of an English jury, and hoped they would not suffer his fate to be decided by the popular prejudice raised against him. The hope of proving his innocence had hitherto sustained him.

' He professed himself the warm friend and admirer of that sex whose cause was now asserted, and concluded with solemnly declaring that the whole prosecution was founded on a dreadful mistake, which, he had no doubt, the evidence he was about to call would clear up to the satisfaction of the Court.'

His counsel then proceeded to call his witnesses.

Mr. Mitchell, the first evidence, was an artificial flower-maker, living in Dover Street, Piccadilly. The prisoner had worked for him nine months in all; he had worked with him on the 18th of January, the queen's birth-day, the day on which Miss Porter had been wounded, from nine o'clock in the morning till one o'clock in the day, and from half past two till twelve at night: he had then supped with the family. He gave the prisoner a good character, as behaving with good nature to the women in the house.

Miss Mitchell, the witness's sister, told the same story.

Two other witnesses, domestics in the same house, likewise appeared on behalf of the prisoner; but the whole of the evidence, on his part, proved rather contradictory.

Mr. Justice Buller, with great accuracy and ability, went through the whole of this extraordinary business, stating, with great clearness and perspicuity, the parts of the evidence that were most material for the consideration of the jury, with many excellent observations.

He said it had been stated, in various ways, that great outrages had been committed by the prisoner at the bar, and therefore, in his defence, he had, very properly, not only applied to the compassion of the jury, to guard against the effects of prejudice, but also to their judgment. It was very proper to do so, and in this he only demanded justice: prejudice often injured, though it could never serve, the cause of justice.

In this the jury would have only to consider what were the facts of which they were to be satisfied, and on which it was their province to decide. This being done by them, and if they should find the prisoner guilty upon the present charge, he would reserve his case for the opinion of the twelve judges of England; and this he should do for several reasons: first, because this was completely and perfectly a new case in itself; and, secondly, because this was the first indictment of the kind that was ever tried. Therefore, although he himself entertained but little doubt upon the first point, yet, as the case was new, it would be right to have a solemn decision upon it. So that hereafter the law, in that particular, may be declared from undoubted authority.

Upon the second point he owned that he entertained some doubts. This indictment was certainly the first of the kind that was ever drawn in this kingdom. It was founded upon the statute of the 6th George I. Upon this statute it must be proved that it was the intent of the party accused, not only to wound the body, but also cut, tear, and spoil the garment; (here the learned judge read the clause of the act:)—one part of this charge was quite clear, namely, that Miss Porter was wounded, and her clothes torn. The first question, therefore, for the consideration of the jury would be, whether this was done wilfully, and with intent to spoil the garment, as well as to wound the body. That was a fact for the jury to decide; and, if they agreed upon this, then, whether the prisoner was the man who did it.

He observed that there might be cases in which the clothes were torn, and yet where this act would not apply; such, for instance, as a scuffle in a quarrel, where clothes might be torn wilfully, but not with that malice and previous intent which this act required.

It should be observed, that here there was a wound given, with an instrument that was not calculated solely for the purpose of affecting the body, such, for instance, as piercing or stabbing, by making a hole; but here was an actual cutting, and the wound was of a very considerable length, and so was the rent in the clothes. It was for the jury to decide whether, as both body and clothes were cut, he who intended the end did not also intend the means.

He left it to the jury to say, upon the whole of the case, whether the prisoner was guilty or innocent.

The jury immediately, without hesitation, found the prisoner guilty.

Mr. Justice Buller then ordered the judgment in this case to be arrested, and the recognizances of the persons bound to prosecute to be respited until the December sessions.

The court was crowded with spectators by nine, when this trial began, which ended at five o'clock at night.

All the witnesses were examined separately.

At the commencement of the sessions at the Old Bailey, on the 10th of December, 1790, Judge Ashurst addressed the prisoner nearly in the following terms: ' You have been capitally convicted under the statute 6 George I. of maliciously tearing, cutting, spoiling, and defacing, the garments of Anne Porter, on the 18th of January last. Judgment has been arrested upon two points—one, that the indictment is informal; the other that the act of parliament does not reach the crime. Upon solemn consideration, the judges are of opinion

319

that both the objections are well founded: but, although you are discharged from this indictment, yet you are within the purview of the common law. You are therefore to be remanded, to be tried for a misdemeanour.'

He was accordingly, on the 13th of the same month, tried at Hicks's Hall for the misdemeanour, in making an assault on Miss Anne Porter.

The trial lasted sixteen hours: there were three counts in the indictment; viz. for assaulting with intent to kill, for assaulting and wounding, and for a common assault.

The charge was that he, on the 18th of January, 1790, made an assault on Anne Porter, and, with a certain knife, inflicted on her person a wound nine inches long, and, in the middle part of it, four inches deep.

The same witnesses were then called in support of the charge as appeared on the trial at the Old Bailey: they gave a very clear, correct, and circumstantial evidence, positively swearing to the person of the prisoner.

The facts proved were nearly the same, with very little variation indeed, with those which were given in evidence on his trial for the felony at the Old Bailey; for which reason we forbear to enter more fully on his trial.

The prisoner produced two witnesses, Miss Amet and Mr. Mitchell, who attempted to prove an *alibi*, and the credit of their testimony was not impeached by any contradiction. The question therefore was, to which the jury would give credit; for the evidence on both sides was equally fair and unexceptionable.

The prisoner was again put to the bar at ten o'clock the next morning, and tried on the remaining indictments, on three of which he was found guilty; when the Court sentenced him two years' imprisonment in Newgate for each, and at the expiration of the time to find security for his good behaviour, himself in two hundred pounds, and two sureties in one hundred pounds each.

Thus ended the case of this man, which had greatly interested every rank of people; but all were by no means satisfied of his guilt, believing that the female witnesses, a circumstance which we have shown too frequently to have happened, mistook the man who wounded and ill treated the prosecutrix. The particulars we have given of the uncommon and brutal attack on the defenceless, by a monster of the stronger sex, with our full report of the trial, will sufficiently prepare our readers to judge for themselves on the case of Renwick Williams, divested of the popular prejudice then strong against him.

FREDERIC LORD BALTIMORE, ELIZABETH GRIFFENBURG, AND ANNE HARVEY,

THE FORMER TRIED FOR COMMITTING A RAPE ON SARAH WOODCOCK, AND THE TWO LATTER AS ACCESSORIES BEFORE THE FACT.

THOUGH conviction did not follow the trials of these presumed offenders, it is our duty to state the affair as it was transmitted to the public at the time.

Frederic Lord Baltimore was the lineal descendant of Mr. Calvert, who was promoted to the degree of a peer of Ireland by King James I. from whom he received the grant of an immense tract of land in America, which has since borne the name of Maryland.

Lord Baltimore's father had a country seat at Epsom, where the object of our present notice was born, and sent for education to Eton School, where he became a great proficient in classical knowledge, and was said to have a singular taste and capacity for the learning and manners of the ancients; and his father dying before he was of age, left him in possession of a most ample fortune.

321

His lordship married the daughter of the Duke of Bridgewater, and was exceedingly unhappy in the nuptial connexion, owing to his unbounded attachment to women. In fact, his passion for the sex was so illiberal and so gross, that his house had the appearance of a Turkish seraglio rather than that of an Englishman of fortune; nor was it reputable for any woman of character to have entered within his walls.

Lord Baltimore, during his residence abroad, sailed

Sarah Woodcock forcibly introduced to Lord Baltimore.

from Naples to Constantinople, where he saw and admired the customs of the Turks; and on his return to England, in 1766, he caused a part of his house to be taken down, and rebuilt in the form of a Turkish harem. He kept a number of women, who had rules given them by which to regulate their conduct; and he had agents, to procure him fresh faces, in different parts of the town.

Elizabeth Griffenburg, wife of Dr. Griffenburg, a native of Germany, and Anne Harvey, a woman of low education, were two of the parties employed by Lord Baltimore in his irregular designs on the sex.

In November, 1767, Mrs. Harvey told his lordship that a young lady named Woodcock, who was very handsome, kept a milliner's shop on Tower Hill. Prompted by curiosity, and a still more ignoble motive, Lord Baltimore went once or twice to the shop, and purchased some trifling articles, by way of making an acquaintance. He then asked her if she would attend him to the play; but this she declined, having never been at a play in her life; and, as she had been bred up among that rigid sect of dissenters called Independents, she had been taught to consider theatrical diversions as incompatible with the duties of Christianity.

Some time afterwards Lord Baltimore went hastily into Miss Woodcock's shop, saying that he had been splashed by mud from a hackney-coach. This was noticed by the young lady, who expressed her surprise that he could be so near the coach as to see, but not avoid it. He answered, 'I was thinking of you, Miss;' but she paid no regard to this compliment, as she considered him as a neighbour, and a married man.

At length Lord Baltimore and his agents had completed the outlines of the ungenerous plan which they had determined, if possible, to carry into execution. Mrs. Harvey, going to Miss Woodcock's shop on the 14th of December, bespoke a pair of laced ruffles, which she desired might be made up against the next day, for the use of a lady, who might be a good customer if she was not disappointed, as she was fond of encouraging persons who were young in trade.

On the following day Mrs. Harvey called and paid for the ruffles, and, having given orders for some other articles, desired that they might be brought to her house in the Curtain Road, near Holywell Mount, Shoreditch, on the succeeding day.

At the time appointed Miss Woodcock went to the house, where Mrs. Harvey received her politely, and desired her to drink tea; but as the days were short, and as she had no friend to attend her, she expressed her wish to decline the invitation. During their conversation one Isaac Isaacs, a Jew, came into the house, and, having paid his respects to Mrs. Harvey, said he was going to the play. Hereupon Mrs. Harvey said ' I was going to attend a lady with some millinery goods;' and then to Isaacs, 'This is the lady I was speaking to you of;' then again to Miss Woodcock, ' I would be glad you would go with me; the lady wants a great many things, and will be a very good customer to you.'

Isaacs now observed, that, as it was necessary for him to have a coach, he could set them both down at the lady's house. This was objected to by Miss Woodcock, on account of her dress; but this objection was overruled by Mrs. Harvey, who said that circumstance could not have any weight with the lady they were about to attend.

At this time Lord Baltimore's coach was waiting in the neighbourhood; and Isaacs, going out under the pretence of calling a coach, gave directions for drawing it to the door. This being done, the parties got into it; but Miss Woodcock did not observe whether it was a hackney-coach or not.

The coachman drove at a great rate; the glasses were drawn up, and at length they arrived in the court-yard of a house, apparently that of a person of fashion. Mrs. Harvey took Miss Woodcock up stairs through a suite of rooms elegantly furnished, in one of which she saw an elderly man sitting, whom she afterwards knew to be Dr. Griffenburg, who politely desired her to repose herself, while he informed the lady of the house of her arrival.

Dr. Griffenburg had not been long absent when Lord Baltimore entered; and Miss Woodcock was much alarmed when she discovered that he was the very person who had repeatedly been at her shop; but he desired her to be appeased, saying that he was steward to the lady on whom she was come to attend. Miss Woodcock desired that she might immediately see the lady; on which Lord Baltimore said he would fetch her; and, soon afterwards bringing in Mrs. Griffenburg, said that she was the lady who had ordered the milinery goods.

Orders were now given for tea; and, when the equipage was taken from the table, Lord Baltimore brought from another room some purses, a ring, some smelling-bottles, and other articles, which he said he had purchased for Miss Woodcock. She seemed to despise the trifles, which she intimated might have pleased her well enough when a child.

As the evening advanced, she seemed importunate to depart, saying that her friends would become uneasy at her long absence; but at this time she had no idea of being forcibly detained.

To divert her from the thought of departing, Lord Baltimore took her to view several apartments in the house. On their coming into one of which, where there was a harpsichord, he proposed to play a tune on that instrument to the young lady; and, when he had so done, and she became still more anxious to depart, he insisted that she should stay to supper, and gave a private intimation to Mrs. Griffenburg to make the necessary preparations.

Mrs. Griffenburg being retired, Lord Baltimore took Miss Woodcock behind the window-curtain, and behaved to her in a manner very inconsistent with the rules of decency. On her making violent opposition to this insult, Dr. Griffenburg and Mrs. Harvey advanced, as if to assist his lordship; but she contested the matter with them all, and, forcing her way towards the door, declared that she would go home immediately: yet still it does not appear that she had any suspicion of sustaining the violence that was afterwards offered her.

After this, Lord Baltimore insisted on her sitting with him at supper; but her mind was too much discomposed to admit of her thinking of taking any refreshment. He offered her a glass of syllabub; but she beat it out of his hand, and ran towards the door, with an intention to have departed: but he told her it was late; that no coach was then to be procured; and at length said positively that she should not go home.

Dr. Griffenburg, with his wife and Mrs. Harvey, now endeavoured to prevail on the young lady to go to bed; but she declared that she would never sleep in that house. On this they conducted her to a room, in which they went to bed: but she continued walking about till the morning, and lamenting her unhappy situation.

Looking out of the window about eight o'clock, she observed a young woman passing, to whom she threw out her handkerchief, which was then heavy with tears. As the party did not see her, she called out ' Young woman! ' on which the other made a motion as if she would fling the handkerchief within the rails.

As Miss Woodcock called to the woman, with an intention of sending her to her father, the two women now jumped out of bed, and forced her from the window, upbraiding her with what they called a rejection of her good fortune, and wishing themselves in so happy a situation.

Her reply was, that all the fortune the man possessed should not prevail on her to think of living with him on dishonourable terms; and she again demanded that liberty to which she had so just a claim.

The women now quitting the room, Lord Baltimore and Dr. Griffenburg came in soon afterwards; when the former said that he was astonished at her outrageous behaviour, as he had promised that she should go home at twelve o'clock. She replied that she would go home directly, as her sister, and particularly her father, would be inexpressibly anxious on occasion of her absence.

Lord Baltimore now conducted her down stairs, and ordered breakfast; but she refused to eat, and wept incessantly till twelve o'clock, when she once more demanded her liberty. His lordship now said that he loved her to excess; that he could not part with her; that he did not intend any injury to her, and that he would write to her father: and on this he wrote a letter, of which the following is a copy; and in it sent a bank-note of two hundred pounds:—

'Your daughter Sally sends you the enclosed, and desires you will not be uneasy on her account, because every thing will turn out well with a little patience and prudence. She is at a friend's house safe and well, in all honesty and honour; nothing else is meant, you may depend on it; and, sir, as your presence and consent are necessary, we beg of you to come, in a private manner, to Mr. Richard Smith's, in Broad Street Buildings.'

Lord Baltimore showed this letter to Miss Woodcock; but so greatly was her mind disturbed, that she knew little of its contents; and so exceedingly was she terrified, that she wrote the following words at the bottom, by his direction: 'Dear father, this is true, and should be glad you would come this afternoon:— From your dutiful daughter.'

After writing the above postscript, she appears to have been convinced of the impropriety of it, and, turning to his lordship, she said 'Can you look me in the face, and say that your name is Richard Smith, or that these are Broad Street Buildings?' Struck with guilt, he acknowledged his name was not Richard Smith, but said that gentleman lived within a few doors; and that the place was not the Broad Street

Buildings in the city, but another of the same name at the west end of the town.

She now wept incessantly at the thought of her unhappy situation, and repeatedly begged for her liberty; but, no sooner did she presume to go towards the window to make her distress evident to any casual passenger, than one or other of the women forced her away.

At length Mrs. Griffenburg gave orders that the window should be nailed up; but Lord Baltimore came in at the juncture, and pretended to be very angry at this proceeding, lest it should be suspected that murder was intended to be committed in the house. His lordship then told Miss Woodcock that if she presumed to pull up the windows, or make any disturbance, he would throw her into the street; a circumstance by which she was greatly terrified.

This happened at the approach of night, and she continued weeping and lamenting her situation, and refused to take any refreshment at supper. When desired to go to bed, she refused to do so, unless Lord Baltimore would solemnly promise not to molest her. On this she spent the night walking about the room, while the two women who were appointed to guard her went to bed.

In the morning she went into a parlour, where Lord Baltimore waiting on her, she endeavoured to represent his ill conduct in the most striking light, and begged that if he had the tenderness of a father for a child he would permit her to depart. He said that she might write to her father, which she did; and, fearful of giving offence, said that she had been treated ' with as much honour as she could expect, and begged her friends would come immediately.' Lord Baltimore was now out of the room; but the women told Miss Woodcock that his lordship had sent two hundred pounds to her father on the preceding day. She seemed amazed at this circumstance, which appears to be a proof of the anxiety of her mind at the time the letter was written.

Soon after this a servant came in with a letter as from the presumed Richard Smith. It was written in a language she did not understand; but Lord Baltimore pretended to explain it to her, saying it intimated that her father had been at Mr. Smith's, but would not wait while she was sent for.

In order to carry on the imposition, his lordship sent for a man who personated the supposed Mr. Smith; but Miss Woodcock was soon convinced that he had never seen her father, from the unsatisfactory answers that he gave to her inquiries.

After this Lord Baltimore played a tune, while the pretended Mr. Smith and Mrs. Harvey danced to the music; but in the mean time Miss Woodcock was tormented by a thousand conflicting passions. She was then shown some fine paintings in the room, one of which being that of a ship in distress, she said it bore a great resemblance to her own unhappy situation.

Then the man called Smith was desired by Lord Baltimore to draw Miss Woodcock's picture; and he instantly pulled out a pencil, and made the drawing, while the young lady sat in a posture of extreme grief and dejection.

At midnight Mr. Broughton, his lordship's steward, brought intelligence that Isaacs, the Jew, having offered a letter to Miss Woodcock's father, was stopped till he should give an account where the young lady was secreted. Lord Baltimore was, or affected to be, in a violent passion, and vowed vengeance against the father; but in the interim the Jew entered, and delivered a letter which he pretended to have received from Miss Woodcock's sister. She took it to read; but she had wept so much that her eyes were sore; and of all she read she could recollect but this passage:—
' Only please to appoint a place where and when we may meet with you.'

The hour of retirement being arrived, Miss Woodcock refused to go up stairs, unless she might be assured of not receiving any insult from his lordship. She had not taken any sustenance since she entered the house. For this night she laid down in her clothes, on a bed in which Mrs. Harvey reposed herself. She asked this bad woman if she had ever been in love; and acknowledged that she herself was addressed by a young fellow, who appeared to be very fond of her, and that they were to settle in business as soon as the marriage should take place; wherefore she desired Mrs. Harvey to show her the way out of a house that had been so obnoxious to her: but the answer of the latter was, that though she had lived in the house several years, she did not herself know the way out of it.

On the following morning, when Miss Woodcock went down stairs, she pleaded earnestly with Lord Baltimore for her liberty; on which he became most violently enraged, called her by the vilest names, and said that, if she spoke to him on the subject any more, he would either throw her out of the window, or send her home in a wheelbarrow, with her petticoats tied over her head; and, turning to Isaacs the Jew, he said, ' Take the slut to a mean house like herself; ' which greatly terrified her, as she presumed he meant a house of ill fame.

The sufferings she had undergone having by this time made her extremely ill, Lord Baltimore mixed a physical draught for her, which he insisted on her drinking.

On the Sunday afternoon he begged her to sit and hear him talk. His discourse consisted of a ridicule on religion, and every thing that was sacred, even to the denying the existence of a soul.

After supper he made six several attempts to ravish her within two hours; but she repulsed him in such a determined manner, that it was impossible for him to accomplish his dishonourable purpose. On that night she lay with Mrs. Harvey; but could get no rest, as she was in perpetual fear of renewed insults from his lordship.

On the Monday morning she was told that she should see her father, if she would dry her eyes, wash herself, and put on clean linen. Mrs. Griffenburg now supplied her with a change of linen; and then she was hurried into the coach with Lord Baltimore, Doctor Griffenburg, and two women. They were carried to Lord Baltimore's country seat at Epsom, where she experienced several fresh acts of indecency from her ignoble tormentor; and, on her again resisting him, he said she must submit that night, with or without her consent; and in this declaration he was supported by the two infamous women.

At supper she ate a few mouthfuls; but declined drinking any thing, lest some intoxicating matter should be mixed with the liquor. Lord Baltimore and his people now diverted themselves with the game of blindman's buff; but Miss Woodcock refused to take any share in their ridiculous folly.

The two women now conducted her to the bedchamber, and began to undress her; nor was she capable of making much resistance, being weak, through want of food and continued grief. Still, however, she begged to be deprived of life, rather than submit to dishonourable treatment.

On the drawing of the curtains she observed that Lord Baltimore was in bed, which added to her former terrors; but she was not suffered to remain long in doubt: the women left her; but, alas! not to her repose; for that night gave rise to the crime which furnished matter for the prosecution of which we are now reciting the particulars.

Twice (according to Miss Woodcock's deposition) was this horrid purpose effected; and, though she called out repeatedly for help, yet she found none; and in the morning, when she went to Mrs. Harvey's room, and told her what had passed, the latter advised her to be quiet, for that she had made noise enough already.

The infamous Harvey now hinting that worse consequences might still be expected, Miss Woodcock determined to seem content with her situation, disagreeable as it was, in the hope of obtaining the protection of her friends.

In this hope she frequently went to the window, flattering herself that she might see some person whom she knew. With the same view she went out once with his lordship, and once with Mrs. Griffenburg; and, having accidentally heard the name of Lord Baltimore mentioned, she presumed this to be the person who had treated her so ill; nor had she a guess who it was till this period.

On the afternoon of the day that she made this discovery they went to London, to the great joy of Miss Woodcock, who hoped now to find an easier communication with her friends. At her request she was permitted to sleep alone; and the next day he introduced her to Madam Saunier, the governess to his lordship's natural daughters, telling her that Miss Woodcock had been recommended as a companion to the young ladies.

On this day he gave her some money, and desired her to dispose of it as she thought proper; and, when night advanced, he sent Mrs. Griffenburg to order her to come to bed. She at first refused to comply, and at length yielded only on conditional terms. What passed this night is too horrid for relation.

On the following day Mrs. Griffenburg told her that she had been preparing another apartment for her, and begged that she would come and see it; and conducted her to a stone garret, which was remarkably cold and damp; and, being among the servants' apartments, she began to apprehend that Lord Baltimore, having gratified his own passion, was disposed to transfer her to his dependents.

Miss Woodcock's friends now began to form some conjectures where she might be secreted; and Mr. Davis, a young fellow who had paid his addresses to her, determined to exert himself to ascertain the fact.

On the Sunday he placed himself under a window of Lord Baltimore's house, and had not been there long before she saw him, and intimated that she did so. On this Davis took out a book, motioning with his hand for her to write. She then waved her hand for him to approach; but, as he did not seem to comprehend her meaning, she ran into another room, and said 'I cannot come to you; is my father well?' He answered that all parties were well, and asked what was become of Mrs. Harvey. The young lady now put down the window, and retired, unable any longer to continue the conversation.

Mr. Davis now went and informed Miss Woodcock's father of the discovery he had made; on which the old gentleman went to Mr. Cay, a baker, in Whitecross Street, to ask his opinion. Mr. Cay went with him to Mr. Watts, an attorney, who advised them to make application to Lord Mansfield for a writ of habeas corpus. But it may be now necessary to take notice of what passed between Lord Baltimore and Miss Woodcock in the mean time.

On the day following that on which she had been seen by Davis, his lordship told her that she should see her father that day, at Dr. Griffenburg's, in Dean Street, Soho; and he said he would make a settlement on her for life if she would acknowledge that she had been well treated. This she agreed to, in the hope of obtaining her freedom. She was then told that her father had caused Mrs. Harvey to be taken into custody.

Lord Baltimore now went to Griffenburg's with Miss Woodcock, taking likewise a young lady, of whom she was to declare herself the companion: but they had been only a few minutes at Griffenburg's when a servant came to apprize his lordship that Sir John Fielding's people had surrounded his house.

Lord Baltimore, having previously sent one of his servants with a letter to Miss Woodcock's father, now ordered a coach; and he, and Dr. Griffenburg and the young lady, now went to a tavern in Whitechapel, in quest of the servant, who told them that Mr. Woodcock having been out all day in search of his daughter, and not being returned, he (the servant) would not leave the letter, from a point of prudence.

Hereupon they drove to a house in Covent Garden, where the servant soon arrived with a note from Sir John Fielding's clerk, desiring Miss Woodcock to come to Bow Street, where her friends were, in expectation of her arrival. Fearful of taking any step that might involve her in still farther difficulties, she showed Lord Baltimore the note, when he declared she should not comply with the contents; and they immediately drove to Dr. Griffenburg's.

At this place they were met by his lordship's steward, who said his house was still surrounded by peace-officers; but, as they went away soon afterwards, this unworthy peer then took Miss Woodcock home in his own carriage.

On their arrival the valet-de-chambre told his master that on the Sunday morning the young lady had spoken to a person from the window. His lordship now demanded if this was fact. She acknowledged that it was; but said she had not acquainted her friends with her distressed situation.

He now tried to calm her mind, but said that she must sleep with him that night, which she positively refused, unless he would engage not to offer her any insult; and this promise was made, and complied with.

In the morning Mr. Watts, the attorney, called at Lord Baltimore's house with a writ of habeas corpus; but the porter would not admit him till he produced the writ; but then he was asked into the house, and Lord Baltimore made acquainted with his business. On this his lordship told his prisoner Mr. Watts's business, and begged she would prepare to see him with all possible composure.

In the interim his lordship waited on the attorney, who demanded whether one Sarah Woodcock was in his house: but, on his declining to give an immediate answer, Watts said that he would serve the writ unless she was instantly produced; and that the consequence would be that all his doors must be broke open till she was found: but he hoped that so violent a procedure would not be necessary.

His lordship now begged his patience for a short time, and his requisition should be complied with. Mr. Watts agreed to wait, and the other, going to Miss Woodcock, requesting her to write to her father, and declare that she had been used with tenderness, and had consented to her then situation; and he desired her to add that she wished to see her father and sisters, but hoped their visit would be of the peaceful kind; and with all this she complied, in hope, as she afterwards declared, of obtaining her liberty.

This letter being sealed, and dispatched by one of his lordship's servants, he introduced the attorney to Miss Woodcock, who asked her if her residence in that house was matter of choice, or whether she was forcibly detained. She replied that she remained there by her own consent, but that she was anxious to see her father.

With this declaration Mr. Watts appeared satisfied, saying that no person had any right to interfere, if she voluntarily consented to her situation.

His lordship then intimated that it would be proper for her to go to Lord Mansfield, and make a similar declaration. She made no hesitation to comply with this proposal; but still appeared exceedingly anxious to have a conference with her father.

On this the parties went to Lord Mansfield's house

in Bloomsbury Square, where they were shown into different apartments; and Miss Woodcock's friends waited in an antechamber, to hear the issue of this extraordinary affair.

The young lady being examined by Lord Mansfield, he inquired minutely into the circumstances respecting her being conveyed to Lord Baltimore's house. She answered every question in the most explicit manner; and, when the judge asked her if she was willing to live with his lordship, she answered in the affirmative; but expressed great earnestness to see her friends first.

On this she was shown into the room where her friends waited; and the first question she asked was ' Who Lord Mansfield was, and whether he had a right to set her at liberty?' She was told that his right was indisputable; and his lordship being again consulted, he inquired if she still adhered to her former opinion; to which she replied that she did not, but desired to go home with her father.

His lordship then asked her how happened the sudden change in her mind. Her answer was ' Because, till I saw them, I did not know you had power to release me.' His lordship then said ' Child, it is in my power to let you go; ' and told her she was at full liberty to go where she pleased'; on which she went into the other room to her friends, but was unable to express her joy on the occasion.

In the interim Lord Mansfield addressed the Reverend Mr. Watson, a dissenting minister, and some other persons present, to the following effect:— ' Gentlemen, I would have you take notice of Miss Woodcock's answers, because possibly this matter may be variously talked of in public, and justice ought to be done to both parties; for, when this lady came before me on her private examination, she expressed a desire to see her father and sister, or sisters: and now she has answered as you have heard.'

On Miss Woodcock's discharge, Mr. Cay, the baker,

in Whitecross Street (to whom her father had delivered the two hundred pound bank-note, which had been enclosed in the letter by Lord Baltimore), conveyed the young lady to Sir John Fielding, before whom she swore to the actual commission of the rape by Lord Baltimore.

At this time Mrs. Griffenburg and Mrs. Harvey were in custody; and a warrant was issued to apprehend Lord Baltimore; but he secreted himself for the present, and surrendered to the Court of King's Bench on the last day of Hilary term, 1768; and the two women being brought thither by habeas corpus, they were all admitted to bail, in order for trial at Kingston, in Surrey, because the crime was alleged to have been committed at his lordship's seat at Epsom.

In the interim Miss Woodcock went to the house of Mr. Cay, in Whitecross Street; but, not being properly accommodated there, she went to the house of a friend, where she lived in great privacy and retirement till the time arrived for the trial of the offending parties.

Bills of indictment being found against Lord Baltimore and the two women, they were all brought to trial before the Lord Chief Baron Smythe; and, after the evidence against them had been given, in substance as may be collected from the preceding narrative, Lord Baltimore made the following defence, which was read in Court by Mr. Hamersley, solicitor to his lordship:—

' My Lord and Gentlemen,
' I have put myself upon my country, in hopes that prejudice and clamour will avail nothing in this place, where it is the privilege of the meanest of the king's subjects to be presumed innocent until his guilt has been made appear by legal evidence. I wish I could say that I had been treated abroad with the same candour. I have been loaded with obloquy, the most malignant libels have been circulated, and every other method which malice could devise has been taken to

337

create general prejudice against me. I thank God that, under such circumstances, I have had firmness and resolution enough to meet my accusers face to face, and provoke an inquiry into my conduct. *Hic murus aheneus esto,—nil conscire sibi.* The charge against me, and against these poor people who are involved with me, because they might otherwise have been just witnesses of my innocence, is in its nature very easy to be made, and hard to be disproved. The accuser has the advantage of supporting it by a direct and positive oath; the defence can only be collected from circumstances.

' My defence is composed, then, of a variety of circumstances, all tending to show the falsity of this charge, the absurdity of it, the improbability that it could be true. It will be laid before the jury under the direction of my counsel; and I have the confidence of an innocent man, that it will be manifest to your lordship, the jury, and the whole world, that the story told by this woman is a perversion of truth in every particular. What could induce her to make such a charge I can only suspect: very soon after she came to my house, upon a representation to me that her father was distressed, I sent him a considerable sum of money: whether the ease with which the money was obtained from me might suggest the idea as a means of obtaining a larger sum of money, or whether it was thought necessary to destroy me, in order to establish the character of the girl to the world, I know not; but I do aver, upon the word of a man of honour, that there is no truth in any thing which has been said or sworn of my having offered violence to this girl. I ever held such brutality in abhorrence. I am totally against all force; and for me to have forced this woman, considering my weak state of health, and my strength, is not only a moral, but a physical, impossibility. She is, as to bodily strength, stronger than I am. Strange opinions, upon subjects foreign to this charge, have been falsely imputed to me, to inflame this accusation. Libertine as I am represented, I hold no such opinions. Much has been said against me, that I seduced this girl from her parents: seduction is not the point of this charge; but I do assure your lordship and the jury this part of the case has been aggravated exceedingly beyond the truth. If I have been in any degree to blame, I am sure I have sufficiently atoned for every indiscretion, which a weak attachment to this unworthy woman may have led me into, by having suffered the disgrace of being exposed as a criminal at the bar in the county which my father had the honour to represent in parliament, and where I had some pretensions to have attained the same honour, had that sort of an active life been my object.

' I will take up no more of your lordship's time than to add that, if I had been conscious of the guilt now imputed to me, I could have kept myself and my fortune out of the reach of the laws of this country. I am a citizen of the world; I could have lived any where: but I love my own country, and submit to its laws, resolving that my innocence should be justified by the laws. I now, by my own voluntary act, by surrendering myself to the Court of King's Bench, stake, upon the verdict of twelve men, my life, my fortune, and, what is dearer to me, my honour.

' BALTIMORE.

' March 25, 1768.'

The substance of the defences of Mrs. Griffenburg and Mrs. Harvey consisted principally in alleging that Miss Woodcock had consented to all that had passed, and that no force had been used towards her either by Lord Baltimore or themselves.

The evidence of Dr. Griffenburg was not admitted, as his name was upon record, on a charge of having been concerned in a crime of a similar nature.

After every thing alleged against the prisoners had

been heard in the most dispassionate manner, the judge addressed himself to the jury in the following terms: —

'Gentlemen of the Jury,

'The prisoner at the bar, Lord Baltimore, stands indicted for feloniously ravishing, and carnally knowing, Sarah Woodcock, spinster, against her will, on the 22d of December last, at Epsom, against the statute which makes this offence felony: and the other two prisoners are indicted as accessories before the fact, by feloniously and maliciously procuring, aiding, and abetting Lord Baltimore to commit the said rape, at the same time and place. To this they have pleaded not guilty, and you are to try if they are guilty. Before I state to you the evidence I will mention to you two or three things: in the first place, my lord complains of libels and printed accounts of this transaction, which have been circulated. It is a most unjustifiable practice, and tends to the perversion of public justice; and, therefore, if you have seen any thing printed on the side of the prosecutrix, or the prisoners, I must desire you to divest yourselves of any prejudice that such publications must have occasioned, and give your verdict only on the evidence now laid before you. Another thing I desire is, that, whichever way the verdict is given, none of the friends of any of the parties will make use of any expressions of approbation or applause, which are extremely improper and indecent in a court of justice, and I shall certainly commit any person whom I know to be guilty of it. The last thing that I shall mention to you is, to desire that no resentment you may feel at the manner in which she was carried to Lord Baltimore's house may have any influence on your verdict; for, however unwarrantable the manner was in which she came into his power, if, at the time he lay with her, it was by her consent, he is not guilty of the offence of which he is indicted; though it was proper to be given in evidence on this trial, to account for her being with him, and his having an opportunity of committing the crime: and to show, from the indirect manner of getting her to his house, the greater probability that her account is true. Having said this, I will now state to you the whole evidence as particularly as I can.'

Mr. Baron Smythe then stated the whole of the evidence to the jury, as before given, which took up three hours, and then concluded thus:—

'In point of law, the fact is fully proved on my lord and the two other prisoners, if you believe the evidence of Sarah Woodcock. It is a crime which in its nature can only be proved by the woman on whom it is committed; for she only can tell whether she consented or no: it is, as my lord observes, very easy to be made, and hard to be disproved; and the defence can only be collected from circumstances; from these you must judge whether her evidence is or is not to be believed. Lord Hale, in his 'History of the Pleas of the Crown,' lays down the rules:—1. If complaint is not made soon after the injury is supposed to be received; 2. If it is not followed by a recent prosecution; a strong presumption arises that the complaint is malicious. She has owned the injury was received December 22; the complaint was not made till December 29; but she has accounted for it in the manner you have heard. The strong part of the case on behalf of the prisoners is her not complaining when she was at Lord Mansfield's, the supreme magistrate in the kingdom in criminal matters. You have heard how she has explained and accounted for her conduct in that particular, which you will judge of. Upon the whole, if you believe that she made the discovery as soon as she knew she had an opportunity of doing it, and that her account is true, you will find all the prisoners guilty; if you believe that she did not make the discovery as soon as she had an opportunity, and from thence, or other circumstances, are not satisfied her account is true, you will find them all not guilty; for, if he is not guilty, they cannot be so; for they cannot be accessory to a crime which was never committed.'

After an absence of an hour and twenty minutes, the jury returned with a verdict that the prisoners were Not Guilty.

This singular affair was tried at Kingston, in Surrey, on the 26th of March, 1768.

Our readers will not be displeased with a few remarks on this very extraordinary transaction—The meanness of Lord Baltimore, and the unreasonable terror and ignorance of Miss Woodcock, will appear to be equal objects of astonishment. His lordship's devices to obtain possession of this woman were beneath the dignity of a nobleman, or, indeed, of any man; and her tame submission to the insult is a proof that she had little idea of the sacred protection which the laws of her country would have afforded her; for Lord Baltimore's house (at the bottom of Southampton Row, Bloomsbury) was not so obscurely situated but that she might have made application to many a passenger.

Something, indeed, must be allowed to feminine fear on such an occasion, after she once found herself in the actual possession of a man from whom she thought it would be dangerous even to attempt an escape.

Miss Woodcock's ignorance of Lord Mansfield's power will appear very extraordinary; but surely not more so than that of a man, who, being an evidence before Sir John Fielding, addressed him successively by the titles of sir! your honour! your worship! your lordship! your grace! and your majesty! These appellations were repeatedly heard to be given within half an hour by the writer of this narrative; and he presumes the circumstance may be considered as an apology for the superlative ignorance of Miss Woodcock.

On the whole, however, this case is of the melancholy

342

kind. What shall we think of a man, of Lord Baltimore's rank and fortune, who could debase himself beneath all rank and distinction, and, by the wish to gratify his irregular passions, submit to degrade himself in the opinion of his own servants and other domestics?

Addison has a fine sentiment, by which our nobility ought to be influenced: —

> ' Honour 's a sacred tie; the law of kings;
> The noble mind's distinguishing perfection:
> It aids and strengthens Virtue where it meets her,
> And imitates her actions where she is not:
> It is not to be sported with.'——

JOHN MILLS

EXECUTED FOR MURDER.

THIS monster was another son of Richard Mills, whose execution has already appeared; and the sequel will show that he was in the habits of cruelty and villainy ' worthy of his sire.'

He also was concerned in the murder of the custom-house officers, but escaped a little longer the hand of justice. He was likewise one of that gang of villains who most daringly broke open the custom-house at Poole; and yet was he reserved to make atonement for

a fresh murder, equally cruel as that for which his
father and brother had forfeited their lives.

John Mills, and some associates, travelling over
Hind Heath, saw the judges on their road to
Chichester, to try the murderers of Chater and Galley;
on which young Mills proposed to rob them; but the
other parties refused to have any concern in such an
affair.

Mills and his Companions whipping Hawkins to Death

Soon after his father, brother, and their accomplices, were hanged, Mills thought of going to Bristol,
with a view of embarking for France; and, having
hinted his intentions to some others, they resolved to
accompany him; and, stopping at a house on the road,
they met with one Richard Hawkins, whom they
asked to go with them; but the poor fellow hesitating,
they put him on horseback behind Mills, and carried

him to the Dog and Partridge, on Slendon Common, which was kept by John Reynolds.

They had not been long in the house when complaint was made that two bags of tea had been stolen, and Hawkins was charged with the robbery. He steadily denied any knowledge of the affair; but this not satisfying the villains, they obliged him to pull off his clothes; and, having likewise stripped themselves, they began to whip him with the most unrelenting barbarity; and Curtis, one of the gang, said he did know of the robbery, and, if he would not confess, he would whip him till he died; for he had whipped many a rogue, and washed his hands in his blood.*

These bloodthirsty villains continued whipping the poor wretch till their breath was almost exhausted: while he begged them to spare his life, on account of his wife and child. Hawkins drawing up his legs, to defend himself in some measure from their blows, they kicked him on the groin in a manner too shocking to be described; continually asking him what was become of the tea. At length the unfortunate man mentioned something of his father and brother; on which Mills and one Curtis said they would go and fetch them; but Hawkins expired soon after they had left the house.

Rowland, one of the accomplices, now locked the door; and, putting the key in his pocket, he and Thomas Winter (who was afterwards admitted evid-

* On the 11th of December, 1750, John Watling, nick-named Peter Jack, a smuggler of Horsey, in Norfolk, was hanged. This villain, among the numerous enormities which he committed, at the head of eleven more smugglers, went in the night to the house of Abraham Bailey, who had been a custom-house watchman, pulled him out of bed, whipped him with their whips until the blood trickled down his body, then hung him by the neck to a tree, but let him down before he was dead. When he recovered his senses they obliged him to answer their questions, and made him swear to his own damnation if he revealed what they had done to him.

ence) went out to meet Curtis and Mills, whom they saw riding up a lane leading from an adjacent village, having each a man behind him. Winter desiring to speak with his companions, the other men stood at a distance, while he asked Curtis what he meant to do with them, who replied, to confront them with Hawkins.

Winter now said that Hawkins was dead, and begged that no more mischief might be done; but Curtis replied, ' By G— we will go through it now; ' but at length they permitted them to go home, saying that when they were wanted they should be sent for.

The murderers now coming back to the public house, Reynolds said ' You have ruined me; ' but Curtis replied that he would make him amends. Having consulted how they should dispose of the body, it was proposed to throw it into a well in an adjacent park; but this being objected to, they carried it twelve miles, and, having tied stones to it, in order to sink it, they threw it into a pond in Parham Park, belonging to Sir Cecil Bishop; and in this place it lay more than two months before it was discovered.

This horrid and unprovoked murder gave rise to a royal proclamation, in which a pardon was offered to any persons, even outlawed smugglers, except those who had been guilty of murder, or concerned in breaking open the custom-house at Poole, on the condition of discovering the persons who had murdered Hawkins, particularly Mills, who was charged with having had a concern in the horrid transaction.

Hereupon William Pring, an outlawed smuggler, who had not had any share in either of the crimes excepted in the proclamation, went to the secretary of state, and informed him that he would find Mills if he could be ascertained of his own pardon; adding, that he believed he was either at Bath or Bristol.

Being assured that he need not doubt of the pardon, he set out for Bristol, where he found Mills, and with him Thomas and Lawrence Kemp, brothers; the former of whom had broken out of Newgate, and the other was outlawed by proclamation. Having consulted on their desperate circumstances, Pring offered them a retreat at his house near Beckenham, in Kent, whence they might make excursions, and commit robberies on the highway.

Pleased with this proposal, they set out with Pring, and arrived in safety at his house; where they had not been long before he pretended that his horse being an indifferent one, and theirs remarkably good, he would go and procure another, and then they would proceed on the intended expedition.

Thus saying, he set out, and they agreed to wait for his return; but, instead of going to procure a horse, he went to the house of Mr. Rackster, an officer of the excise at Horsham, who, taking with him seven or eight armed men, went to Beckenham at night, where they found Mills and the two brothers Kemp just going to supper on a breast of veal. They immediately secured the brothers by tying their arms; but Mills, making resistance, was cut with a hanger before he would submit.

The offenders, being taken, were conducted to the county gaol for Sussex; and, being secured till the assizes, were removed to East Grinstead, where the brothers Kemp were tried for highway robberies, convicted, sentenced, and executed.

Mills, being tried for the murder of Hawkins, was capitally convicted, and received sentence of death, and to be hung in chains near the place where the murder was committed.

After conviction he mentioned several robberies in which he had been concerned, but refused to tell the names of any of his accomplices; declaring that he thought he should merit damnation if he made discoveries by means of which any of his companions might be apprehended and convicted.

The country being at that time filled with smugglers, a rescue was feared; wherefore he was conducted to the place of execution by a guard of soldiers; and, when there, prayed with a clergyman, confessed that he had led a bad life, acknowledged the murder of Hawkins, desired that all young people would take warning by his untimely end, humbly implored the forgiveness of God, and professed to die in charity with all mankind.

He was executed on Slendon Common on the 12th of August, 1749, and afterwards hung in chains near the same spot.

HANNAH DAGOE,

EXECUTED FOR ROBBING A POOR WOMAN.

WE have adduced many instances of the hardness of heart, and contempt of the commandments of God, in *men* who have undergone the last sentence of the law; but we are of opinion that in this *female* will be found a more relentless heart, in her last moments, than any criminal we have yet recorded.

Hannah Dagoe was born in Ireland, and was one of that numerous class of women who ply at Covent Garden Market, to the exclusion of poor Englishwomen.

She became acquainted with a poor and industrious woman of the name of Eleanor Hussey, who lived by herself in a small apartment, in which was some creditable household furniture, the remains of the worldly goods of her deceased husband. Seizing an opportunity, when the owner was from home, this daring woman broke into Hussey's room, and stripped it of every article which it contained.

For this burglary and robbery she was brought to trial at the Old Bailey, found guilty, and sentenced to death.

She was a strong masculine woman, the terror of her fellow-prisoners, and actually stabbed one of the men who had given evidence against her; but the wound happened not to prove dangerous.

On the road to Tyburn she showed little concern at her miserable state, and paid no attention to the exhortations of the Romish priest who attended her.

Hannah Dagoe resisting her execution.

When the cart in which she was bound was drawn under the gallows she got her hands and arms loose, seized the executioner, struggled with him, and gave him so violent a blow on the breast as nearly knocked him down. She dared him to hang her, and took off her hat, cloak, and other parts of her dress, and disposed of them among the crowd, in despite of him.*

* The clothes in which criminals die are claimed as the perquisite of the executioner, unless a full equivalent is given him by the friends of the deceased.

349

After much resistance he got the rope about her neck, which she had no sooner found accomplished, than, pulling a handkerchief, bound round her head, over her face, she threw herself out of the cart, before the signal given, with such violence, that she broke her neck, and died instantly, on the 4th of May, 1763.

JOHN CROUCH AND WIFE,

TRIED FOR OFFERING TO SELL A YOUNG GIRL.

THOUGH our laws punish more than one hundred and sixty offences with death, and though a statute is made against almost every species of crime, still the depravity of man is ever practising some turpitude not, perhaps, fully comprised in our penal code. A flagitious crime, for instance, of the following nature, could hardly be contemplated, in a land of liberty and affection, by any set of legislators, and punishment must consequently be resorted to from those laws against petty offences.

On the 15th of January, 1766, an elderly man and woman were observed on the Royal Exchange, London, with a fine young girl, apparently fourteen years of age, but thinly and shabbily clothed; and, consequently, shivering with cold in that inclement season of the year. So uncommon an appearance in that scene of bustle and business, it being then what is called nearly 'High 'Change,' attracted considerable attention.

It was first conceived that they were asking charity, as the man had addressed two or three gentlemen, from whom he received a contemptuous denial. At length he accosted an honest captain of a ship, who instantly gave publicity to the base proposal which had been made to him—namely, to purchase the unfortunate and innocent girl!

The parties were immediately taken into custody by the beadles of the Exchange, and carried before the

sitting magistrate at Guildhall, who committed t.
man and woman to prison as vagrants, and ordere
the girl to be taken care of in the London Workhouse.

On their examination they persisted that the girl
was their own child; but it appeared so unnatural
that parents in Britain should offer for sale their
offspring, that an inquiry into the transaction was set
on foot.

At the general sessions of the peace, held at Guildhall, on the 12th of May following, this unnatural
man and woman were brought to the bar.

It appeared that the man was named John Crouch,
and that his residence was at Bodmin, in Cornwall.
The woman was his wife; the unfortunate girl his
niece; and having heard ' that young maidens were
very scarce in London, and that they sold for a good
price,' he took her out of the poor-house there, and,
accompanied by his wife, had set off, and travelled on
foot from Bodmin to London, two hundred and thirty-
two miles, in order to mend their fortune by her sale!

The jury found the man guilty on an indictment
presented against him for an offence far short of his
crime; but, considering the woman under his influence,
acquitted her. The husband was sentenced to six
months' imprisonment in Newgate, and to pay a fine
of one shilling.

ELIZABETH BROWNRIGG,

EXECUTED FOR TORTURING HER FEMALE APPRENTICES TO DEATH.

THE long scene of torture in which this inhuman
woman kept the innocent object of her remorseless
cruelty, ere she finished the long-premeditated murder,
engaged the interest of the superior ranks, and roused
the indignation of the populace more than any

MRS BROWNRIGG.

criminal occurrence in the whole course of our melancholy narratives.

This cruel woman, having passed the early part of her life in the service of private families, was married to James Brownrigg, a plumber, who, after being seven years in Greenwich, came to London, and took a house in Flower-de-Luce Court, Fleet Street, where he carried on a considerable share of business,

Elizabeth Brownrigg cruelly flogging her Apprentice, Mary Clifford.

and had a little house at Islington for an occasional retreat.

She had been the mother of sixteen children; and, having practised midwifery, was appointed by the overseers of the poor of St. Dunstan's parish to take care of the poor women who were taken in labour in the workhouse, which duty she performed to the entire satisfaction of her employers.

Mary Mitchell, a poor girl, of the precinct of White

Friars, was put apprentice to Mrs. Brownrigg in the year 1765; and about the same time Mary Jones, one of the children of the Foundling Hospital, was likewise placed with her in the same capacity; and she had other apprentices.

As Mrs. Brownrigg received pregnant women to lie-in privately, these girls were taken with a view of saving the expense of women servants. At first the poor orphans were treated with some degree of civility; but this was soon changed for the most savage barbarity.

Having laid Mary Jones across two chairs in the kitchen, she whipped her with such wanton cruelty that she was occasionally obliged to desist through mere weariness.

This treatment was frequently repeated; and Mrs. Brownrigg used to throw water on her when she had done whipping her, and sometimes she would dip her head into a pail of water. The room appointed for the girl to sleep in adjoined the passage leading to the street door; and, as she had received many wounds on her head, shoulders, and various parts of her body, she determined not to bear such treatment any longer, if she could effect her escape.

Observing that the key was left in the street door when the family went to bed, she opened it cautiously one morning, and escaped into the street.

Thus freed from her horrid confinement, she repeatedly inquired her way to the Foundling Hospital till she found it, and was admitted after describing in what manner she had been treated, and showing the bruises she had received.

The child having been examined by a surgeon, (who found her wounds to be of a most alarming nature,) the governors of the hospital ordered Mr. Plumbtree, their solicitor, to write to James Brownrigg, threatening a prosecution, if he did not give a proper reason for the severities exercised toward the child.

No notice of this having been taken, and the governors of the hospital thinking it imprudent to indict at common law, the girl was discharged, in consequence of an application to the chamberlain of London. The other girl, Mary Mitchell, continued with her mistress for the space of a year, during which she was treated with equal cruelty, and she also resolved to quit her service. Having escaped out of the house, she was met in the street by the younger son of Brownrigg, who forced her to return home, where her sufferings were greatly aggravated on account of her elopement. In the interim, the overseers of the precinct of White Friars bound Mary Clifford to Brownrigg; nor was it long before she experienced similar cruelties to those inflicted on the other poor girls, and possibly still more severe. She was frequently tied up naked, and beaten with a hearth-broom, a horsewhip, or a cane, till she was absolutely speechless. This poor girl having a natural infirmity, the mistress would not permit her to lie in a bed, but placed her on a mat, in a coal-hole that was remarkably cold: however, after some time, a sack and a quantity of straw formed her bed, instead of the mat. During her confinement in this wretched situation she had nothing to subsist on but bread and water; and her covering, during the night, consisted only of her own clothes, so that she sometimes lay almost perished with cold.

On a particular occasion, when she was almost starving with hunger, she broke open a cupboard in search of food, but found it empty; and on another occasion she broke down some boards, in order to procure a draught of water.

Though she was thus pressed for the humblest necessaries of life, Mrs. Brownrigg determined to punish her with rigour for the means she had taken to supply herself with them. On this she caused the girl to strip to the skin, and during the course f a whole day, while she remained naked, she repeatedly beat her with the butt-end of a whip.

In the course of this most inhuman treatment a jack-chain was fixed round her neck, the end of which was fastened to the yard door, and then it was pulled as tight as possible without strangling her.

A day being passed in the practice of these savage barbarities, the girl was remanded to the coal-hole at night, her hands being tied behind her, and the chain still remaining about her neck.

The husband having been obliged to find his wife's apprentices in wearing apparel, they were repeatedly stripped naked, and kept so for whole days, if their garments happened to be torn.

The elder son had frequently the superintendence of these wretched girls; but this was sometimes committed to the apprentice, who declared that she was totally naked one night when he went to tie her up. The two poor girls were frequently so beaten that their heads and shoulders appeared as one general sore; and, when a plaster was applied to their wounds, the skin used to peel away with it.

Sometimes Mrs. Brownrigg, when resolved on uncommon severity, used to tie their hands with a cord, and draw them up to a water-pipe which ran across the ceiling in the kitchen; but that giving way, she desired her husband to fix a hook in the beam, through which a cord was drawn, and, their arms being extended, she used to horsewhip them till she was weary, and till the blood followed at every stroke.

The elder son having one day directed Mary Clifford to put up a half-tester bedstead, the poor girl was unable to do it; on which he beat her till she could no longer support his severity; and at another time, when the mother had been whipping her in the kitchen till she was absolutely tired, the son renewed the savage treatment. Mrs. Brownrigg would sometimes seize the poor girl by the cheeks, and, forcing the skin down violently with her fingers, cause the blood to gush from her eyes.

Mary Clifford, unable to bear these repeated severities, complained of her hard treatment to a French lady who lodged in the house; and she having represented the impropriety of such behaviour to Mrs. Brownrigg, the inhuman monster flew at the girl, and cut her tongue in two places with a pair of scissors.

On the morning of the 13th of July this barbarous woman went into the kitchen, and, after obliging Mary Clifford to strip to the skin, drew her up to the staple, and, though her body was an entire sore from former bruises, yet this wretch renewed her cruelties with her accustomed severity.

After whipping her till the blood streamed down her body, she let her down, and made her wash herself in a tub of cold water; Mary Mitchell, the other poor girl, being present during this transaction. While Clifford was washing herself Mrs. Brownrigg struck her on the shoulders, already sore with former bruises, with the butt-end of a whip; and she treated the child in this manner five times in the same day.

The poor girl's wounds now began to show evident signs of mortification. Her mother-in-law, who had resided some time in the country, came about this time to town, and inquired after her. Being informed that she was placed at Brownrigg's, she went thither, but was refused admittance by Mr. Brownrigg, who even threatened to carry her before the lord mayor if she came there to make further disturbances. Upon this the mother-in-law was going away, when Mrs. Deacon, wife of Mr. Deacon, baker, at the adjoining house, called her in, and informed her that she and her family had often heard moanings and groans issue from Brownrigg's house, and that she suspected the apprentices were treated with unwarrantable severity. This good woman likewise promised to exert herself to ascertain the truth.

At this juncture Mr. Brownrigg, going to Hampstead on business, bought a hog, which he sent home. The hog was put into a covered yard, having a skylight, which it was thought necessary to remove, in order to give air to the animal.

As soon as it was known that the sky-light was removed, Mr. Deacon ordered his servants to watch, in order, if possible, to discover the girls. Accordingly, one of the maids, looking from a window, saw one of the girls stooping down, on which she called her mistress, and she desired the attendance of some of the neighbours, who having been witnesses of the shocking scene, some men got upon the leads, and dropped bits of dirt, in order to induce the girl to speak to them; but she seemed wholly incapable. Mrs. Deacon then sent to the girl's mother-in-law, who immediately called upon Mr. Grundy, one of the overseers of St. Dunstan's, and represented the case. Mr. Grundy and the rest of the overseers, with the women, went and demanded a sight of Mary Clifford; but Brownrigg, who had nicknamed her Nan, told them that he knew no such person; but, if they wanted to see Mary (meaning Mary Mitchell), they might, and accordingly produced her. Upon this Mr. Deacon's servant declared that Mary Mitchell was not the girl they wanted. Mr. Grundy now sent for a constable, to search the house, but no discovery was then made.

Mr. Brownrigg threatened highly; but Mr. Grundy, with the spirit that became the officer of a parish, took Mary Mitchell with him to the workhouse, where, on the taking off her leathern bodice, it stuck so fast to her wounds that she shrieked with the pain; but, on being treated with great humanity, and told that she should not be sent back to Brownrigg's, she gave an account of the horrid treatment that she and Mary Clifford had sustained, and confessed that she had met the latter on the stairs just before they came

358

to the house. Upon this information Mr. Grundy and some others returned to the house, to make a stricter search; on which Brownrigg sent for a lawyer, in order to intimidate them, and even threatened a prosecution unless they immediately quitted the premises. Unterrified by these threats, Mr. Grundy sent for a coach, to carry Brownrigg to the Compter; on which the latter promised to produce the girl in about half an hour, if the coach was discharged. This being consented to, the girl was produced from a cupboard under a beaufet in the dining-room, after a pair of shoes, which young Brownrigg had in his hand during the proposal, had been put upon her. It is not in language to describe the miserable appearance this poor girl made; almost her whole body was ulcerated.

Being taken to the workhouse, an apothecary was sent for, who pronounced her to be in danger.

Brownrigg was therefore conveyed to Wood Street Compter; but his wife and son made their escape, taking with them a gold watch and some money. Mr. Brownrigg was now carried before Alderman Crossby, who fully committed him, and ordered the girls to be taken to St. Bartholomew's Hospital, where Mary Clifford died within a few days; and the coroner's inquest, being summoned, found a verdict of Wilful Murder against James and Elizabeth Brownrigg, and John their son.

In the mean time Mrs. Brownrigg and her son shifted from place to place in London, bought clothes in Rag Fair to disguise themselves, and then went to Wandsworth, where they took lodgings in the house of Mr. Dunbar, who kept a chandler's shop.

This chandler, happening to read a newspaper on the 15th of August, saw an advertisement, which so clearly described his lodgers, that he had no doubt but they were the murderers.

On this he went to London the next day, which was

unday, and, going to church, sent for Mr. Owen, the churchwarden, to attend him in the vestry, and gave him such a description of the parties that Mr. Owen desired Mr. Deacon and Mr. Wingrave, a constable, to go to Wandsworth, and make the necessary inquiry.

On their arrival at Dunbar's house, they found the wretched mother and son in a room by themselves, who evinced great agitation at this discovery. A coach being procured, they were conveyed to London, without any person in Wandsworth having knowledge of the affair, except Mr. and Mrs. Dunbar.

At the ensuing sessions at the Old Bailey, the father, mother, and son, were indicted; when Elizabeth Brownrigg, after a trial of eleven hours, was found guilty of murder, and ordered for execution; but the man and his son, being acquitted of the higher charge,* were detained, to take their trials for a misdemeanour, of which they were convicted, and imprisoned for the space of six months.

After sentence of death was passed on Mrs. Brownrigg she was attended by a clergyman, to whom she confessed the enormity of her crime, and acknowledged the justice of the sentence by which she had been condemned. The parting between her and her husband and son, on the morning of her execution, was affecting beyond description. The son falling on his knees, she bent herself over him and embraced him; while the husband was kneeling on the other side.

On her way to the fatal tree the people expressed their abhorrence of her crime in terms which, though not proper at the moment, testified their detestation of her cruelty. Before her exit, she joined in prayer

---

* It seems the child was looked upon as the apprentice of the wife, and not the husband; though the husband was obliged to find her apparel: however, accessories in murder are equally guilty, and it is strange that the man and his son should have been acquitted.

with the Ordinary of Newgate, whom she desired to declare to the multitude that she confessed her guilt, and acknowledged the justice of her sentence.

After her execution, which took place at Tyburn, September the 14th, 1767, her body was put into a hackney-coach, and conveyed to Surgeons' Hall, where it was dissected, and her skeleton hung up.

That Mrs. Brownrigg, a midwife by profession, and herself the mother of many children, should wantonly murder the offspring of other women, is truly astonishing, and can only be accounted for by that depravity of human nature which philosophers have always disputed, but which true Christians will be ready to allow.

Let her crimes be buried, though her skeleton be exposed; and may no one hereafter be found wicked enough to copy her vile example!

Women who have the care of children from parish workhouses or hospitals should consider themselves at once as mistresses and as mothers; nor ever permit the strictness of the former character to preponderate over the humanity of the latter.